𝕮𝕳𝖊 𝕳𝖚𝖙𝖍 𝕷𝖎𝖇𝖗𝖆𝖗𝖞.

THE WORKS

OF

GABRIEL HARVEY, D.C.L.

IN THREE VOLUMES.

FOR THE FIRST TIME COLLECTED AND EDITED
WITH MEMORIAL-INTRODUCTION, NOTES AND ILLUSTRATIONS, ETC.,

BY THE REV:
ALEXANDER B. GROSART, LL.D. (EDIN.), F.S.A. (SCOT.),
St. George's, Blackburn, Lancashire.

VOL. II.

PRECURSOR OF PIERCE'S SUPEREROGATION.
AND
PIERCE'S SUPEREROGATION, OR A NEW PRAYSE OF
THE OLD ASSE. A PREPARATIUE TO CERTAINE
LARGER DISCOURSES, INTITULED
NASHES S. FAME.

1593.

PRINTED FOR PRIVATE CIRCULATION ONLY.
1884.
50 *Copies.*]

AMS PRESS, INC.
NEW YORK
1966

AMS PRESS, INC.
New York, N.Y. 10003
1966

Manufactured in the United States of America

The Huth Library

OR

ELIZABETHAN-JACOBEAN

Unique or Very Rare

BOOKS

IN

VERSE AND PROSE

LARGELY

From the Library of

Henry Huth Esqʳ.

(*Engraved by W. J. Alais from a Photograph.*)

Edited with Introductions, Notes and Illustrations, etc.

BY THE

Rev. Alexander B. Grosart. LL.D. F.S.A.

FOR PRIVATE CIRCULATION ONLY

CONTENTS.

———

Foolifh he that feares, and.faine would ftop
An inundation working on apace ;
Runs to the breach, heapes mighty matter vp,
Throwes indigefted burthens on the place,
Loades with huge waights, the outfide and the top,
But leaues the inner parts in feeble cafe:
Thinking for that the outward forme feemes ftrong
'Tis fure inough, and may continue long.

But when the vnderworking waues come on,
Searching the fecrets of vnfenced waies,
The full maine Ocean following hard vpon,
Beares downe that idle frame, fkorning fuch ftaies ;
Proftrates that fruftrate paines as if not done,
And proudly on his filly labors plaies,
Whilft he perceiues his error, and doth finde
His ill proceeding contrary to kind.

So fares it with our indirect diffeignes,
And wrong-contriued labors at the laft,
Whilft working Time or Iuftice vndermines
The feeble ground-worke, Craft thought laid fo faft:
Then when out-breaking vengeance vncombines
The ill-ioynd plots fo fairely ouercaft,
Turnes vp thofe ftrong-pretended heapes of fhowes,
And all thefe weake illufions ouerthrowes.

DANIEL'S *Civill Warres* (1599), B. iii., 4–6.

THE HUTH LIBRARY.

THE WORKS

OF

GABRIEL HARVEY, D.C.L.

VOL. II.

PRECURSOR OF PIERCE'S SUPEREROGATION.

AND

PIERCE'S SUPEREROGATION, OR A NEW PRAYSE OF
THE OLD ASSE.

1593.

Looke how a Tygreſſe that hath loſt her whelpe,
Runs fiercely raging through the woods aſtray :
And ſeeing her ſelfe depriu'd of hope or helpe,
Furiously aſſaults what's in her way,
To ſatisfie her wrath, (not for a pray ;)
    So ſell ſhe on me in outragious wiſe ;
    As could diſdaine and iealouſie deuiſe.
             DANIEL'S *The Complaint of Roſamond.*

V.

PRECURSOR

OF

PIERCE'S SUPEREROGATION OR A NEW PRAYSE OF THE OLDE ASSE.

1593.

NOTE

This precursor of the larger 'Pierce's Supererogation' was separately published and in anticipation of its publication. When the latter appeared such copies of the former as remained unsold were bound up with it. But very few must so have remained over, as the present tractate is rarely found prefixed or affixed. Not more than three complete copies seem to be known.

Mr. J. Payne Collier—who reprinted both, like his other reprints of the Harvey-Greene books, with deplorable inaccuracy—supposed that Harvey or his friends suppressed or withdrew the precursor, because he had been so "much laughed at for the vanity and egotism" shown therein. But, seeing that the Printer in his Epistle at the close of the present tractate expressly states that it was to precede the other and larger—incidentally letting out that the so-called 'Preparatiue' was all of 'Nashes S. Fame' intended, for the Letters and Sonnets named are found appended to the larger 'Pierce's Supererogation'—ours is the true explanation, *i.e.*, separate and prior publication. Harvey's "selfe-admiration" might or might not be "so impervious that it could scarcely distinguish between applause and irony"; but *certes* none of the (high-flown) laudation was ironical, albeit obtained in part at least under misrepresentation and published without the authors' consent.

For the text of both I am indebted again to the Huth Library. There is a second complete exemplar of precursor and sequel in the British Museum; an incomplete in the Bodleian. See Memorial-Introduction for more of these books.   A. B. G.

Pierces Supererogation

OR

A NEW PRAYSE OF THE
OLD ASSE.

A Preparatiue to certaine larger Difcourfes, intituled
NASHES S. FAME.

Gabriell Haruey.

Il vostro Malignare Non Giova Nvlla.

LONDON
Imprinted by Iohn Wolfe.
1593.

TO MY VERY GENTLE AND LIBE-
rall frendes, M. Barnabe Barnes, M. Iohn
Thorius, M. Antony Chewt, and
euery fauorable Reader.

OUING M. Barnabe, M. Iohn, and
M. Antony, (for the reſt of my
partiall Cōmenders muſt pardon
me, till the Print be better ac-
quainted with their names) I haue
lately receiued your thriſe-curteous Letters, with
the Ouerplus of your thriſe-ſweet Sonets annexed:
the liberalleſt giftes, I beleeue, that euer you be-
ſtowed vpon ſo ſlight occaſion, and the very prodi-
galleſt fruites of your flooriſhing wittes. Whoſe
onely default is, not your, but my default, that
the matter is nothing correſpondent to the manner;
and miſelfe muſt either groſely forget miſelfe, or
franckly acknowledge mi ſimple ſelfe an vnworthy

fubiect of fo worthy commendations. Which I
cannot read without blufhing, repeate without
fhame, or remember without griefe, that I come
fo exceeding-fhort in fo exceffiue great accountes;
the fummes of your rich largeffe, not of my poore
defert; and percafe deuifed to aduertife me what
I fhould be, or to fignifie what you wifh [me] to
be; not to declare what I am, or to infinuate what
I may be. Eloquence, and Curtefie were euer
bountifull in the amplifying veine: and it hath
bene reputed a frendly Pollicy, to encourage their
louing acquaintance to labour the attainement of
thofe perfections, which they blafon in them, as
already atcheiued. Either fome fuch intention
you haue, by / way of Stratageme, to awaken my
negligence, or enkindle my confidence; or you are
difpofed by way of Ciuility, to make me vnreafon-
ably beholding vnto you for your extreme affec-
tion. Which I muft either leaue vnrequited; or
recompenfe affection with affection, & recommende
me vnto you with your owne Stratageme, fitter to
animate frefher fpirites, or to whet finer edges.
Little other vfe can I, or the world reape of thofe
great-great commendations, wherewith you, and
diuers other Orient wittes haue newly furcharged
me, by tendring fo many kinde Apologies in my
behalfe, and prefenting fo many fharpe inuectiues
againft my aduerfaries: vnleffe alfo you purpofed

to make me notably afhamed of my cōfeffed in-
fufficiency, guilty of fo manifold imperfectiōs, in
refpect of the leaft femblance of thofe imputed
fingularities. Whatfoeuer your intendment in an
ouerflowing affection was, I am none of thofe,
that greedily furfet of felfe-conceit, or fottifhly
hugge their owne babyes. *Narciffus* was a fayre
boy, but a boy: *Suffenus* a noble braggard, but
a braggard: *Neftor* a fweet-tongued old-man, but
an Old-man: and *Tully* (whom I honour in his
vertues, and excufe in his ouerfightes) an eloquent
Selfe-loouer, but a Selfe-loouer. He that thought
to make himfelfe famous with his ouerweening
and brauing *Il'e, Il'e, Il'e,* might perhaps nourrifh
an afpiring imagination to imitate his *Ego, Ego,
Ego,* fo glorioufly reiterated in his gallant Orations.
Some fmirking minions are fine fellowes in their
owne heades, and fome cranke Princockes iolly
men in their owne humours: as defperate in refo-
lution, as the dowtieft ranke of Errant knightes;
and as coye in phantafie, as the niceft fort of
fimpring damofels, that in their owne glaffes find
no creature fo bewtifull, or amiable, as their deli-
tious felues. I haue beheld, / & who hath not
feene fome lofty conceites, towring very high, &
coying themfelues fweetly on their owne amount-
ing winges, young feathers of old Icarus? The
gay Peacocke is woondroufly inamored vpon the

glittering fanne of his owne gorgious taile, and
weeneth himfelfe worthy to be crowned the Prince
of byrdes, and to be enthronifhed in the chaire
of fupreme excellency. Would Chrift, the greene
Popiniay, with his newfangled ieftes, as new as
Newgate, were not afmuch to fay, as his owne
Idol. Queint wittes muft haue a Priuiledge to
prank-vp their dainty limmes, & to fawne vpon
their owne trickfie deuifes. But they that vnpar-
tially know themfelues, feuerely examine their
owne abilities; vprightly counterpoife defectes
with fufficiencies; frankly confeffe the greateft
part of their knowledge, to be the leaft part of
their ignorance; aduifedly weigh the difficulties
of the painfull and toylefome way, the hard
maintenance of credit eafely gotten, the impoffible
fatisfaction of vnfatisfiable expectation, the vncer-
taine fickleneffe of priuate Phantafie, & the cer-
taine brittleneffe of publique Fame; are not lightly
bewitched with a fonde doting vpon their owne
plumes. And they that deepely confider vpon
the weakeneffe of inward frailty, the cafualtie of
outward fortune, the detraction of Enuie, the
virulency of Malice, the counter-pollicy of Am-
bition, and a hundred-hundred empeachments of
growing reputation: that afwell diuinely, as philo-
fophically haue learned to looue the gentleneffe of
Humanity, to embrace the mildneffe of Modeftie,

to kiſſe the meekeneſſe of Humilitie, to loath the odioufneſſe of Pride, to aſſuage the egrenefs of Spite, to preuent the vengeance of Hatred, to reape the ſweet fruites of Temperance, to tread the ſmooth Path of Securitie, to take the firme courſe of Aſſuraunce, / and to enioy the felicitie of Contentment: that iudicioufly haue framed themſelues to carry Mindes, like their Bodies, and Fortunes, as apperteineth vnto them, that would be loth to ouerreach in preſumptuous conceit: they I ſay, and all they that would rather vnderly the reproche of obſcuritie, then ouercharge their mediocritie with an illuſiue opinion of extraordinary furniture, and I wott not what imaginarie complementes: are readier, and a thouſand times readier, to returne the greateſt Prayſes, where they are debt, then to accept the meaneſt, where they are almes. And I could nominate ſome, that in effeꝗ make the ſame reckoning of Letters, Sonets, Orations, or other writinges commendatory, that they do of meate without nouriſhment, of hearbes without vertue, of plants without fruite; of a lampe without oyle, a linke without light, or a fier without heate. Onely ſome of vs are not ſo deuoide of good manner, but we conceiue what belongeth to ciuill duty, and will euer be preſt to interteine Curteſie with curteſie, & to requite any frendſhip with frendſhip: vnfainedly deſirous,

rather to recompenfe in deedes, then to glofe,
or paint in wordes. You may eafely perfuade
me to publifh, that was long fithence finifhed in
writing, and is now almoft difpatched in Print:
(the amendes muft be addreffed in fome other
more materiall Treatife, or more formal Difcourfe :
and haply *Nafhes S. Fame* may fupply fome
defectes of Pierces Supererogation :) but to fuffer
your thrife-affectionate Letters and Sonets, or
rather your thrife-lauifh beneuolences to be pub-
lifhed, which fo farre furmount not onely the
mediocrity of my prefent endeuour, but euen the
poffibility of any my future emproouement; I
could not be perfuaded by any eloquence, or im-
portunacy in the world, were I not as monftroufly /
reuiled by fome other without reafon, as I am
exceffiuely extolled by you without caufe. In
which cafe he may feeme to a difcreet enemy
excufable, to an indifferent frend iuftifiable, that is
not tranfported with his owne paffion, but relyeth
on the iudgement of the learnedeft, and referreth
himfelfe to the Practife of the wifeft. In the one,
efteeming *Plutarch* or *Homer* as an hundred Autors:
in the other, valuing *Cato*, or *Scipio*, as a thoufand
Examples. I neuer read, or heard of any re-
fpectiue, or confiderate perfon, vnder the degree
of thofe that might reuenge at pleafure, contemne
with autority, affecure themfelues from common

obloquy, or commande publique reputation,
(mighty men may finde it a Pollicy, to take a
fingular, or extraordinary courfe), fo carelefle of
his owne credit : fo recklefle of the prefent time,
fo fenfelefle of the pofterity, fo negligent in
occurents of confequence, fo diffolute in his
proceedings, fo prodigall of his name, fo deuoide
of all regarde, fo bereft of common fenfe, fo vilely
bafe, or fo hugely hawtie of minde ; that in cafe
of infamous imputation, or vnworthy reproch,
notorioufly fcattered-abroad, thought it not requi-
fite, or rather neceffary, to ftand vpon his owne
defence according to Equity, and euen to labour
his owne commendation according to the prefented
occafion. Difcourfes yeeld plenty of Reafons : and
Hiftories affourde ftore of Examples. It is no
vain-glory to permit with confideration, that abufed
Modefty hath affected with difcretion. It is vanity
to controwle, that true honour hath practifed : and
folly to condemne, that right wifedome hath
allowed. If any diflike Immodefty indeede, de-
fpife vanity indeede, reprooue Arrogancy indeede,
or loath Vainglory indeede ; I am as forward with
Tongue and Hart as the foremoft of the forwardeft :
and were / my pen anfwerable, perhaps at occafion
it fhould not greatly lagge behinde. To accom-
plifh, or aduaunce any vertuous purpofe, (fith it is
now enforced to be fturring), it might eafely be

entreated, euen to the vttermoſt extent of that
little-little Poſſibility, wherewith it hath pleaſed
the Greateſt to endowe it.   Howbeit Curteſie is as
ready to ouerloade with prayſe, as Malice eger to
ouerthrow with reproch.   Both ouerſhoote, as the
manner is ; but malice is the Diuell.   For my
poore part, I hope the One ſhall do me as little
harme, as fayre weather in my iorney : I am ſuer,
the other hath done me more good, then was
intended, and ſhall neuer puddle or annoy the
courſe of the cleere running water.   Albeit I haue
ſtudied much, and learned little: yet I haue
learned to gleane ſome handfulls of corne out-of
the rankeſt cockle : to make choice of the moſt
fragrant flowers of *Humanitie,* the moſt vertuous
hearbes of *Philoſophie,* the moſt ſoueraine fruites
of *Gouernment,* and the moſt heauenly manna of
Diuinitie : to be acquainted with the fayreſt,
prouided for the fowleſt, delighted with the
temperateſt, pleaſed with the meaneſt, and con-
tented with all *weather.*   Greater men may
profeſſe, and can atchieue greater matters: I
thanke God, I know the lēgth, that is, the ſhortnes
of mine owne foote. If it be any mans pleaſure
to extenuate my ſufficiēcy in other knowledge, or
practiſe, to empeach my ability in wordes, or
deedes, to debaſe my fortune, to abridge my
commendations, or to annihilate my fame, he

fhall finde a cold aduerfary of him, that hath layed hoat paffions awatering, and might eafely be induced to be the Inuectiue of his owne Non-proficiency. Onely he craueth leaue to eftimate his credit, and to value his honefty, as behooueth euery man, that regardeth any good : and if withall it be his / vnfained requeft, that Order fhould repeale diforder ; moderation reftraine licentioufneffe ; difcretion abandon vanity ; mildneffe affuage choller; meekneffe alay arrogancy ; confideration reclaime rafhneffe ; indifferency attemper paffion ; Curtefie mitigate, Charity appeafe, & Vnity attone debate : pardon him. Or, in cafe nothing will preuaile with fury but fury, and nothing can winne defired amity, but pretended hoftility, that muft driue-out one naile with another, & beat-away one wedge with another, according to the Latin Prouerbe : Pardon him alfo, that in the refolution of a good minde, will commaund, what he cannot entreat ; and extort, what he cannot perfuade. That little may be done with no great adoo : and, feeing it may as furely, as eafely be done, I am humbly to befeech eftablifhed Wifedome, to winke at one experiment of aduenturous Folly ; neuer before embarked in any fuch actiō, and euer to efchewe the like with a chary regard, where any other mediation may purchafe redreffe. I will not vrge what conniuence hath been noted in as

diffauorable cafes : it is fufficient for me to pleade
mine own acquittall. Other prayfe he affecteth
not, that in a deepe infight into his innermoft
partes, findeth not the higheft pitch of his Hope,
equiualent to the loweft pit of your commendation.
And if by a gentle conftruction, or a fauorous
encouragement, he feemeth any thing in others
opinion, that is nothing in his owne Cenfure, the
leffer his merite, the greater their mercy ; and the
barrainer his defert, the frutefuller your liberality.
Whofe vnmeafurable prayfes I am to interpret, not
as they may feeme in fome bounteous conceit,
but as they are in mine owne knowledge ; good
wordes, but vnfitly applied ; frendly beneuolences,
but waftfully beftowed ; gallant amplifications, but
flenderly defer/ued : what but termes of Ciuility,
or fauours of Curtefie, or hyperboles of Looue :
whofe franke allowance I fhall not be able to earne
with the ftudy of twenty yeares more : in briefe,
nothing but partiall witneffes, preiudicate iudge-
ments, idle preambles, and in effect meere wordes.
And euen fo as I found them, I leaue them. Yet
let me not difmiffe fo extenfiue curtefie with an
empty hand. Whatfoeuer I am, (that am the
leaft little of my thoughtes, and the greateft
contempt of mine owne hart) *Parthenophill* and
Parthenophe embellifhed, the *Spanifh Counfellour*
Inglifhed, and *Shores Wife* eternifed ; fhall euer-

laftingly teftifie what you are : go forward in
maturity, as ye haue begun in pregnancy, and
behold *Parthenopoeus* the fonne of the braue
Meleager, *Homer* himfelfe, and of the fwift
Atalanta *Calliope* herfelfe : be thou, Barnabe, the
gallant Poet, like Spencer, or the valiant fouldiour,
like Bafkeruile ; and euer remember thy *French
feruice* vnder the braue Earl of Effex. Be thou,
Iohn, the many-tongued Linguift, like Andrewes,
or the curious Intelligencer, like Bodley ; and
neuer forget *thy Netherlandifh traine* vnder Him,
that taught the Prince of Nauarre, now the
valorous king of Fraunce. Be thou Antony, the
flowing Oratour, like Dooue, or the fkilfull Heralde,
like Clarentius ; and euer remember *thy Portugall
voyage* vnder Don Antonio. The beginning of
vertuous Proceedings, is the one halfe of honorable
actions. Be yourfelues in hope, and what your-
felues defire in effect : and I haue attained fome
portion of my requeft. For you cannot wifh fo
exceeding-well vnto me, but I am as ready with
tongue, and minde, to wifh a great-deale better
vnto you, and to reacquite you with a large vfury
of moft-affectionate prayers, recommending you to
the diuine giftes, and gratious bleffings of Heauen.

May / it pleafe the fauorable Reader, to voutfafe
me the Curtefie of his Patience, vntill he hath
thoroughly perufed the whole Difcourfe at his

howers of leyfure (for fuch fcriblings are hardly
worth the vacanteft howers): I am not to im-
portune him any farther ; but would be glad, he
might finde the Whole, leffe tedious in the end,
then fome Parts in the beginning, or midft ; or,
at-leaft, that one peece might helpe to furnifh-out
amendes for an other. And fo taking my leaue
with the kindeft Farewell of a moft thankfull
minde, I defift from wearying him with a tedious
Preface, whom I am likely to tire with fo many
fuperfluous Difcourfes. Howbeit might it happely
pleafe the fweeteft Interceffour, to enfweeten the
bittereft gall of Spite, and to encalme the rougheft
tempeft of Rage ; I could cordially wifh, that
Nafhes S. Fame might be the Period of my
Inuectiues : and *the excellent Gentlewoman*, my
patroneffe, or rather Championeffe in this quarrel,
is meeter by nature, and fitter by nurture, to be
an enchaunting Angell, with her white quill, then
a tormenting Fury with her blacke inke. It re-
maineth at the election of one, whom God indue
with more difcretion.

At London: this 16. of July, 1593. The in-
uiolable frend of his entire frendes, Gabriell
Haruey. /

Her owne Prologue, or Demurr.

O Mufes, may a wooman poore, and blinde,
A Lyon-draggon, or a Bull-beare binde ?
Ift poffible for puling wench to tame
The furibundall Champion of Fame ?
He brandifheth the whurlewinde in his mouth,
And thunderbolteth fo-confounding fhott :
Where fuch a Bombard-goblin, North, or South,
With drad Pen-powder, and the conquerous pott ?
Silly it is, that I can fing, or fay :
And fhall I venture fuch a bluftrous fray ?
Hazard not, panting quill, thy afpen felfe :
Hel'e murther thy conceit, and braine thy braine.
Spare me, ô fuper domineering Elfe,
And moft, railipotent *for euer raine.*

Si Tibi vis ipfi parcere, parce Mihi.

Her Counter-fonnet, or Correction of her owne Preamble.

Scorne *frump the meacock Verfe that dares not fing,*
Drouping, fo like a flagging flowre in raine :
Where doth the Vrany *or* Fury *ring,*
That fhall enfraight my ftomacke with difdaine ?
Shall Frend put-vp fuch braggardous affrontes ?
Are milkfop Mufes fuch whiteliuer'd Trontes ?
Shall Boy the gibbet be of Writers all,
And none hang-vp the gibbet on the wall ?

If | dreery hobbling Ryme hart-broken be,
And quake for dread of Danters fcarecrow Preſſe :
Shrew Proſe, thy pluckcrow implements addreſſe,
And pay the hangman pen his double fee.
Be Spite a Sprite, a Termagant, a Bugg :
Truth feares no ruth, and can the Great Diu'll tugg
          ——*Ultrix accincta flagello.*

Her old Comedy, newly intituled.

My Proſe is reſolute, as Beuis ſworde :
March rampant beaſt in formidable hide :
Supererogation Squire on cockhorſe ride :
Zeale ſhapes an aunſwer to the blouddieſt worde.
If nothing can the booted Souldiour *tame,*
Nor Ryme, nor Proſe, nor Honeſty, nor Shame,
But Swaſh *will ſtill his trompery aduaunce,*
Il'e leade the gagtooth'd fopp *a new-founde daunce.*
Deare howers were euer cheape to pidling me :
I knew a glorious, and brauing Knight,
That would be deem'd a truculentall wight :
Of him I fcrauld a dowty Comedy.
Sir Bombarduccio *was his cruell name :*
But Gnaſharduccio *the ſole brute of* Fame.

L'Enuoy.

See, how He brayes, and fumes at me poore laſſe,
That muſt immortaliſe the killcowe Aſſe. *|*

TO THE RIGHT WORSHIPFVLL, his efpeciall deare frend, M. Gabriell Haruey, Doctour of Lawe.

SWEET M. Doctour Haruey, (for I cannot intitule you with an Epithite of leffe value then that which the Grecian, and Roman Oratours afcribed to Theophraftus, in refpect of fo many your excellent labours, garnifhed with the garland of matchleffe Oratory) : if at any time either the moft earneft perfuafion of a deare frend, and vnufually moft deare, and conftant, adiured therevnto by the fingular vertue of your moft prayfe-worthy, and vnmatchable wit : or the woonderful admiration of your peerleffe conceit, embraued with fo many gorgeous ornamentes of diuine Rhetorique : or the doubtleffe fucceffiue benefit thereof, deuoted to the glory of our Englifh Eloquence, and our vulgar Tufcanifme (if I may fo terme it) ; may worke any plaufible or refpective motions with you to bewtifie, and enrich our age, with thofe moft praife-moouing workes, full of gallanteft difcourfe, and reafon, which I vnderftand by fome affured intelligence be now glowing vpon the anvile, ready to receiue the right artificiall forme of diuineft workemāfhip: thē let I befeech you, nay; by all our mutuall frendfhips I coniure you (loue and admiration of them arming me with the placarde of farther confidence) thofe, and other your incomparable writings, fpeedily, or rather pre/fently, fhew thēfelues in the fhining light of the Sunne. That, by this Publication of fo rare, & rich Difcourfes, our Englifh Rauens, the fpitefull, enemyes to all birdes of more bewtifull wing, and more harmonious note then themfelues, may fhroude themfelues in their nefts of bafeft obfcurity, & keepe hofpitality with battes, and owles, fit conforts for fuch vile carions. Good Sir, arife, and confound thofe Viperous Cryticall monfters, and thofe prophane Atheiftes of our Commonwealth ; which endeuour with their mutinous and Serpentine hiffing, like geefe, not to arme the Senatours and Oratours of Rome, but to daunt, aftonifh, and, if it were poffible, to ouerthrow them. And fithence the very thunder-lightning of your admirable Eloquence, is fufficiētly auailable to ftrike them with a lame Palfie of tongue, (if they be not already fmitten with a fenceleffe Apoplexy in head, which may eafely enfewe fuch contagious Catharres and Reumes, as I am priuy fome of them haue been grieuoufly diffeafed withall), miffe not, but hitt them feurly home, as they deferue with Supererogation. You haue bene reputed euermore, fince firft I heard of you in Oxford and elfewhere, to haue bene as much giuen to fauour, commende, and frequent fuch as were approoued, or toward in learning,

witt, kinde behauiour, or any good quality, as
may be required in any man of your demerit :
an vndoubted figne, how much you loath In-
uectiues or any needeles contētions. I would
(as many your affectionate frēds would) it had
bene your fortune to haue encountred fome
other Paranymphes, then fuch as you are now to
difcipline : moft vnwillingly, I perceiue, but moft
neceffarily, & not without efpeciall confideration,
being fo manifeftly vrged, and grofely prouoked
to defend yourfelfe. But you haue ere now bene
acquainted / with patience perforce : and I hope
the moft defperate fwafher of them will one day
learne to fhew himfelf honefter or wifer. And
thus recommending your fweete endeuours, with
your grauer ftudies, to the higheft treafury of
heauenly Mufes; I right hartely take my leaue
with a Sonnet of that Mufe, that honoreth the
Vrany of du Bartas, and yourfelfe : of du Bartas
elfewhere ; here of him, whofe excellent Pages of
the French King, the Scottifh King, the braue
Monfieur de la Nöe, the aforefayd Lord du Bartas,
Sir Philip Sidney, and fundry other worthy perfon-
ages, deferue immortall commendation. I thanke
him very hartely that imparted vnto me thofe fewe
fheetes : and if all be like them, truly all is paffing
notable, and right fingular.

SONNET:

Thofe learned Oratours, *Roomes auncient fages,*
　Perfuafions Pith, directours of affection,
　The mindes chief counfail, rhetoriques perfection,
　The pleafaunt baulms of peace, warres fierce
　　outrages:
Sweet Grecian Prophets, *whofe fmooth Mufe affuages*
　The Furies powerfull wrath, poifons infection :
　Philofophers *(by Caufes due connexion,*
　Match't with th' Effects of Nature) future ages
Embrauing with rich documents of Art : |
　The wifeft States-men *of calme Commonweales :*
　The learned Generall Councels, *which impart*
　Diuineft laws, whofe wholefome Phyfique Heales
　　Both Church, and Layety : All in one *beholde*
　　Ennobled Arts, as Precious ftones in golde.

From my lodging in Holborne: this of June.
1593. Your moft affectionate,

　　　　　　　　　　　Barnabé Barnes.

Hauing perufed my former Sonet, if it may
pleafe you, Sir, to do afmuch for your deare
frends *Parthenophill,* and *Parthenophe,* they fhall
haue the defired fruite of their fhort exercife, and
will reft beholding to your curteous acceptance:
which they would be glad to reacquite in the
loouingeft manner they may. And fo moft affec-

tionatly recommend themfelues vnto your good felf: whofe vnblemifhed fame they will euermore maintaine with the beft bloud of their hartes, tongues, and Pennes. We will not fay, how much we long to fee the whole Prayfes of your two notorious enemyes, the *Affe* and the *Foxe*.

Sonet.

Nafh, or the confuting Gentleman.

The Mufes fcorne ; the Courtiers laughing-ftock ;
  The Countreys Coxecombe ; Printers proper new ;
  The Citties Leprofie ; the Pandars ftew ;
  Vertues difdayne ; honefties aduerfe rock ;
Enuies vile champion ; flaunders ftumblingblock.
  Graund | Oratour of Cunny-catchers crew ;
  Bafe broaching tapfter of reports vntrue ;
  Our moderne Viper, and our Countryes mock ;
True Valors Cancer-worme, fweet Learnings ruft.
  Where fhall I finde meete colours, and fit wordes,
  For fuch a counterfaict, and worthleffe matter ?
Him, whom thou rayleft on at thine owne luft,
  Sith Bodine *and fweet* Sidney *did not flatter,*
  His Inuectiue thee too much grace affordes.
                                    Parthenophil.

SONET.

Haruey, or the fweet Doctour.

Sidney, *fweet Cignet, pride of Thamefis ;*
   Apollos laurell ; Mars-his proud prowefe :
Bodine, *regifter of Realmes happinefe,*
   Which Italyes, and Fraunces wonder is :
Hatcher, *with filence whom I may not mife :*
   Nor Lewen, *Rhetoriques richeft noblefe :*
Nor Wilfon, *whofe difcretion did redrefe*
   Our Englifh Barbarifme : adioyne to this
Diuineft morall Spencer *: let thefe fpeake*
   By their fweet Letters, which do beft vnfould
Harueys *deferued praife : fince my Mufe weake*
   Cannot relate fomuch as hath bene tould
By thefe Fornam'd *: then, vaine it were to bring*
   New feather to his Fames fwift-feathered wing.
                             Parthenophe.

THE PRINTERS ADUERTISSE-
ment to the Gentleman Reader.

Curteous Gentlemen, it feemed good to M. Doctour
Haruey, for breuity-fake, and becaufe he liked not
ouer-long Preambles, or Poftambles, to fhort dis-
courfes, to omit the commendatorie Letters, and Son-
nets of M. Thorius, M. Chewt, and diuers other
his affectionate frendes of London, and both the

Vniuerſities. Which neuertheleſſe, are reſerued to be prefixed, inſerted, or annexed, either in his defenſiue Letters, *enlarged with certaine new Epiſtles of more ſpeciall note; or in his* Diſcourſes of Naſhes S. Fame, *already finiſhed, & preſently to be publiſhed, as theſe ſhall like their interteinement: of whoſe fauorable & plauſible Welcome, diuers learned and fine wittes haue preſumed the beſt. Howbeit finally it was thought not amiſſe, vpon conference with ſome his aduiſed acquaintance, to make choice of ſome two or three of the reaſonableſt, and temperateſt Sonnets (but for variety, & to auoyde tedioufneſſe in the entrance, rather to be annexed in the end, then prefixed in the beginning of the preſent Diſcourſes): one of the foreſayd* M. Thorius, *an other of* M. Chewt, *and the third of a learned French gentleman,* Monſieur Fregeuill Gautius, *who hath publiſhed ſome weighty Treatiſes, aſwell Politique as Religious, both in Latin and French; and hath acquainted* M. Doctour Haruey *with certaine moſt profitable Mathematicall deuiſes of his own inuention. The reſidue is not added by me, but annexed by the Autor himſelfe: whom I humbly recommende to your curteous Cenſure, and ſo reſt from ouertroubling you with my vnpoliſhed lines.*

VI.

PIERCE'S SUPEREROGATION OR A NEW PRAYSE OF THE OLDE ASSE.

1593.

NOTE.

It will be noticed that the title-page of 'Pierce's Supererogation' is identical with that of its slender precursor (see relative Note, page 2). So that the precursor was a 'preparative' to a 'preparative,' although the Printer in his Epistle to the former deals with the so-called 'Preparative' as really 'Nashes S. Fame,' by appending to it the Letters and Sonnets specified by him. As stated in Note before the Precursor, I am indebted for our text to the Huth Library. See Memorial-Introduction for more.

A. B. G.

Pierces Supererogation

OR

A NEW PRAYSE OF THE
OLD ASSE.

A Preparatiue to certaine larger Difcourfes, intituled
NASHES S. FAME.

Gabriell Haruey.

IL VOSTRO
MALIGNARE NON
GIOVA NVLLA.

(*Touch, and respectfully,
the tree.*)

LONDON
Imprinted by Iohn Wolfe.
1593.

Pierces Supererogation.

OR

A NEW PRAYSE OF THE

OLD ASSE.

A Preparatiue to certaine larger Difcourses, intituled

NASHES S. FAME.

 Was euer vnwilling to vndertake any enterprife, that was vnmeete for me ; or to play any part, either in earneft, or in ieft, that might ill befeeme me : and neuer more vnwilling then at this in-ftant, when I muft needes do it, or put fomething in hazard, that I would be loth to commit to the curtefie of aduenture. Not becaufe my Confuters fwordes, or my enemies daggers carry any credite with the wife ; or becaufe my Letters feare any

difcredite with the honeft ; or becaufe I cannot
abide to be confuted, that daily confute my felfe,
and condemne euery mine owne default with
rigour : but becaufe Silence may feeme fufpicious
to many ; Patience contemptible to fome ; A good
minde, A bad hart to thofe, that value all by
courage ; A knowne forbearer of Libellers, A
continuall bearer of coales ; and there is no end
of abufes vpon abufes, of iniuries vpon iniuries,
of contempt vpon contempt, where prefumptuous
Impudency, and odious Slaunder, the two errantift
vagabonds in the world, may fafe conduct them-
felues, and franckely paffe vncontrolled.   Yet were
that, either / all, or the worft of all, I could ftill
vow filence in brawles, and would ftill profeffe
Patience in wronges : (I hate brawles with my
hart : and can turne-ouer A volume of wronges
with a wett finger :) but fome cunning men, that
carry hooney in their mouthes, and gall in their
hartes, not fo fweete in the Premiffes, as bitter in
the Conclufion, can fmoothly, and finely defcant
vpon the leaft aduantage, howfoeuer iniurious :
and certaine pretty Experiences, by way of fenfible
inftruction, haue taught fome, that Malice was
neuer fuch an hypocrite, as now ; and the world
neuer fuch a Scoggin, as now ; & the Diuell neuer
fuch a knaue, as now : & what a defperate
diffoluteneffe were it in him, that regardeth his

good name, to abandon himſelfe, or to relinquiſh the deereſt thing in this life, (I know no deerer thing, then honeſt credite) to the fauour of Enuy, or to the diſcretion of Fortune? Gentlemen, he is hardly beſtead for a Patrone, that relyeth on the tuition of Enuy, or repoſeth his affiance in the protection of Fortune: and he muſt not take it vnkindely, to bee forſaken of other by the way, that forſaketh himſelfe in the way. Euen he that loueth not to be his owne defender, much leſſe his owne prayſer (do him no wrong, my Maſters, though ye doe him no right) yet hateth to be his owne traytor: and hath reaſon to experimente ſome rounde concluſions, before hee offer his throte to the blade of villany, or his forhead to the brand of diffamation. And although he be the ſubiect of his own contempt, and the argument of his owne Satyres: (ſurely no man leſſe doteth vpon himſelfe, or more ſeuerely cenſureth his own imperfections:) yet he in ſome reſpects diſdayneth to be reuiled by the abiects of the world. Whoſe diſpraiſe in ſome age were a commendation, and whoſe praiſe an inuectiue: but this is a queint world, and needeth no Aprill / ſhowers, to furniſh May-games. I proteſt, I haue theſe many yeeres, not in pride, but in iudgement, ſcorned, to appeere in the rancke of this ſcribling generation: and could not haue bene hired with a

great fee, to publifh any Pamflet of whatfoeuer
nature, in mine owne name, had I not bene in-
tollerably prouoked, firft by one rakehell, and now
by an other, the two impudenteft mates, that
euer haunted the preffe: (fome haue called them
knaues in grofe: I haue found them fooles in
retayle:) but when it came to this defperate point,
that I muft needes either bee a bafe writer, or a
vile Affe in printe, the leffe of the two euils was
to be chofen : and I compelled rather to alter my
refolution for a time, then to preiudice my felfe
for euer.   They that lift may feede at the manger
with the fonnes of the Mule : it is another Table-
Philofophy, that I fanfie.   Howbeit amongft all
the misfortunes, that euer happened vnto me, I
account it my greateft affliction, that I am con-
ftrained to bufy my penne, without ground, or
fubftance of difcourfe, meete for an actiue and
induftrious world.   Euery man hath his croffes
in one accident, or other : but I know not a
greeuouffer perfecution, then a bafe employment
of precious time, neceffarily enforced.   Other
croffes may fomeway edifie : this is a plague
without remedy ; a torment without end ; a hell
without redemption.   As in the courfe of my
ftudy, it was allwayes my reckoning ; He loofeth
nothing, whatfoeuer he lofeth, that gaineth Time :
fo in the tafke of my writing, or other exercife,

it is my account ; He gayneth nothing, whatfoeuer
he gayneth, that loofeth Time. A good matter,
deliuered in good manner, winneth fome eftimation
with good mindes: but no manner fufficient to
countenance a contemptible Theame : & a rafcall
fubiect abafeth any forme : or what hath drowned
the / memory of the trimmeft, and daintieft trifles,
that fine conceit hath deuifed ?   Were it mine
owne election, I might worthily incurre many
reproofes, and iuftly impute them to my fimple
choyce : but Neceffity hath as little free will, as
Law ; and compelleth like a Tyrant, where it
cannot perfwade, like an Oratour, or aduife like a
Counfellour. Any Vertue, an honourable Common-
place, and a flourifhing braunch of an heauenly
tree : Politique, and militar affaires, the woorthieft
matters of confultation, and the two Herculean
pillers of noble ftates : the priuate liues of
excellent perfonages in fondry courfes, and the
publike actions of puiffant nations in fondry
gouernementes, fhining mirrours of ' notable vfe
for the prefent time, and future ages.   Were it
at my appointment, to difpofe freely of mine
owne howers : O how willingly, and cheerefully
could I fpend the frefheft & deereft part of my
life, in fuch argumentes of valour?   Learninge is
a goodly and gallant Creature in many partes : &
diuers members of that beautifull body vpbraide

the moſt-exquiſite penne, and moſt-curious pencil
of inſufficiency : no diligence too-much, where no
labour inough : the fruitefulleſt ſciences require
painefulleſt induſtry, and ſome liuely principles
would be touched to the quicke : whatſoeuer
booke-caſe, or ſchole-point is found by experience
to be eſſentiall, and practicable in the world,
deſerueth to be diſcuſſed with ſharpe inuention,
and found iudgement.   I could yet take pleaſure,
and proffite, in canuaſſing ſome Problems of
naturall Philoſophy, of the Mathematiques, of
Geography, and Hydrography, of other com-
modious experimentes, fit to aduaunce many
valorous actions : and I would, vppon mine owne
charges, trauaile into any parte of Europe, to
heare ſome pregnant Paradoxes, and certaine
ſingular queſtions in the / higheſt profeſſions of
Learning, in Phyſick, in Law, in Diuinity,
effectually and thoroughly diſputed *pro, & contra :*
and would thinke my trauaile as aduantageouſly
beſtowed to ſome purpoſes of importance, as they
that haue aduenturouſly diſcouered new-found
Landes, or brauely ſurprized Indies.   What con-
ferences, or diſputations, what Parliaments, or
Councels, like thoſe, that deliberate vpon the beſt
gouernement of Commonwealthes, and the beſt
diſcipline of Churches ; the dubble anchor of the
mighty ſhipp, and the two great Luminaries of

the world? Other extrauagant difcourfes, not materiall, or quarrelous contentions, not auaileable, are but waftinge of winde, or blotting of paper. What fhould Exercife, or ftuddy, burne the Sunne or the candle in vaine? or what fhould I doe againft my felfe, in fpeakinge for my felfe, if outward refpectes did not inwardly gripe, and a prefent exigence lay violent handes vpon me? Though extremity be powerable, yet an vnwilling will is excufable. Philofophers, and Lawyers can beft argue the cafe of inuoluntary actes: but what fo forcible, as compulfion: or fo pardonable, as a paffiue action? Blame him not, or blame him gently, that would be a little loth, to be dieted at the racke of the old Affe, or to be bitten of the young dog. He is no party in the caufe, that pleadeth thus againft *Ariftogiton.* Sweet Gentlemen, imagine it to be a fpeech, addreffed vnto your felues. *Peraduenture the viper did neuer bite any of you; and the Gods forbid, it fhould euer bite you: but when you efpie any fuch pernicious creature, you prefently difpatch it: in like manner when you behold a Sycophant, and a man of a viperous nature, looke not till he hath bitten fome of you, but fo foone as he ftarteth-vp, pull him downe.* And againe in another place of the fame fententious, and politique Oration: *Hee that | mainetayneth a Sycophant, is by nature and kinde an ennemy of the good:*

vnleſſe ſome-body imagine, that the ſeede and roote of a naughty Sycophant ought to remaine in the Citty, as it were for ſtore, or good huſbandry. Demoſthenes was as deepely wiſe, as highly eloquent : and hath many ſuch notable ſentences, as it were Caueats, or Prouiſoes, againſt the daungerous ennemies of that flouriſhing Citty, and eſpecially againſt Calumnia-tours, whoſe viperous ſting hee could by no meanes auoide : albeit otherwiſe ſuch an Oratour, as could allure heartes with perſwaſion, or coniure mindes with aſtoniſhment. I would no other Citty loued figges: or muſt an other Citty of neceſſity loue figges, becauſe it is growne an other Athens, a mother of eloquence, a nurſe of learning, a grandame of valour, a ſeat of honor, and as Ariſtotle termed Athens, a garden of Alcinous, wherein one fruite ripeneth vpon an other, one peare vppon an other, one grape vpon an other, and one figge vppon an other. The Sycophant be his owne interpreter : & if he may be licenſed, or permitted to bee his owne caruer too, much good may it doe him, and ſweete digeſtion geue him ioy of his dainety figg. I muſt haue a little care of one, that cãnot eaſily brucke vnreaſonable ſawcineſſe : & would be loth to ſee the garden of Alcinous made the garden of Greene, or Motley. It was wont to be ſaid by way of a Prouerbe ; Hee that will be made a ſheepe, ſhall find wolues inough : but forſooth this

exceeding-wife worlde, is a great Affe-maker: and
he that will fuffer himfelfe to be proclaimed an
Affe in printe, fhall bee fure neuer to want loade
and loade inough. Who fo ready to call her
neighbour, a fkold, as the rankeft fkold of the
parifh : or who fo forward to accufe, to debafe, to
reuile, to crow-treade an other, as the arranteft
fellow in a country? Let his owne mouth / be his
pafport, or his owne penne his warrant: & who
fo leawd as his greateft aduerfary, modefty: or fo
honeft, as his deereft frend, villany : or fo learned,
as his learnedeft counfell, vanity : or fo wife, as
his profoundeft Autor, young Apuleius. What
familiar fpirite of the Ayre, or fire, like the
glibb, & nimble witt of young Apuleius? or
where is the Eloquence that fhould defcribe the
particular perfections of young Apuleius? Pru-
dence, may borrow, difcretion: Logique, argu-
ments ; Rhetorique, coulours ; Phantafy, conceites;
Steele, an edge ; and Gold, a lufter, of young
Apuleius. O the rare, and queint Inuention, ô
the gallant, and gorgeous Elocution : ô the braue,
and admirable amplifications : ô the artificiall, and
fine extenuations : ô the liuely pourtraitures of
egregious prayfes, and difprayfes : ô the cunning,
and ftraunge mingle-mangles : ô the pithy ieftes,
and maruelous girdes of yong Apuleius : the very
prodigality of Art, and Nature. What greater

impoffibility, then to decipher the high, and mighty
ftile of young Apuleius, without a liberall portion
of the fame eleuate fpirite? Happy the old father,
that begat, and thrife happy the fweete Mufes,
that fuckled, and foftered young Apuleius. Till
Admiration hath found-out a fmoother and trickfier
quill for the purpofe : Defire muft be content to
leaue the fupple and tidy conftitution of his omni-
fufficient Witt, vndifplayed. Onely it becommeth
gentle mindes to yeeld themfelues thanckefull ; and
to tender their bounden duety to that ineftimable
pearle of Eloquence, for this precious glimze of
his incomprehenfible valour ; one fhorte Maxime,
but more worth, then all the Axioms of Ariftotle ;
or the Idees of Plato ; or the Aphorifmes of
Hippocrates ; or the Paragraphes of Iuftinian.
He knoweth not to manage his penne, that was
not born with an Affe / in his mouth; a foole in
his throate ; and a knaue in his whole body.
Simple men may write againft other, or pleade for
themfelues : but they cannot confute cuttingly,
like a hackfter of Queen-Hith, or bellow luftely,
like the foreman of the Heard. I goe not about
to difcouer an Affe in an Oxes hide : hee needeth
no other to pull him by the famous eares, that is
fo hafty to defcry, and fo bufy to beftirre his wifeft
partes: but what a notable Affe indeede was I,
that fought the winges of a mounting Pegafus, or

a ftying Phenix, where I found the head, & feete
of a braying creature? Some promifes, are des-
perate debtes: and many threatninges, empty
cloudes ; or rather armies fighting in the ayre,
terrible vifions. Simplicity cannot dubble: and
plaine dealing will not diffemble. I looked either
for a fine-witted man, as quicke as quick-filuer,
that with a nimble dexterity of liuely conceite, and
exquifite fecretaryfhip, would out-runne mee many
hundred miles in the courfe of his dainty deuifes ;
a delicate minion : or fome terrible bombarder of
tearmes, as wilde as wild-fire, that at the firft flafh
of his fury, would leaue me thunder-ftricken vpon
the ground, or at the laft volley of his outrage,
would batter me to duft, and afhes. A redoubted
aduerfary. But the trimme filke-worme, I looked
for, (as it were in a proper contempt of common
fineneffe) prooueth but a filly glow-woorme : and
the dreadfull enginer of phrafes, in fteede of
thunderboltes, fhooteth nothing but dogboltes, and
catboltes, and the homelieft boltes of rude folly.
Such arrant confuting ftuffe, as neuer print faw
compiled together, till maifter Villany became an
Autor; and Sir Nafh a gentleman. Printers, take
hede how ye play the Heralds : fome lufty gentle-
men of the maker, can no fooner bare a Goófe-
quill, or a Woodcockes feather in their fhield, but
they / are like the renowmed Lobbelinus, when hee

had gotten a new coate: and take vpon them, without pitty, or mercy, like the onely Lordes of the field. If euer Efquier raued with conceit of his new Armes, it is Danters gentleman : that mightily defpifeth, whatfoeuer hee beholdeth from the high turret of his creaft, and cranckly fpitteth vppon the heads of fome, that were not greatly acquaynted with fuch familiar enterteinement. His beft frende, be his Iudge : and I appeale to my worft ennemy, whether he neuer read a more peftilent example of proftituted Impudency? Were hee not a kinfeman of the forefayd viper, a Dog in malice, a Calfe in witt, an Oxe in learning, and an Affe in difcretion : (time fhall cronicle him, as he is :) was it poffible, that any mã fhould haue beftowed fome broad, and loud tearmes, as he hath done? Who could abide it, without actuall reuenge, but hee, that enterteineth fpite with a fmile, maketh a paftime of Straunge Newes ; turneth choler into fanguine, vineger into wine, vexation into fport, and hath a falue for a greater fore.

Come young Sophifters, you that affecte raylinge in your difputations, and with a clamorous howte would fet the Philofophy fchooles *non plus* : come olde cutters, you that vfe to make dowty frayes in the ftreetes, and would hack-it terribly : come hee- and fhee-fcoldes, you that loue to pleade-it-out

inuincibly at the barre of the dunghill, & will
rather loofe your liues, then the laft word: come
bufy commotioners, you that carry a world of
quarrelous wits, and mutinous tounges in your
heads : come moft-redowted Momus, you that
will fternely keepe heauen, and earth in awe :
come running heads, and giddy pennes of all
humours, you that daunce attendance vpon oddeft
fafhions : and learne a perfect methode, to paffe
other, and to excell your / felues : fuch a new-
deuifed modell, as neuer faw Sun before, & may
make the gayeft mold of antiquity to blufh. Old
Archilochus, and Theon, were but botchers in
their rayling faculty : Stefichorus, but a grofe
bungler : Ariftarchus but a curious, and nice foole :
Ariftophanes and Lucian but merry iefters : Ibis
againft Ouid ; Meuius againft Horace ; Carbilius
Pictor againft Virgill ; Lauinius againft Terence ;
Crateua againft Euripides ; Zoilus againft Homer,
but ranke fowters. Saluft did but dally with
Tully : Demades but toy with Demofthenes :
Pericles but fporte with Thucydides, and fo foorth.
For examples are infinite : and no exercife more
auncient, then Iambiques amongft Poetes ; In-
uectiues amongft Oratours ; Confutations amongft
Philofophers ; Satyres amongft Carpers ; Libels
amongft factioners; Pafquils amongft Malcontentes;
and quarrells amongft all. But the Olde Affe was

an Infante in Witt, and a Grammer Scholler in Arte :
Lucians Rhetor, neuer fo brauely furnifhed, will
be heard with an Eccho : Iulian will rattle Chris-
tendome : Arrius will fhake the Church : Mac-
chiauell will yerke the Commonwealth: Vnico
Aretino will fcourge Princes : and heere is a lufty
ladd of the Caftell, that will binde Beares, and ride
golden Affes to death.   Were the pith of courage
loft, it might be founde in his penne : or were
the marrow of conceite to feeke, where fhould witt
looke for witt, but in his Inckebottle ? Arte was
a Dunfe, till Hee was a writer : and the quickeft
Confuter, a drowfy dreamer, till he put a life into
the dead quill, & a flye into the woodden boxe of
forlorne Pandora.   A pointe for the Satyrift, whofe
conceite is not a Ruffian in folio : and a figg for
the Confuter, that is not a Swafhbucler with his
pen.   Old whimwhams haue plodded on, long
enough : frefh inuention from the tapp, muft /
haue his frifkes, & careers an other while : and
what comparable to this fpowte of yarking elo-
quence ? Giue me the fellow, that is as Peerelefle,
as Pennylefle ; and can oppofe all the Libraries
in Poules Churchyard, with one wonderfull work
of Supererogation ; fuch an vnmatcheable peece
of Learning, as no bookes can counteruaile, but
his owne ; the onely recordes of the fingularities
of this age.   Did I fpeake at a venture, I might

deceiue, and be deceiued : but where Experience is a witneffe, and iudgement the Iudge, I hope the errour will not be vnreafonably great.

There was a time, when I floted in a fea of encountring waues; and deuoured many famous confutations, with an eager, and infatiable appetite: efpecially Ariftotle againft Plato, and the old Philofophers: diuers excellent Platoniftes, indued with rare, & diuine wittes, (of whome elfewhere at large,) Iuftinus Martyr, Philoponus, Valla, Viues, Ramus, againft Ariftotle: oh but the great maifter of the fchooles, and high Chauncellour of Vniuerfities, could not want pregnant defence : Perionius, Gallandius, Carpentarius, Sceggius, Lieblerus againft Ramus: what? hath the royall Profeffour of Eloquence, and Philofophy, no fauourites? Talæus, Offatus, Freigius, Minos, Rodingus, Scribonius, for Ramus againft them; and fo foorth, in that hott contradictory courfe of Logique, and Philofophy. But alas filly men, fimple Ariftotle, more fimple Ramus, moft fimple the reft, either ye neuer knew, what a fharpe-edged, & cutting Confutation meant: or the date of your ftale oppofitions is expired; and a new-found land of confuting commodities difcouered, by this braue Columbus of tearmes, and this onely marchant venturer of quarrels ; that detecteth new Indies of Inuention, & hath the winds of Æolus

at commaundement. Happy, you flourifhinge
youthes, / that follow his incomparable learned
fteps: and vnhappy we old Dunfes, that wanted
fuch a worthy Prefident of all nimble and liuely
dexterities. What fhould I appeale infinite other
to their perpetuall fhame: or fummon fuch, and
fuch to their foule difgrace? Erafmus in Latine,
and Sir Thomas More in Englifh, were fuppofed
fine, and pleafant Confuters in their time, and were
accordingly embraced of the forwardeft and trim-
meft wittes: but alacke how vnlike this dainty
minion? Agrippa was reputed a gyant in con-
futation; a demi-god in omnifufficiency of know-
ledge; a diuell in the practife of horrible Artes:
oh, but Agrippa was an vrcheon, Copernicus a
fhrimpe, Cardan a puppy, Scaliger a baby, Para-
celfus a fcab, Eraftus a patch, Sigonius a toy,
Cuiacius a bable to this Termagant; that fighteth
not with fimple wordes, but with dubble fwordes:
not with the trickling water of Helicon, but with
piercing Aqua fortis: not with the forry powder
of Experience, but with terrible gunpowder: not
with the fmall fhott of contention, but with the
maine ordinaunce of fury. For breuity I ouerfkip
many notable men, and valorous Confuters in their
feuerall vaines: had not affection otherwhiles
fwinged their reafon, where reafon fhould haue
fwayed their affection. But Partiality, was euer

the busiest Actour; and Passion, the whottest
Confuter: whatsoeuer plausible cause otherwise
pretended: and hee is rather to bee esteemed an
Angell, then a man, or a man of Heauen, not of
Earth, that tendereth integrity in his hart; equity
in his tounge; and reason in his penne. Flesh,
and bloud are fraile Creatures, and partiall dis-
coursers: but he approacheth neerest vnto God,
& yeeldeth sweetest fruite of a diuine disposition,
that is not transported with wrath, or any blinde
passion, but guided with cleere, / and pure Reason,
the soueraigne principle of sound proceeding. It
is not the Affirmatiue, or Negatiue of the writer,
but the trueth of the matter written, that carryeth
meat in the mouth, and victory in the hande.
There is nothing so exceeding foolish, but hath
beene defended by some wise man: nor any thinge
so passinge wise, but hath bene confuted by some
foole. Mans will, no safe rule, as Aristotle sayth:
good Homer sometime sleepeth: S. Augustine was
not ashamed of his retractations: S. Barnard saw
not all thinges: and the best chart may eftsoones
ouerthrow. He that taketh a Confutation in
hand, must bringe the standard of Iudgement
with him; & make Wisedome the moderatour of
Wit. But I might aswell haue ouerpassed the
censure, as the persons: & I haue to do with a
party, that valueth both alike, and can phansy no

Autor, but his owne phanfy.   It is neyther reafon,
nor rime, nor witt, nor arte, nor any imitation, that
hee regardeth : hee hath builded towers of Super-
arrogation in his owne head, and they muft ftand,
whofoeuer fall.   Howbeit I cannot ouerflipp fome
without manifeft iniury, that deferue to haue their
names enrolled in the firft rancke of valiant Con-
futers : worthy men, but fubieƈt to imperfeƈtions,
to errour, to mutuall reproofe ; fome more, fome
leffe, as the manner is.   Harding, and Iewell, were
our Efchines, and Demofthenes : and fcarfely any
language in the Chriftian world, hath affoorded a
payre of aduerfaries, equiualent to Harding, and
Iewell ; two thundring and lightning Oratours in
diuinity : but now at laft infinitely ouermatched by
this hideous thunderbolt in humanity ; that hath
the onely right tearmes inueƈtiue, and triumpheth
ouer all the fpirites of Contradiƈtion.   You that
haue read Luther againft the Pope : Sandolet,
Longolius, Omphalius, Oforius, againft / Luther :
Caluin againft Sadolet : Melanchthon againft Lon-
golius : Sturmius againft Omphalius : Haddon
againft Oforius : Baldwin againfte Caluin : Beza
againfte Baldwin : Eraftus againft Beza : Trauers
againft Eraftus : Sutcliff againft Trauers : and fo
foorth : (for there is no ende of endleffe con-
trouerfies : nor Bellarmine fhall euer fatisfye the
Proteftantes : nor Whittaker contente the Papiftes :

nor Bancroft appeafe the Precifians: nor any reafon
pacify affection: nor any authority refolue obfti-
nacy:) you that haue moft diligently read thefe,
and thefe, and fundry other, reputed excellente in
their kindes, caft them all away, and read him
alone: that can fchoole them all in their tearmes
inuectiue, and teacheth a new-found Arte of con-
futing, his all-onely Arte.   Martin himfelfe but
a meacocke: and Papp-hatchet himfelfe but a
milkefop to him: that inditeth with a penne of
fury, and the incke of vengeance; and hath cart-
loades of paperfhot, and chainfhot at commaunde-
ment.   Tufh, no man can blafon his Armes,
but himfelfe.   Behold the mighty Champion, the
dubble fword-bearer, the redowtable fighter with
both handes, that hath robbed William Conquerour
of his furname, and in the very firft page of his
Straunge Newes, choppeth-off the head of foure
Letters at a blow.   Hee it is, that hath it rightly
in him indeede; and can roundly doe the feate,
with a witneffe.   Why, man, he is worth a
thoufand of thefe pidlinge and driblinge Con-
futers, that fitt all day buzzing vpon a blunt
point, or two: and with much adoe drifle out
as many fentences in a weeke, as he will powre-
downe in an howre.   It is not long, fince the
goodlyeft graces of the moft-noble Common-
wealthes vpon Earth, Eloquence in fpeech, and

Ciuility in manners, arriued in thefe remote parts
of the world: it was a happy reuolution of the /
heauens, and worthy to be chronicled in an Eng-
lifh Liuy, when Tiberis flowed into the Thames;
Athens remoued to London; pure Italy, and fine
Greece planted themfelues in rich England; Apollo
with his delicate troupe of Mufes, forfooke his old
mountaines, and riuers; and frequented a new
Parnaffus, and an other Helicon, nothinge in-
feriour to the olde, when they were moft folemnely
haunted of diuine wittes, that taught Rhetorique
to fpeake with applaufe, and Poetry to fing with
admiration.   But euen fince that flourifhing trans-
plantation of the daintieft, and fweeteft lerning,
that humanitie euer tafted; Arte did but fpringe
in fuch, as Sir Iohn Cheeke, and M. Afcham: &
witt budd in fuch, as Sir Phillip Sidney, & M.
Spencer; which were but the violetes of March,
or the Primerofes of May: till the one begane to
fprowte in M. Robart Greene, as in a fweating
Impe of the euer-greene Laurell; the other to
bloffome in M. Pierce Pennileffe, as in the riche
garden of pore Adonis: both to growe to per-
fection, in M. Thomas Nafhe; whofe prime is a
harueft, whofe Arte a mifterie, whofe witt a miracle,
whofe ftile the onely life of the preffe, and the very
hart-blood of the Grape.   There was a kind of
fmooth, and clenly, and neate, and fine elegancy

before : (proper men, handfome giftes :) but alacke,
nothinge liuelie, and mightie, like the braue *vino
de monte*, till his frifking penne began to playe the
Sprite of the buttry, and to teach his mother-
tongue fuch lufty gambolds, as may make the
gallanteft French, Italian, or Spanifh gagliards to
blufhe, for extreame fhame of their ideot fim-
plicitie. The difference of wittes is exceeding
ftraung, and almoft incredible. Good lord, how
may one man paffe a thoufand, and a thoufande
not compare with one? Arte may giue out pre-
cepts, and directoryes / in *communi forma :* but it
is fuperexcellent witt, that is the mother pearle
of precious Inuention; and the goulden mine of
gorgeous Elocution. Na, it is a certaine pregnant,
and liuely thing without name, but a queint miftery
of mounting conceit, as it were a knacke of dex-
terity, or the nippitaty of the nappieft grape, that
infinitly furpaffeth all the Inuention, and Elocution
in the world; and will bunge Demofthenes owne
mouth with new-fangled figures of the right ftampe,
maugre all the thundering, and lightninge Periodes
of his eloquenteft orations, forlorne creatures. I
haue had fome prettie triall of the fineft Tufcanifme
in graine; and haue curioufly obferued the cun-
ningeft experiments, and braueft complements of
afpiring emulation: but muft geeue the bell of
fingularity, to the humorous witt; and the gar-

land of victory, to the *dominiering Eloquence.* I
come not yet to the Praife of the olde Affe: it
is young Apuleius, that feedeth vpon this glory:
and hauing enclofed thefe rancke commons, to
the proper vfe of himfelfe, & the capricious flocke;
adopteth whom he lifteth, without exception: as
Alexander the great, had a huge intention, to haue
all men his fubiectes, and all his fubiectes called
Alexanders.   It was ftrange newes for fome, to be
fo affefied: and a worke of Supererogation for
him, fo bountifully to voutchfafe his golden name:
the appropriate cognifance of his noble ftile.   God-
night poore Rhetorique of forry bookes: adieu
good old Humanity: gentle Artes, and Liberall
Sciences content your felues: Farewell my deere
moothers, fometime floorifhing Vniuerfities: fome
that haue long continued your fonnes in Nature ;
your apprentifes in Arte; your feruauntes in Exer-
cife; your louers in affection; and your vaffalles
in duety: muft either take their leaues of their
fweeteft freendes; or become / the flaues of that
dominiering eloquence, that knoweth no Art but
the cutting Arte; nor acknowledgeth any fchoole,
but the Curtifan fchoole.   The reft is pure
naturall, or wondrous fupernaturall.   Would it
were not an infectious bane, or an incroching
pocke.   Let me not bee miftaken by finifter con-
ftruction, that wreafteth and wrigleth euery fillable

to the worft.   I haue no reference to my felfe ;
but to my fuperiours by incomparable degrees.
To be a Ciceronian, is a flowting ftocke: poore
Homer, a wofull wight, may put his finger in a
hole, or in his blind eye: the excellenteft hiftories,
and woorthieft Chronicles, (ineftimable monu-
mentes of wifdome, and valour,) what but ftale
Antickes?   the flowers, and fruites of delicate
humanity, that were wont to be dainetily and
tenderly conferued, now preferued with duft, as
it were with fugar, and with hoare, as it were
with hoony.   That frifking wine, & that liuely
knacke in the right capricious veine, the onely
booke, that holdeth-out with a countenance ; and
will be heard, when woorme-toungued Oratours,
duft-footed Poets, and weatherwife hiftorians fhall
not bee allowed a woord to caft at a dogg.   There
is a fatall Period of whatfoeuer wee terme flourifh-
inge: the worlde runneth on wheeles: and there
muft be a vent for all thinges.   The Ciceronian
may fleepe, til the Scogginift hath plaid his part:
One fure Conny-catcher, woorth twenty Philofo-
phers: A phantafticall rimefter, more vendible,
then the notableft Mathematician : no profeffion,
to the faculty of rayling: all harfh, or obfcure,
that tickleth not idle phantafies with wanton
dalliance, or ruffianly ieftes.   Robin Good-fellow
the meeteft Autor for Robin Hoodes Library: the

leſſe of Cambridge, or Oxforde, the fitter to
compile woorkes of Supererogation: and wee
that were ſimply trayned after the / Athenian, and
Romane guiſe, muſt bee contente to make roome
for roiſters, that know their place, and will take it.
Titles, and tearmes are but woordes of courſe: the
right fellow, that beareth a braine, can knocke
twenty titles on the head, at a ſtroke; and with
a iugling ſhift of that ſame inuincible knacke,
defende himſelfe manfully at the Paper-barre.
Though I be not greatly employed, yet my
leiſure will ſcarſely ſerue, to moralize Fables of
Beares, Apes, and Foxes: (for ſome men can
giue a ſhrewd geſſe at a courtly allegory:) but
where Lordes in expreſſe tearmes are magnifically
contemned, Doctours in the ſame ſtile may be
courageouſly confuted. Liberty of Tounge, and
Pen, is no Bondman: nippitaty will not be tied
to a poſt: there is a cap of mainetenaunce, called
Impudency: and what ſay to him, that in a ſuper-
abundaunce of that ſame odd capricious humour,
findeth *no ſuch want in England as of an Aretine,*
that might ſtrip theſe golden Aſſes out-of their gay
trappinges, and after he had ridden them to death
with rayling, leaue them on the dunghill for carrion?
A frolicke mind, and a braue ſpirite to bee em-
ployed with his ſtripping inſtrument, in ſupply
of that onely want of a diuine Aretine, the

great rider of golden Affes. Were his penne
as fupererogatory a woorkeman, as his harte ; or
his lines fuch tranfcendentes, as his thoughtes:
Lord, what an egregious Aretine fhould we fhortly
haue : how exceffiuely exceeding Aretine himfelfe ;
that beftowed the furmountingeft amplifications at
his pleafure, and was a meere Hyperbole incarnate?
Time may worke an accomplifhment of woonders:
and his graund intentions feeme to prognofticate
no leffe, then the vttermoft poffibilities of capacity,
or fury extended : would God, or could the Diuell,
giue him that vnmeafurable allowance of witt, and
Arte, that he extreamely / affecteth, and infinitely
wanteth, there were no encounter, but of admira-
tion, and honour. But it may very-well befeeme
me to conceale defectes : and I were beft to let
him runne out his iolly race, and to attende hys
pleafure at all affayes, for feare hee degrade mee,
or call mee a Letter-monger. Oh, would that
were the worft. Gallant Gentlemen, did you euer
fee the blades of two brandifhed fwordes in the
handes of a Fury? See them now : and Lo how
the victorious Duellift ftretcheth-out the armes of
his Proweffe, to runne vppon thofe poore Letters
with a maine carreere. *Aut nunc, aut nunquam:*
now the deadly ftroke muft be ftricken: now,
now he will furely lay about him, like a lufty
throffher, and beate all to powder, that commeth

in the mighty fwinge of his dubble flayle.   But I
know not what aftonifhing terror may bedimm my
fight : and peraduenture the one of thofe vnlawfull
weapons is no fword, but a fhaken firebrand in the
hand of Alecto.   All the worfe : and he twice wo-
begon poore foule, that is at once affaulted with
Fier, and Iron, the twoo vnmercifull inftrumentes
of Mars enraged.   God fhield quiet men from the
handes of fuch cruell Confuters : whofe argumentes
are fwoordes ; whofe fentences, murthering bullets ;
whofe phrafes, crofbarres ; whofe tearmes no leffe,
then ferpentine powder ; whofe very breath, the
fier of the match : all exceedingly fearefull, faue
his footinge, which may haply giue him the flipp.
Hee that ftandeth vppon a wheele, let him beware
he fall not.   I haue heard of fome feate Strata-
gems, as fly, as the flyeft in Frontine, or Polyen :
& could tell you a pretty Tale of a flippery
grounde, that woulde make fome bodies eares
glow : but hee that reuealeth the fecrete of his
owne aduauntage, may haue fcope enough to
befhrew himfelfe.   The Ægyptian Mercury would
prouide / to plant his foote vpon a fquare ; and
his Image in Athens was quadrangular, whatfoeuer
was the figure of his hatt : and although he were
fometime a Ball of Fortune, (who can affure him-
felfe of Fortune?) yet was he neuer a wheele of
folly, or an eele of Ely.   The glibbeft tunge muft

confult with his witt; & the roundeft head with
his feete: or peraduenture hee will not greatly
thanke his tickle deuife. The Wheelewright may
bee as honeft a man, as the Cutler: the Drawer, as
the Cutter: the Deuifer, as the Printer: the worft
of the fix, as the Autor: but fome tooles are falfe
Prophets; and fome fhoppes fuller of fophiftry,
then Ariftotles Elenches, and if neuer any witty
deuifer did futtelly vndermine himfelfe, good
enough. I can tell you, the Wheele was an
auncient Hieroglyphique of the moft-conning
Ægyptians; & figured none of their higheft
myfteries of triumph, or glory. But when againe
I lift-vp mine eyes, and behold the glorious picture
of that moft-threatning Slaffher: is it poffible, fo
couragious a Confuter, fhould bee leffe terrible,
then the Bafilifke of Orus Apollo, that with his
onely hiffing, killed the poore fnakes, his neigh-
bours? can any Letters liue, that hee will flay?
Were not Patience, or Submiffion, or any courfe
better, then farther difcourfe? what fonder bufi-
neffe, then to troble the Printe with Pamphlets,
that cannot poffibly liue, whiles the Bafilifke
hiffeth death? Was I woont to ieft at Elder-
tons ballatinge; Gafcoignes fonnettinge; Greenes
pamphletting; Martins libelling: Hollinfheads
engrofing; fome-bodies abridging; and whatchi-
caltes tranflating: & fhall I now become a fcribling

Creature with fragmentes of fhame, that might long fithence haue beene a frefh writer with discourfes of applaufe? The very whole matter, what but a thinge of nothinge? the Methode, what but a hotchpot / for a gallimafry? by the one, or other, what hope of publike vfe, or priuate credite? Socrates minde could as lightly digeft poifon, as Mithridates boddy : and how eafely haue the greateft ftomackes of all ages, or rather the valianteft courages of the worlde, concoƈted the harfheft, and rankeft iniuries? Politique Philip, viƈtorious Alexander, inuincible Scipio, triumphant Cæfar, happy Auguftus, magnificent Titus, and the flower of the nobleft mindes, that Immortality honoureth, with a fweete facility gaue many bitter reprehenfions the flip, and finely ridd their handes of rougheft obloquies. Philofophy profeffeth more: and the Philofopher of Emperours, or rather the Emperour. of Philofophers, Marcus Antoninus, when hee deferued beft, could with a felicity heare the woorft. Cherrifh an inward contentment in thy felfe, my minde : and outward occurrences, whome they will not make, fhall not marre. It is as great a prayfe, to be difcommended of the difhoneft, as to be commended of the vertuous : fay, affirme, confirme, approoue, iuftify what you can, the Captaine-fcolde hath vowed the laft word : none fo bolde to aduenture any thinge, as he that

hath no good thinge to loofe: let him forge, or
coyne, who will beleeue him? Lay-open his
vanity, or foolery, who knoweth it not? yet who
fo eager to defende, or offende, with tooth, or
nayle, by hooke or crooke? The Arte of figges,
hadd euer a dapper witt, a deft conceite, a flicke
forhead, a fmugg countenaunce; a ftinginge tongue;
a nippinge hande; a bytinge penne ; and a
bottomleffe pitt of Inuention, ftoared with neuer-
fayling fhiftes of counterfeite cranckes : and my
betters by many degrees, haue bene faine to bee the
Godfonnes of young Apuleius. Diuers excellente
men haue prayfed the old Affe : giue the young
Affe leaue to praife himfelfe, / and to practife his
minion Rhetorique vppon other. There is no
dealinge, where there is no healinge. To ftriue
with dirt, is filthy : to play with edged tooles,
daungerous: to trie mafteries with a defperate
aduerfary, hazardous : to encounter Demofthenes
Viper, or Apolloes Bafilifke, deadly. To intende
your owne intentions with an inuiolable conftancy,
and to leuell continually at your owne determined
fcope, without refpecte of extrauagant endes, or
cumberfome interruptions : the beft courfe of
proceeding, and onely firme, cheerefull, gallant
and happy refolution. Euery by-way, that ftrayeth
or gaddeth from that direct Path, a wandring
errour : and a perillous or threatninge by-way, a

forreſt of wilde beaſtes. Handle, touch not the ranckeling byle; and throw away the launcing inſtrument.

I could conceiue no leſſe, then thus, and thus, when I beganne firſt to ſuruiew that brauing Empreſe: and euer me thought, *Aut nunc, aut nunquam,* ſeemed to prognoſticate greate tempeſtes at hande, and euen ſuch valorous workes of Supererogation, as would make an employed man of Florence, or Venice, to breake day with any other important buſineſſe of ſtate, or traffique. I went on, & on, ſtill, and ſtill loking for thoſe preſaged woondermentes: & thought it Platoes great yeare, till I hadd runne-thorough the armed pikes, and felte the whole dinte of the two vengeable vnlawfull weapons. But I beleeue, neuer poore man found his Imagination ſo hugely mocked, as this cõfuting Iugler cooſened my expectation without meaſure: as if his whole drift had bene nothinge elſe, but with a pleaſurable Comedy, or a mad Stratagem, (like thoſe of Bacchus, and Pan) queintelye deuiſed to defeate the opinion of his credulous reader, and to ſurpriſe ſimple minds with a moſt vnlikely / euent. A fine peece of conueiance in ſome pageantes: and a braue deſeigne in fitt place. Arte knoweth the pageants: and pollicy the place. In erneſt, I expected nether an Oratour of`the Stewes: nor a

Poet of Bedlam : nor a knight of the alehowfe :
nor a quean of the Cuckingftole : nor a broker of
baggage ftuffe : nor a pedler of ftraunge newes:
nor anye bafe trumperye, or meane matters, when
Pierce fhould racke his witt, and Penniles ftretch-
out his courage, to the vttermoft extent of his
poffibility. But without more circumlocution,
pryde hath a fall : and as of a A Catt, fo of
Pierce himfelfe, howfoeuer infpired, or enraged,
you can haue but his fkinne, puffed vp with winde,
and bumbafted with vanitye. Euen when he
ftryueth for life, to fhewe himfelfe braueft in the
flaunt-aflaunt of his courage ; and when a man
would verily beleeue he fhould nowe behold the
ftately perfonage of heroicall Eloquence face to
face ; or fee fuch an vnfeene Frame of the
miracles of Arte, as might amaze the heauenly eye
of Aftronomy : holla fir, the fweete Spheres are
not too prodigall of their foueraine influences.
Pardon mee S. Fame. What the firft pang of his
diuine Furie, but notable Vanitie : what the fecond
fitte, but woorthy vanity? what the thirde career,
but egregious vanity? what the glory of his
ruffian Rhetorique, and curtifan Philofophy, but
excellent villany ? That, that is Pierces Superero-
gation : and were Penniles a perfon of any reckon-
ing, as he is a man of notorious fame, that, that
perhaps, in regard of the outragious fingularity,

might be fuppofed a Tragicall, or Heroicall villany,
if euer any villany were fo intituled. The prefent
confideration of which fingularity, occafioneth me
to bethinke me of One, that this other day very
foberlie commended fome extraordinary giftes in
Nafhe : and when he / had grauelie maintayned,
that in the refolution of his confcience, he was
fuch a fellowe, as fome wayes had few fellowes;
at laft concluded fomewhat more roundly.

*Well, my maifters, you may talke your pleafures
of Tom Nafh ; who yet fleepeth fecure, not without
preiudice to fome, that might be more ielous of their
name : but affure your felues, if M. Penniles had
not bene deepely plunged in a profound extafie of
knauery, M. Pierce had neuer written that famous
worke of Supererogation, that now ftayneth all the
bookes in Paules-churchyard, and fetteth both the
vniuerfities to fchoole. Till I fee your fineft humanitie
beftow fuch a liberall exhibition of conceit, and
courage, vpon your neateft wittes ; pardon me though
I prefer one fmart Pamflet of knauery, before ten
blundring volumes of the nine Mufes. Dreaming,
and fmoke amount alike : Life is a gaming, a
iugling, a fcoulding, a lawing, a fkirmifhing, a
warre ; a Comedie, a Tragedy : the fturring witt, a
quinteffence of quickfiluer ; and there is noe dead
flefhe in affection, or courage. You may difcourfe of
Hermes afcending fpirit ; of Orpheus enchãting*

harpe ; of Homers diuine furie ; of Tyrtæus enrag-
ing trumpet ; of Pericles bounſinge thunderclaps ; of
Platos enthuſiaſticall rauiſhment ; and I wott not
what maruelous egges in mooneſhine : but a flye for
all your flying ſpeculations, when one good fellow
with his odd ieſtes, or one madd knaue with his
awke hibber-gibber, is able to putt downe twentye of
your ſmuggeſt artificiall men, that ſimper it ſo nicely,
and coylie in their curious pointes. Try, whē you
meane to be diſgraced : & neuer giue me credit, if
Sanguine witt putt not Melancholy Arte to bedd. 1
had almoſt ſaid, all the figures of Rhetorique muſt
abate me an ace of Pierces Supererogation : and
Penniles hath a certayne nimble and climbinge reach
of Inuention, as good as a long pole, and a hooke, that
neuer fayleth at a pinch. It were vnnaturall, as
the ſweete Emperour, Marcus Antoninus ſaid, that
the fig-tree ſhould euer want iuice./ You that
purpoſe with great ſummes of ſtuddy, & candles to
purchaſe the worſhipfull names of Dunſes, &
Dodipoles, may cloſely ſitt, or ſokingly ly at your
bookes : but you that intende to be fine companionable
gentlemen, ſmirkinge wittes, and whipſters in the
world, betake yee timely to the liuely praꞔtis of the
minion profeſſion, and enure your Mercuriall fingers
to framé ſemblable workes of Supererogation. Certes
other rules are fopperies : and they that will ſeeke
out the Arꞔhmiſtery of the buſieſt Moderniſtes, ſhall

*find it nether more, nor leſſe, then a certayne prag-
maticall ſecret, called Villany, the verie ſcience of
ſciences, and the Familiar Spirit of Pierces Supererо-
gation. Cooſen not your ſelues with the gay-nothings
of children, & ſchollers: no priuitie of learning, or
inſpiration of witt, or reuelation of miſteryes, or
Arte Notory, counteruayleable with Pierces Supererо-
gation: which hauing none of them, hath them all,
and can make them all Aſſes at his pleaſure. The
Book-woorme was neuer but a pick-gooſe: it is the
Multiplying ſpirit, not of the Alchimiſt, but of the
villaniſt, that knocketh the naile one the head, and
ſpurreth cutt farther in a day, then the quickeſt
Artiſt in a weeke. Whiles other are reading,
wryting, conferring, arguing, diſcourſing, experimēt-
ing, platforminge, muſing, buzzing, or I know not
what: that is the ſpirrit, that with a woondrous
dexterity ſhapeth exquiſite workes, and atchieueth
puiſſant exploites of Supererogation. O my good
frends, as ye loue the ſweete world, or tender your
deare ſelues, be not vnmindfull what is good for the
aduauncemente of your commendable partes. All is
nothing without aduancement. Though my experiēce
be a Cipher in theſe cauſes, yet hauing ſtudiouſly
peruſed the newe Arte-notory, that is, the foreſaid
ſupererogation; and hauing ſhaken ſo many learned
aſſes by the eares, as it were by the hands: I could
ſay no leſſe, and might think more.*

Something elfe was vttered the fame time
by the fame Gentleman, afwell concerning the
prefent ftate of France, which / he termed the
moft vnchriftian kingdome of the moft chriftian
kinge ; as touching certaine other newes of I
wott not what dependence : but my minde was
running on my halfpeny, and my head fo full of
the forefaid round difcourfe, that my hand was
neuer quyet, vntill I had altered the tytle of this
Pamphlet, and newlie chriftened it *Pierces Super-
erogation :* afwell in remembrance of the faid dis-
courfe, as in honour of the appropriate vertues of
Pierce himfelfe ; who aboue all the writers that
euer I knew, fhall go for my money, where the
curranteft forgery, impudency, arrogancy, phan-
tafticalitie, vanity ; and great ftore of little
difcretion may go for payment ; and the filthieft
corruption of abhominable villany paffe vnlaunced.
His other miraculous perfections are ftill in abey-
ance : and his monftrous excellencyes in the
predicament of Chimera. The birde of Arabia
is longe in hatchinge : and mightye workes of
Supererogation are not plotted, & accomplifhed
attonce. It is pittie for fo hyperbolicall a conceite,
ouer-hawty for the furmounting rage of Taffo
in his furious agony, fhould be humbled with fo
diminitiue a witt ; bafe enough for Elderton, and
the riffe-raffe of the fcribling rafcality. I haue

heard of many difparagementes in felowfhip :
but neuer fawe fo great Impudency married to
fo little witt ; or fo huge prefumption allyed to
fo petty performance. I muft not paint, though
hee dawbe. Pontan decipher thy vauntinge
Alopantius Aufimarchides anew : and Terence
difplay thy boaftinge Thrafo anew : and Plautus
addreffe thy vaine-glorious Pyrgopolinices anew :
heere is a bratt of Arrogancy, a gofling of the
Printing-houfe, that can teach your braggardes to
play their partes in the Printe of woonder, & to
exploit redowtable workes of Supererogation ;
fuch as neuer were atchieued in Latin, or /
Greeke. Which deferue to bee looked-for with
fuch a longing expectation, as the Iewes looke
for their kingly Meffias : or as I looke for
Agrippas dreadfull Pyromachy : for Cardans
multiplied matter, that fhall delude the force of
the Canon : for Acontius perfect Arte of forti-
fieng little townes againft the greateft Battery :
for the Iliades of all Courtly Stratagems, that
Antony Riccobonus magnifically promifeth : for
his vniuerfall Repertory of all Hiftories, con-
tayning the memorable actes of all ages, all
places, and all perfons : for the new Calepine of
all learned, and vulgar languages, written, or
fpoken, whereof a loud rumour was lately pub-
lifhed at Bafill : for a generall Pandectes of the

Lawes, and ftatutes of all nations, and common-
wealthes in the worlde, largely promifed by
Doctor Peter Gregorius, but compendioufly
perfourmed in his *Syntagma Iuris vniuerfi :* for
fundry fuch famous volumes of hugy miracles in
the cloudes. Do not fuch Arch-woondermentes
of Supernaturall furniture, deferue arch-expecta-
tion? What fhould the Sonnes of Arte, dreame
of the Philofophers Stone, that like Midas, turneth
into golde, whatfoeuer it toucheth : or of the
foueraine, and diuine Quinteffence, that like Efcu-
lapius reftoreth health to fickneffe ; like Medea,
youth to Olde-age ; like Apollonius, life to death?
No Philofophers Stone, or foueraine Quinteffence,
howfoeuer precioufly precious, equiualent to fuch
diuine woorkes of fupererogation. O high-minded
Pierce, hadd the traine of your woordes, and
fentences bene aunfwearable to the retinue of
your bragges, and threates, or the robes of your
apparaunce in perfon, futeable to the weedes of
your oftentation in tearmes : I would furely haue
beene the firft, that fhould haue proclaimed you,
the moft-finguler Secretary of this language,
and / the heauenlieft creature vnder the Spheres.
Sweete M. Afcham, that was a flowing fpring
of humanity, and worthy Sir Phillip Sidney, that
was a florifhing fpring of nobility, muft haue
pardoned me : I would directly haue difcharged

my confcience. But you muft giue plaine men leaue to vtter their opinion without courtinge : I honor high heads, that ftand vpon low feet ; & haue no great affection to the gay fellowes, that build vp with their clãbring hartes, and pull downe with their vntoward hands. Giue me the man that is meeke in fpirit, lofty in zeale : fimple in prefumption, gallant in endeuour : poore in pro- feffion, riche in performance. Some fuch I knowe, and all fuch I value highly. They glory not of the golden Stone, or the youthfull Quinteffence : but Induftrie is their goulden Stone ; Action their youthfull Quinteffence ; and Valour their diuine worke of Supererogation. Euerye one may thinke as he lifteth ; & fpeake as he findeth occafion : but in my fancy, they are fimply the fimpleft fellows of al other, that boaft they will exploite miracles, & come fhort in ordinarie reckonings. Great matters are no woonders, when they are menaced, or promifed with big othes : and fmall thinges are maruels, when they are not expected, or fufpected. I wondred to heare, that Kelly had gotten the Golden Fliece, and by vertue thereof was fodenly aduaunced into fo honorable reputation with the Emperours maieftye ; but would haue woondred more, to haue feene a woorke of Supererogation from Nafhe : whofe witt muft not enter the liftes of comparifon

with Kelleyes Alchimy : howfoeuer he would
feeme to haue the Greene Lion, and the Flying
Eagle in a boxe. But Kelley will bidd him looke
to the fwolne Toade, & the daunfing Foole.
Kelly knoweth his *Lutum Sapientiæ,* and vfeth
his termes of Arte. Silence / is a great mifterye :
and lowde wordes but a Coweherds horne. He
that breedeth mountaynes of hope, and with
much adoe begetteth a molehill (fhall I tell
him a newe tale in ould Inglifhe?) beginneth
like a mightie Oxe, & endeth like a fory
Affe. To atchieue it without oftentation is a
notable prayfe : but to vaunt it without atcheue-
ment, or to threaten it without effecte ; is but a
dubble-proofe of a fimple witt. Execution fheweth
the hability of the man : prefumption bewraieth
the vanitie of the mind. The Sunne fayth not ;
I will thus, and thus difplaye my glorious beames,
but fhineth indeede : the fpringe braggeth not of
gallant flowers, but florifheth indeede : the Harueft
boafteth not of plentifull fruit, but fructifieth in-
deede. Æfops fellowes being afked, what they
could doe, anfwered they could doe any thing ;
but Æfope making a fmall fhowe, could doe much
indeede : the Greeke Sophifters knowing nothinge
in comparifon, (knowledge is a dry water) pro-
feffed a fkill in all thinges ; but Socrates knowing
in a manner all things, (Socrates was a fpringing

rocke) profeſſed a ſkill in nothinge : Lullius, and
his ſectaryes, haue the ſignet of Hermes, and the
admirable Arte of diſputinge infinitly *de omni
ſcibili ;* but Agrippa, one of the vniuerſalleſt
ſchollars, that Europe hath yeelded, and ſuch a
one, as ſome learned men of Germany, France, &
Italie, intituled The Omniſcious Doctour, Socrati-
callie declameth againſt the vanitye of ſciences, and
for my comforte penneth the Apology of the
Aſſe. Neuer any of theſe prating vagabundes
had the vertuous Elixir, or other important ſecret :
(yet who ſuch monarches for Phiſique, Chirurgery,
Spagirique, Aſtrology, Palmaſtry, naturall & ſuper-
naturall Magique, Necromancy, Familiar-ſpiritſhipp,
and all profound cunninge, as ſome of theſe arrant
Impoſtours?) / hee is a Pythagorean, and a cloſe
fellow of his tongue, & pen, that hath the right
magiſterium indeede ; and can diſpatch with the
finger of Art, that they promis with the mouth
of coſenage. They that vaunt, do it not ; & they
that pretend leaſt, accompliſh moſt. High-ſpirited
Pierce doe it indeede, that thou crakeſt in vaine ;
and I will honour thy worke, that ſcorne thy
worde. When there was no neede, thy breath
was the mouth of Ætna ; & like a Cyclops,
thou didſt forge thunder in Mongibello : now the
warringe Planet was expected in perſon, and the
Fiery Trigon ſeemed to giue the Alarme ; *thou*

talkeſt of Cattes meate and Dogges meate enough:
and wilt try it out by the teeth at the ſigne of
the Dogs-head in the pot.   Oh, what a chatering
Monky is here : & oh what a dog-fly, is the dog-
ſtarr proued?   Elderton would haue anſwered this
geere out-of-cry : or had I the witt of Scoggin, I
could ſay ſome thing to it : but I looked for Cattes
meate in *aqua fortis,* & Dogs meat in Gunpowder;
& can no ſkill of theſe termes, ſteeped in thy
mothers gutter, & thy fathers kennel.   Na, if
you will needes ſtrike it as dead as a dore naile ;
and run vpon me with the blade of Cattes meate,
& the fierbrond of Dogges meate : I haue doone.
Or in caſe your meaning be, as you ſtoutely pro-
teſt, to trounce me after twenty in the hundred, *and*
to haue about with me, with two ſtaues, and a pyke,
like a tall fellowe of Cracouia: there is no dealing
for ſhort weapons.   Young Martin was an ould
hackſter : & had you plaid your maiſters prizes
in his time, he peraduenture durſte haue looked
thoſe two ſtaues in the face, and would haue
deſired that pike of ſome more acquaintance : but
Truce keepe me out of his handes, that fighteth
furiouſly with two ſtaues of Cattes meate and a
pyke of Dogges meate : and is reſolutely bente,
the beſt blood / of the brothers ſhall pledge him
in vineger.   Happy, it is noe worſe, then vineger;
a good ſawce for Cattes meate, and Dogges meate.

Gentlemen, you that thinke prommiſſe a bonde, and vſe to performe more, then you threaten ; neuer beleeue Braggadocio againe for his ſake. When he hath done his beſt, and his worſt : truſt me, or credit your owne eies, his beſt Beſt is but Cattes meate, & his worſt Worſt but Doggs meate enough.   What ſhould I goe circuiting about the buſhe ?   He taketh the ſhorteſt cutt to the wood, and diſpatcheth all controuerſies in a fewe ſignificant termes : not thoſe of Gunpowder, which would aſke ſome charging, and diſcharging : but theſe of dogges-meat, which are vp with a vomit.   He that is not ſo little, as the third Cato from heauen, or the eight wiſeman vpon earth, may ſpeake with authority ; and chriſten me a *Dunſe, a foole, an ideot, a dolt, a gooſe-cappe, an aſſe,* and I wot not what, as filthy, as filthy may be.   Dogged Impudḗcy hath his proper Idiotiſme ; & very clarkly ſchooleth the eares of Modeſtie, to ſpell, Fa-fe-fi-fo-fu.   Simple wittes would be dealt playnly withall : I ſtand not vpon coye or nice poyntes ; but am one of thoſe, that would gladlie learne their owne imperfeĉtions, errours, and follies, *in ſpecialliſſima ſpecie :*   Be it knowne vnto all men by theſe preſentes, that Thomas Naſhe, from the top of his witte looking downe vpon ſimple creatures, calleth Gabriell Haruey a Dunſe, a foole, an ideot, a dolt, a gooſe-capp, an aſſe, and ſoe fourth : (for fome of the refidue, is not to be fpoken but with his owne manerly mouth) : but the wife man in printe, fhould haue doone well in his learned Confutation, to haue fhewed particulerlie, which woords in my Letters, were the wordes of a Dunfe : which Sentences, the fentences of a foole : which Arguments, the arguments of / an Ideot : which Opinions, the opinions of a dolt : which Iudgements, the iudgements of a goofe-cap : which Conclufions, the conclufions of an Affe. Eyther this wold be dun, (for I fuppofe, he would be loth to proue fome Affes, that in fauour haue written otherwife, and in reafon are to verify their owne teftimonies) : or he muft be fayne himfelfe, to eate his owne Cattes-meate, & Dogges-meat : and fwallow-downe a Dunfe, a foole, an ideot, a dolt, a goofe-cap, an affe in his owne throate; the proper cafe of his filthieft excrements, and the finke of the famous rafcal ; that had rather be a Poulcatt with a ftinking ftur, then a mufk-cat with gratious fauor. Pardon me gentle Ciuilitie : if I did not tender you, & difclame impudency, I could do him fome peece of right; & fhew him his well fauored face in a Criftall, as true as Gafcoignes fteele-glas. But *truft him not for a dodkin* (it is his owne requeft) *if euer I did my Doctors Actes :* which a thowfand heard in Oxforde; and fome knew to be done with as little premedita-

tion, as euer such actes were done : (for I answered
vpon the questions, that were giuen me by Doctor
Cathedræ, but two dayes before; and read my
Cursory Lecture with a dayes warning :) or if I be
not *A Fawne-guest Messenger betweene M. Chris-
topher Bird*, in whose company, I neuer dined,
or supped these six yeares, *and M. Emmanuell
Demetrius*, with whom I neuer dranke to this day.
Other matters, touching *her Highnesse affabilite
toward Schollers*, (so her Maiesties fauour towards
mee must bee interpreted :) the *Priuy watch-word
of honourable men* in their Letters Commendatory,
euen in the highest degree of praysing, (so our high
Chauncellours commendation must bee quallified :)
Nashes graue Censure of *Publicke Inuectiues, and
Satyres*, (so Harueyes slight opinion of contentious,
and seditious Libels must / be crosbitten :) his
testimony of *Ciceroes consolation ad Dolabellam*,
which he will needes father vpon me in re-
proch, though his betters will neuer pen such a
peec of Latin, whosoeuer wer the Stepp-Tully :)
his derision of the most profitable, and valorous
Mathematical Arts, (whose industrie hath atcheeued
woonders of mightier puissance, then the labours of
Hercules :) his contempt of *the worthiest persons*
in euery faculty, (which he alwayes censureth as
his punyes, and vnderlinges :) *his palpable Atheisme,
and drinkinge a cupp of Lammeswool to the Lambe*

of God : his gibinge at *Heauen*, (the hauen, where
my deceafed brother is arriued,) with a deepe cut
out-of his Gramer rules ; *Aftra petit difertus :* the
very ftarres, are fcarres, where he lifteth : and a
hundred fuch, and fuch Particularities ; that re-
quier fum larger Difcourfe; fhew him to be a
youngman of the greeneft fpringe, as beardles in
iudgement, as in face ; and as Penniles in witt, as
in purfe.   It is the leaft of his famous aduentures,
that hee vndertaketh to be *Greenes aduocate :* as
diuine Plato affayed to defend Socrates at the
Bar : and I knowe not whether it be the leaft of
his dowtye exploites, that he falueth his frendes
credit, as that excellent difciple faued his maifters
life.   He may declare his deere affection to his
Paramour : or his pure honeftye to the world; or
his conftant zeale to play the Diuels Oratour : but
noe Apology of Greene, like *Greenes grotes-worth
of witt :* and when Nafh will indeede accomplifh
a worke of Supererogation, let him publifh, Nafhes
Penniworth of Difcretion.   If he be learneder, or
wifer then other, in fo large an affife, as fhould
appeare by the reporte of his owne mouth ; it is
the better for him : but it were not amiffe, he
fhould fumtime looke-backe to the budget of
Ignorance, and Folly, that hangeth behind him ;
as otherwhiles he condefcendeth to glaunce / at the
fatchell of his grammar bookes.   Calumny & her

coofen-german Impudency, wil not alwaies hould-
out rubbers: and they neede not greatlie bragge
of their harueft, that make Phantafie the roote,
Vanity the ftalke, Follye the eare, Penury the cropp,
and Shame the whole fubftance of their ftuddies.
To be ouer-bould with one, or two, is fomething:
to be fawcy with many, is much: to fpare fewe,
or none, is odious: to be impudent with all, is
intollerable. There were fayre playe enough,
though foule play were debarred: but Boyes,
fooles, and knaues, take all in fnuffe, when the
variance might be debated in the language of
Curtefie: and nothing but horfeplay will ferue,
where the colt is difpofed to play the iade. Did I
lift to perfecute him in his owne vaine, or were
I not reftrained with refpectiue termes of diuine,
and ciuill moderation: ô Aretin, how pleafurably
might I canuas the bawling cur, in a toffing fheete
of paper: or ô Gryfon, who could more eafilie
difcouer a new Arte of riding a headftrong beafte?
But that which Nafhe accounteth the brauery of
his witt, and the dubble creaft of his ftyle, I am in
difcretion to cut-of: and in modefty yeeld it his
onely glorye, to haue the fowleft mouth, that I
euer fawe, and the ftrongeft breath, that I euer
fealt. When witty girding faileth, as it pitifully
fayleth in euery page of that Superarrogatory
worke: Lord, what odious baggage, what rafcal

ftuffe, what villanous trumpery filleth-vpp the
leafe : and howe egregioufly would he playe the
vengeable Sycophant, if the conueiance of his Arte,
or witt, were in anye meafure of proportion,
correfpondent to his peftilent ftomacke? But in
the felleft fitt of his Furye, euen when he runneth
vpon me with openeft mouth, & his Spite like a
poyfonous toade, fwelleth in the full : as if fome
huge timpany / of witt would prefentlye poffeffe
his braine ; or fome horrible Fiery Spright would
flye in my face, and blaft me to nothing : then
good Dick Tarleton is dead, & nothing aliue but
Cattes-meat, & Dogges-meat enough. Na, were
it not, that hee hadd dealt politiquely, in prouiding
himfelfe an autenticall fuerty, or rather a mighty
protedour at a pinch, fuch a deuoted freend, and
infeparable companion, as Æneas was to Achates,
Pylades to Oreftes, Diomedes to Vlyffes, Achilles
to Patroclus, and Hercules to Thefeus : doubtleffe
he had beene vtterly vndone. Compare old, and
new hiftories, of farr, & neere countries: and you
fhall finde the late manner of *Sworne Brothers*, to
be no new fafhion, but an auncient guife, and
heroicall order ; dcuifcd for neceffity, continucd
for fecurity, and mainetayned for proffite, and
pleafure. In braueft actions, in weightieft nego-
tiations, in hardeft diftreffes, in how many cafes,
One man, no-boddy ; and a dayly frend, as neces-

fary, as our dayly bread. No treafure, more pre-
cious : no bonde, more indefefible : no caftle, more
impregnable : no force, more inuincible : no trueth,
more infallible : no element, more needefull ; then
an entire, & affured affociate ; euer preft, afwell in
calamity to comfort, or in aduerfity to relieue, as
in profperity to congratulate, or in aduauncemente
to honour. Life is fweet, but not without fweete
focietie : & an inward affectionate frend, (as it
were *an other The fame, or a fecond Selfe,*) the
very life of life, and the fweet-harte of the hart.
Nafhe is learned, & knoweth his Leripup. Where
was Euryalus, there was Nifus : where Damon,
there Pythias : where Scipio, there Lælius : where
Apollonius, there Damides : where Proclus, there
Archiadas : where Pyrocles, there Mufidorus :
where Nafhe, there his Nifus, his Pythias, his
Lælius, his Dami / des, his Archiadas, his Mufi-
dorus ; his indiuifible companion, with whofe
puiffant helpe hee conquereth, wherefoeuer he
raungeth. Na, Homer not fuch an author for
Alexander : nor Xenophon for Scipio : nor Virgil
for Auguftus : nor Iuftin for Marcus Aurelius :
nor Liuy for Theodofius Magnus : nor Cæfar for
Selymus : nor Philip de Comines for Charles the
fift : nor Macchiauell for fome late princes : nor
Aretin for fome late Curtefans ; as his Authour
for him ; the fole authour of renowned victorie.

Maruel not, that Erafmus hath penned the En-
comium of Folly; or that fo many fingular learned
men haue laboured the commendation of the Affe:
he it is, that is the godfather of writers, the fuper-
intendent of the preffe, the mufter-maifter of in-
numerable bands, the Generall of the great feilde:
hee, and Nafhe will confute the world. And wher
is the Ægles quill, that can fufficiently aduance the
firft fpoiles of their new conqueftes? Whift fory
pen, and be aduifed how thou prefume aboue the
higheft pitch of thy poffibility. Hee that hath
chriftened fo many notable authours; cenfured fo
many eloquent pennes; enrowled fo many worthy
garrifones; & encamped fo many noble, and reue-
rend Lordes, may be bould with me. If I be an
Affe, I haue company enough: and if I be no
Affe, I haue fauour to be enftalled in fuch com-
panye. The name will fhortly grow in requeft, as
it fomtime florifhed in glorious Roome: and who
then will not fue, to be free of that honorable
Company? Whiles they are ridden, I defire not
to be fpared: when the hott-fpurr is aweary with
tyring them, he wil fcarfly troble himfelf with a
fkin. Or if he do, I may chance acquaint him
with a fecret indiftillation; He that drinketh Oyle
of prickes, fhall haue much adooe to voide fyrup
of rofes; and he that eateth nettles for pro-
uander, / hath a priuiledge to piffe vpon Lillyes

for litter.   Poules wharfe honour the memorye
of oulde Iohn Hefter, that would not fticke with
his frende for twentye fuch experimentes; & would
often tell me of *A Magiftral Vnguent* for all fores.
Who knoweth not that Magiftrall vnguent, knoweth
nothing: and who hath that magiftral vnguent,
feareth no gunfhott.   The Confuter meant to be
famous, like Poggius, that altobe-affed Valla,
Trapezuntius, and their defendantes, many learned
Italians: or might haue giuen a geffe at fome
poffible afterclaps, as good as a prognoftication
of an after-winter.   Though Pierce Penniles, for
a fpurt were a ranke rider, and like an arrant
knight ouerran nations with a carreer; yet Thomas
Nafhe might haue beene aduifed, and in pollicy
haue fpared them, that in compaffion fauoured
him; and were vnfaynedlye fory, to finde his
miferable eftate, afwell in his ftyle, as in his
purfe, and in his wit, as in his fortune.   Some
complexions haue much adooe to alter their
nature: & Nafhe wil carrie a tache of Pierce
to his graue, (we haue worfe prouerbes in eng-
lifhe:) yet who feeith not, what apparent good,
my Letters haue done him, that before ouer-
crowed all commers, and goers with like difcre-
tion, but nowe forfooth hath learned fome fewe
handfome termes of refpecte, and verye manerly
beclaweth a fewe, that he might the more

licentioufly befmeere one. S. Fame giue him
ioye of his blacke, and his white chalke.

Who is not limed with fome default; or who
reddier to confeffe his own imperfections, then
mifelfe? but when in profeffed hatred, like a
mortal feudift, he hath vttered his very vttermoft
fpite, & wholy difgorged his racorous ftomacke :
yet can he not, fo much as deuife any particular
action of trefpas, or obiect any certaine vice againft
me, but onely / one greuous crime, called Pumps,
& Patofles, (which indeede I haue worne, euer
fince I knewe Cambridge,) & his owne deereft
hart-root, Pride : which I proteft before God, and
man, my foule in indgment as much detefteth, as
my body in nature lotheth poyfon ; or anything
abhorreth his deadlye enemy, euen amongft thofe
creatures, which are found fatally contrary by
naturall Antipathy. It is not exceffe, but defecte
of pride, that hath broken the head of fome mens
preferment. Afpiring mindes can foare aloft : and
Selfe-conceit, with the countenaunce of Audacity,
the tongue of Impudency, & the hand of Dexterity,
preafeth bouldly into the forwardeft throng of the
fhouldring ranke : whiles Difcretion hath leafure
to difcourfe, whether fomedeale of Modefty were
meeter for manye, that prefume aboue their con-
dition ; and fome deale of Selfe-liking fitter for
fome, that haue fealt no greater want, then want

of Pride. It may feeme a rude difpofition, that
forteth not with the quality of the age : & Pollicy
deemeth that vertue a vice, that modefty, fimplicity,
that refolutenes, diffolutenes, that conformeth not
it felfe, with a fupple & deft correfpõdence to the
prefent time : but no fuch oxe in my mind, as
Tarquinius Superbus: no fuch calfe, as Spurius
Mælius : no fuch colt, as Publius Clodius ; no
fuch Ape, as Lucians Rhetorician, or the Diuels
Oratour. Blind ambition, a noble bayarde: proud
arrogancy, a goulden Affe : vaine conceit, a gaudy
Peacocke : all brauery, that is not effectuall, a gay
nothing. He vpbraideth me with his own good
nature : but where fuch an infolent braggard, or
fuch a puffing thing, as himfelfe ? that in magnify-
ing his owne bable, & debafing me, reuileth them,
whofe bookes, or pantofles he is not worthy to
beare. If I be an Affe, what affes were thofe
curteous frendes, thofe excellent learned men, /
thofe worfhipfull, & honorable perfonages, whofe
Letters of vndeferued, but fingular cõmendation
may be fhewen? What an affe was thifelfe, whẽ
thou didft publifh my praife amongft the notableft
writers of this realme ? or what an Affe art thifelf,
that in the fpitefulleft outrage of thy maddeft
Confutatiõ, doft otherwhiles enterlace fome remem-
brances of more account, then I can acknow-
ledge without vanity, or defier without ambition?

The truth is, I ſtande as little vpon others
commendation, or mine owne titles, as any man
in England whofoeuer ; if there be nothing els to
folicite my caufe : but being fo fhamefully and
intollerably prouoked in the moſt villanous termes
of reproch, I were indeede a notorious infenfate
affe, in cafe I fhould eyther fottiſhly negleſt the
reputation of foe worthy fauorers, or vtterly abandō
mine owne credit. Sweet Gentlemen, renowned
knightes, and honorable Lordes, be not aſhamed
of your Letters, vnprinted, or written : if I liue,
feeing I muſt eyther liue in *tenebris* with obloquy,
or in *luce* with proofe ; by the leaue of God, I
will prooue mifelfe no Affe. I fpeake not onely
to M. Bird, M. Spencer, or Monfieur Bodin,
whom he nothinge regardeth : (yet I would his
owne learning, or iudgmente were anye way
matchable with the worſt of the three :) but
amongſt a number of fundrie other learned, and
gallant Gentlemē, to M. Thomas Watfon, a notable
Poet ; to M. Thomas Hatcher, a rare Antiquary ;
to M. Daniel Rogers of the Court ; to Doſtor
Griffin Floyd, the Queenes profeſſour of lawe at
Oxforde ; to Doſtor Peter Baro a profeſſour of
diuinity in Cambridge ; to Doſtor Bartholmew
Clark, late Deane of the Arches ; to Doſtor
William Lewen, Iudge of the prerogatiue Court ;
to Doſtor Iohn Thomas Freigius, a famous writer

of Germany : to Sir Philip Sidney ; to / M. Secre-
tary Wilſon ; to Sir Thomas Smith ; to Sir Walter
Mildmay ; to milord the biſhop of Rocheſter ; to
milord Treaſurer ; to milord the Earle of Leiceſter:
Vnto whoſe worſhipfull and honorable fauours I
haue bene exceedingly beholding for letters of
extraordinary commendation ; ſuch, as ſome of
good experience haue doubted, whether they euer
voutſafed the like vnto any of either vniuerſity.   I
beſeech God, I may deſerue the leaſt parte of their
good opinion, eyther in effectuall proofe, or in
dutifull thankefullneſſe : but how little ſoeuer I
preſume of mine owne ſufficiency, (he that knoweth
himſelfe, hath ſmal cauſe to conceiue any high hope
of low meanes :) as in reaſon I was not to flatter
miſelfe with their bountifull commendation : So
in iudgement I am not to agreeue miſelfe with the
odious detraction of this peſtilent libeller, or any
like deſpiteous ſlanderer : but in patience am to
digeſt the one with moderation, as in temperance
I qualified the other with modeſty.   Some would
ſay, what is the peeuiſhe grudge of one beggarly
rakehell, to ſo honorable liking of ſo many
excellẽt, & ſome ſingular mẽ ? but god in heauẽ,
teach me to take good by my aduerſaries inuectiue ;
and no harme by my fauourers approbation.   It
is neither the one, nor the other, that deſerueth
euill, or well ; but the thing it ſelfe, that edifieth ;

without which, praife is fmoke ; and with which,
difpraife is fyer. Let me enioy that effential point:
& hauke, or hunt, or fifhe after praife, you that
lift. Many contumelious, and more glorious re-
ports haue paffed from Enemies, & Frends,
without caufe, or vpon fmal occafion : that is the
onely infamy, that cannot acquit it felfe from guilti-
neffe ; & that the only honor, that is grounded
vpō defert. Other winds of diffamation, want
matter to vpholde it ; and other fhadowes of glory,
lacke / a body to fupport it. In vnhappineffe they
are happy, of whofe bad amounteth good ; & in
happineffe they vnhappy, whofe good prooueth
bad : as glory eftfoones followeth them, that fly
from it, & flyeth from them, that followe it.
There is a Terme Probatory, that wil not ly : and
commendations are neuer autenticall, vntill they bee
figned with the feale of approoued Defert, the
only infallible Teftimoniall. Defert, (maugre Enuy,
the companion of Vertue) Socrates highwaye to
Honour ; & the totall fumme of Oforius *De
Gloria.* I will not enter into Macchiauels dis-
courfes, Iouius Elogyes, Cardãs natiuities, Cofmopo-
lites Dialogues, or later Hiftories in dyuers
languages : but fome worthelye continue honorable,
whom they make difhonorable, & contrariwife.
Reafon hath an euen hande, and difpenfeth to
euerye one his right : Arte amplifieth, or extenu-

ateth at occafion : the refidue, is the liberality of
the pen, or the poyfon of the inke : in Logique,
Sophiftrie ; in law, iniury ; in hiftorie, a fable ; in
diuinity, a lye.   Horace, a fharpe, and fententious
Poet, after his pithy manner, comprizeth much in
fewe wordes :

> *Falfus honor iuuat, & mendax infamia terret,*
> *Quem nifi mendacem, & mendofum ?*

For mine owne part, I am reafonably refolute
both wayes, & ftand affraide of phantafticall dis-
credit, as I efteeme imaginatiue credit, or a
contemplatiue banquett.   It fitteth not with the
profeffion of a Philofopher, or the conftancie of a
man, to carrye the minde of a childe, or an youth,
or a woman, or a flaue, or a tyrant, or a beaft.
That refteth not in my power, to reforme, or
alter, I were very vnwife if I fhould not endure
with patience, mittigate with reafon, & contemne
with pleafure.   Onely I can be content in certain
behoouefull refpects, to yeeld a peece of a fatis-
faction vnto fome, that / requier it in affectionate
termes : and what honeft minde, in cafe of mor-
talitie, hath not a care, how the pofterity may be
informed of him ?   Other reafons I haue elfwhere
affigned : and am here to prefent a vowe to
Humilitie, in deteftatiō of that, which my difpofi-
tion abhorreth.

As for his lewd fuppofals, & imputations of counterfait prayfes, without anye probability of circumftance, or the leaft fufpition, but in his owne vengeable malitious head, the common forge of peftilent furmyzes, and arrant flaunders ; they are like my imprifonment in the Fleete of his ftrong Fantafie, and doe but intimate his owne fkill in falfifying of euidence, and fuborning of witneffes to his purpofe : he mufeth, as he vfeth ; & the goodwife her mother would neuer haue fought her daughter in the Oouen, if herfelfe had not beene well acquainted with fuch fhiftes of cunninge conueiance. He was neuer a *non proficient* in good matters ; and hath not ftudied his fellowes Arte of Cunnycatching for nothinge. Examine the Printers gentle Preamble before the Supplication to the Diuell: and tell me in good footh, by the verdicte of the Tuchftone, whether Pierce Penniles commende Pierce Penniles, or no ; and whether that fory praife of the Authour Thomas Nafhe, be not lothfome from the mouthe of the Printer Thomas Nafhe. In coniectural caufes I am not to auouch any thinge; and I mentioned not anye fuch fuppofition before : but the tenour of the ftyle, & as it were the identitye of the phrafe, togither with this newe defcant of his profound infight into forgery, may after a fort tel tales out of the tytle *De Secretis non reuelandis* ;

& yeld a certain ftrong fauour of a vehement
prefumption. There is pregnant euidence enough,
though I leaue probable cōiectures, & violent pre-
fumptions wher I found them. His Life daily
feedeth his Stile ; and his Stile notorioufly be-
wraieth his Life. But / what is that to me, or the
world, howe Nafhe liueth ; or howe the poore
fellowe his father hath put him to his foifting, and
fcribling fhiftes ; his onely *gloria patri*, when all
is done. Rule thy defperate infamous penne ; &
bee the fonne of a mule, or the Printers Gentle-
man, or what thou wilt for me. If thou wilt
needs deriue thy pettigree frō the noble blood of
the Kilprickes, and Childeberds, kinges of France :
what commiffion haue I to fitt vpō Genealogies,
or to call nobilitie in queftion ? If thou beift
difpofed to fpeake as thou liueft, & to liue like
Tonofconcoleros, the famous Babilonian king : in
curtefy, or in pollicy forbeare one, that is not
ouer-hafty to troble himfelfe with trobling other.
What I haue heard credibly reported, I can yet be
cōtent to fmother in filence: & nether threaten
thee with Tiburne, nor Newgate, nor Ouldgate,
nor Counter, nor Fleete, nor any publique penance ;
but wifhe thy amendment : and dare not be too-
fawcy with your good qualities, les[t] you confute
my Maifterfhip of Arte, as you haue done my
Doctorfhip of Lawe. Neuer poore Doctorfhip

was fo confuted. The beft is, I dote not vpon
it ; and would rather be actually degraded, then
any way difparage the degree, or derogate from
them, that are worthier of it. Reft you quiet ;
and I will not onely not ftruggle with you for
a tytle ; but offer here to renounce the whole
aduantage of a late inquifition, vpon a clamorous
denunciation of S. Fame herfelfe : who prefumed
fhe might be as bould to play the blab with you,
as you were to play the flouen with her. Or if
your pen be fo ranke, that it cannot ftande vpon
any ground, but the foile of Calumny, in the
muck-yard of Impudency: or your tongue foe
laxatiue, that it muft vtterly vtter a great horrible
deale more then all; whuift a while : and for
your inftruction, til fome pregnanter / leffons come
abrode, I wil breefely tell you in your eare, A
certaine familiar hiftory, of more then one or two
breakefaftes, wherein fome eight or nine eggs, &
a pound of butter for your pore part, with Gods
plenty of other victuals, & wine enough, powred-
in by quartes, and pottels, was a fcant pittance
for an inuincible ftomack, two houres before his
ordinary. I haue readd of Apicius, and Epicures
Philofophy: but I perceaue you meane not to be
accounted a Pythagorean, or a Stoique. What?
gorge vpon gorge, egges vpon egges, & fack vpō
facke at thefe yeares ? Berlady, Sir Kilpricke, you

muſt prouide for a hott kitchin againſte you growe
ould ; if you purpoſe to liue Doctor Pernes, or
Doctor Kenols yeares. Such egging and whitling
may happen bring you acquainted with the
triumphant chariot of rotten egges ; if you take
not the better order in tyme, with one, or two of
the feuē deadly finnes. I will not offend your
ſtomacke with the nice and queint regiment of
the dainty Platoniſtes, or pure Pythagoreans: fine
Theurgy, too-gant and meager a doctrine for the
Diuels Oratour: if the Arte Notory, cannot be
gotten without faſting, and praying, muchgo-
ditch-them that haue it: let phantaſticall, or
ſuperſtitious Abſtinence, daunce in the aier, like
Ariſtophanes clowdes, or Apuleius witches: your
owne method of thoſe deadly finnes, be your
Caſtell of Health. No remedy, you muſt be
dieted ; & lett-blood in the Cephalica veine of
Aſſes, fooles, doltes, ideots, Dunſes, dodipoules,
and ſo foorth infinitly: & neuer truſt me, if you
be not as tame-tonged, and barren-witted, as other
honeſt men of Lumbardy, & the Low-Cuntries.
Tuſhe man, I ſee deeper into thee, then thou ſeeiſt
into thyſelfe: thou haſt a ſuperficiall tange of ſome
little ſomethinge, as good as nothing ; and a runing
witt, as fiſking as any fiſgig, but / as ſhallow as
Trumpington foorde, and as ſlight as the newe
workemanſhip of guegawes to pleaſe children, or

of toys to mocke apes, or of trinketts to conquer
fauages. Only in that fingular veine of affes, thou
art incomparable ; and fuch an egregious arrant
foole-munger, as liueth not againe. She knew
what fhe faid, that intituled Pierce, the hoggefhead
of witt: Penniles, the tofpot of eloquence: &
Nafhe, the verye inuentor of Affes. She it is,
that muft broach the barrell of thy frifking con-
ceite, and canonife the Patriarke of newe writers.

I will not heere decipher thy vnprinted packet
of bawdye, and filthy Rymes, in the naftieft kind:
there is a fitter place for that difcouery of thy
fouleft fhame, & the whole ruffianifme of thy
brothell Mufe, if fhe ftill proftitute her obfcene
ballatts, and will needes be a young Curtifan of
ould knauery. Yet better a Confuter of Letters,
then a counfounder of manners : and better the
dogges-meate of Agrippa, or Cattes-meat of Pog-
gius, then the fwines-meate of Martial, or goates-
meate of Arretine. Cannot an Italian ribald, vomit-
out the infectious poyfon of the world, but an
Inglifh horrel-lorrel muft licke it vp for a reftora-
tiue ; and attempt to putrify gentle mindes, with
the vileft impoftumes of lewde corruption? Phy
on impure Ganimeds, Hermaphrodits, Neronifts,
Meffalinifts, Dodecomechanifts, Capricians, Inuen-
tours of newe, or reuiuers of old leacheries, and
the whole brood of venereous Libertines, that

knowe no reafon, but appetite, no Lawe but
Lufte, no humanitie, but villanye, noe diuinity
but Atheifme.   Such riotous, and inceftuous
humours would be launced, not feafted: the
Diuell is eloquent enough, to play his owne
Oratour: his Damme an old bawde, wanteth
not the broccage of a young Poet: Wanton
fprites / were alwayes bufie, & Duke Allocer on
his luftye Cocke-horfe, is a whot Familiar: the
fonnes of Adam, & the daughters of Eue, haue
noe neede of the Serpentes carowfe to fet them
agogg: Sodome ftill burneth; and although fier
from heauen fpare Gomorra, yet Gomorra ftil
confumeth itfelfe.   Euen amorous Sonnets, in the
gallanteft and fweeteft ciuill veine, are but dain-
tyes of a pleafurable witt, or iunkets of a wanton
liuer, or buddes of an idle head: whatfoeuer
fprowteth farther, would be lopped.   Petrarckes
Inuention, is pure Loue it felfe ; and Petrarckes
Elocution, pure Bewty it felfe: His *Laura* was
the Daphne of Apollo, not the Thifbe of Pyramus:
a delitious Sappho, not a lafciuious Lais ; a fauing
Hefter, not a deftroying Helena; a nimph of
Diana, not a Curtifan of Venus.   Aretines mufe
was an egregious bawd, & a haggifhe witch of
Theffalia: but Petrarcks verfe, a fine loouer, that
learneth of Mercury, to exercife his fayreft giftes
in a faire fubiect ; & teacheth Wit to be inamored

vpon Beautye : as Quickſiluer embraſeth gold ;
or as vertue affecteth honour ; or as Aſtronomy
gazeth vpon heauen ; to make Arte more excellent
by contemplation of excellenteſt Nature. Petrarck
was a delicate man, and with an elegant iudge-
ment gratiouſly confined Loue within the limits of
Honour ; Witt within the boundes of Diſcretion ;
Eloquence within the termes of Ciuility : as not
many yeares ſithence, an Ingliſhe Petrarck did,
a ſingular Gentleman, and a ſweete Poet ; whoſe
verſe ſingeth, as valour might ſpeake ; and whoſe
ditty, is an Image of the Sun, voutſafing to repre-
ſent his glorious face in a clowde. What ſpeake
I of one, or two Ingliſh Paragons ? or what ſhould
I blaſon the gallant, and braue meeters of Arioſto,
and Taſſo, alwayes notable, ſometimes admirable ?
All the nobleſt Italian, French, and Spaniſh Poets,
haue in their ſeuerall / Veines Petrarchiſed, that is,
looued wittily, not groſely, liued ciuilly, not lewdly,
and written deliciouſly, not wantonly. And it is
no diſhonour for the daintyeſt, or diuineſt Muſe,
to be his ſcholler, whom the amiableſt Inuen-
tion, and bewtifulleſt Elocution acknowledge
their maſter. All poſterity honour Petrarck,
that was the harmony of heauen ; the lyfe of
Poetry ; the grace of Arte ; a precious tablet of
rare conceits, & a curious frame of exquiſite
workemanſhip ; / nothing but neate Witt, and re-

fined Eloquence. Were the amorous mufe of my
enemy, fuch a liuely Spring of fweeteft flowres, &
fuch a liuing Harueft of ripeft fruits; I would
abandon other loues, to dote vpon that moft-louely
mufe, and would debafe the Dyamant in com-
parifon of that moft Dyamant mufe. But out-
vpon ranke, & lothfome ribaldry, that putrifieth,
where it fhould purify, and prefumeth to deflowre
the mofte florifhinge wittes, with whom it con-
forteth, eyther in familiarity, or by fauour. One
Ouid was too-much for Roome; and one Greene
too-much for London: but one Nafhe more intol-
lerable then both: not bicaufe his witt is anye
thinge comparable, but bicaufe his will is more
outragious. Ferraria could fcarcely brooke Ma-
nardus, a poyfonous Phifitian: Mantua hardly
beare Pomponatius, a poyfonous Philofopher:
Florence more hardly tollerate Macchiauel, a
poyfonous politician: Venice moft hardly endure
Arretine, a poyfonous ribald: had they liued in
abfolute Monarchies, they would haue feemed
vtterly infupportable. Germany, Denmarke,
Sweden, Polony, Boemia, Hungary, Mofcouy,
are no foiles of any fuch wittes: but neither
Fraunce, nor Spaine, nor Turky, nor any puiffant
kingdom, in one, or other Monarchy of the old,
or new world, could euer abide any fuch per-
nicious writers, deprauers of cōmon difcipline.

Ingland, fince it was Inglãd, neuer bred more
honorable mindes, more aduenturous hartes, more
valorous handes, or more excellent wittes, then of-
late : it is enough for Filly-folly to intoxicate it
felfe, though it be not fuffered to defyle the lande,
which the water enuironeth, the Earth enritcheth,
the aier enfweeteneth, and the Heauen blefeth.
The bounteous graces of God are fowen thicke,
but come vp thin : corruption had little need to
be / foftred : wantonneffe wilbe a nurfe, a bawde,
a Poet, a Legend to itfelfe: vertue hath much-
adoe to hold-out inuiolably her purpofed courfe :
Refolution is a forward fellow, and Valour a braue
man ; but affections are infectious, and appetite
muft fometime haue his fwinge. Were Appetite
a loyall fubiect to Reafon, and Will an affectionate
feruant to Wifdom; as Labour is a dutifull vaffal
to Commodity, and Trauail a flying poft to
Honour; ô heauens, what exploites of worth,
or rather what miracles of excellency, might be
atcheeued in an age of Pollicy, & a world of
Induftry. The date of idle vanityes is expired :
awaye with thefe fcribling paltryes: there is
another Sparta in hande, that indeede requireth
Spartan Temperance, Spartan Frugality, Spartan
exercife, Spartan valiancye, Spartan perfeuerance,
Spartan inuincibility: and hath no wanton leafure
for the Comedyes of Athens; nor anye bawdy

howers for the fonges of Priapus, or the rymes
of Nafhe. Had he begun to Aretinize, when
Elderton began to ballat, Gafcoine to fonnet,
Turberuille to madrigal, Drant to verfify, or
Tarleton to extemporife; fome parte of his phan-
tafticall bibble-bables, and capricious panges, might
haue bene tollerated in a greene, and wild youth:
but the winde is chaunged, & there is a bufier
pageant vpon the ftage. M. Afchams Toxophilus
long fithence fhot at a fairer marke: and M.
Gafcoigne himfelfe, after fome riper experience,
was glad to trye other conclufions in the Lowe
Countryes; and beftowed an honorable com-
mendation vpon Sir Humfrye Gilbertes gallant
difcourfe, of a difcouery for a newe paffage to
the Eaft Indyes. But read the report of the
worthy Wefterne difcoueries, by the faid Sir
Humfry Gilbert: the report of the braue Weft-
Indian voyage by the conduction of Sir Frauncis
Drake: the report / of the horrible Septentrionall
difcoueries by the trauail of Sir Martin Forbifher:
the report of the politique difcouery of Virginia,
by the Colony of Sir Walter Raleigh: the report
of fundry other famous difcoueryes, & aduentures,
publifhed by M. Rychard Hackluit in one volume,
a worke of importance: the report of the hoatt
wellcom of the terrible Spanifhe Armada to the
coaft of Inglande, that came in glory, and went in

diſhonour: the report of the redoubted voyage
into Spaine, and Portugall, whence the braue Earle
of Eſſex, and the twoo valorous Generals, Sir Iohn
Norris, and Sir Frauncis Drake returned with
honour: the report of the reſolute encounter
about the Iles Azores, betwixt the Reuenge of
Ingland, and an Armada of Spaine ; in which
encounter braue Sir Richard Grinuile moſt vigor-
ouſly & impetuouſly attempted the extreameſt
poſſibilities of valour and fury: for breuity I
ouerſkipp many excellent Traicts of the ſame, or
the like nature: but reade theſe, and M. William
Borrowghes notable diſcourſe of the variation of
the compas, or magneticall needle ; annexed to
the new Attractiue of Robert Norman Hydro-
grapher: vnto which two, Ingland in ſome re-
ſpectes is as much beholding, as Spayne vnto
Martin Cortes, & Peter de Medina, for the Arte
of Nauigation : and when you haue obſerued the
courſe of Induſtry ; examined the antecedents,
and conſequents of Trauail ; compared Ingliſh,
and Spaniſh valour ; meaſured the Forces of both
parties ; weighed euery circumſtance of Aduantage :
conſidered the Meanes of our aſſurance: and
finally found proffit to be our pleaſure, prouiſion
our ſecurity, labour our honour, warfare our wel-
fare : who of reckoning, can ſpare anye lewde, or
vaine tyme for corrupt pamphlets ; or who of

iudgment, will not cry? away with thefe paultringe
fidle-fadles. / When Alexander in his conquerous
expeditions vifited the ruines of Troy, and reuolued
in his minde the valiant actes of the Heroicall
Woorthies there atchieued ; One offered to bring
his Maiefty, the Harpe of Paris: Let it alone,
quoth hee, it is the Harpe of Achilles, that muft
ferue my turne. Paris vppon his harpe, fang
voluptuous, & lafciuious Carols : Achilles harpe
was an inftrument of glory, and a quier of diuine
Hymnes, confecrated to the honour of valorous
Captaines, and mighty Conquerours. He regarded
not the dainety Lydian, Iönian, or Æolian Melody:
but the braue Dorian, and impetuous Phrygian
Mufique : and waged Zenophantus to enflame
and enrage his courage with the furious notes of
Battail. One Alexander was a thoufand Examples
of Proweffe : but Pyrrhus, the redoubted king of
the Epirots, was an other Alexander in tempeftuous
execution : and in a moft-noble refolution con-
temned the Vanities of vnnoble Paftimes: in fo
much that, when one of his Barons afked his
Maieftie, whether of the twoo Mufitians, Charifius,
or Python, pleafed his Highneffe better : Whether
of the two, quoth Pyrrhus: marry Polyfperces
fhall go for my money. He was a braue Captaine
for the eie, & a fitt Mufitian for the eare of
Pyrrhus. Happy Polyfperces, that ferued fuch a

mafter: and happy Pyrrhus that commaunded
fuch a feruaunt. Were fome demaunded, whether
Greenes, or Nafhes Pamflets, were better penned :
I beleeue they would aunfweare; Sir Roger
Williams Difcourfe of War for Militare Doctrine
in Effe ; and M. Thomas Digges Stratioticos, for
Militare Difcipline in Effe. And whiles I re-
member the Princely care of Gelo, a famous
Tyrant of Sicill, (many tyrants of Sicill were very
politique) that commaunded his great horfe to be
brought into the banquetting houfe, where other /
Lordes called for the Harpe, other Knights for
the Waites : I cannot forget the gallant difcourfe
of Horfemanfhip, penned by a rare gentleman,
M. Iohn Aftely of the Court : whom I dare intitle
our Inglifh Xenophon ; and maruell not, that
Pietro Bizzaro, a learned Italian, propofeth him
for a perfect Patterne of Caftilios Courtier. And
thinking vpon worthy M. Aftely, I cannot ouer-
paffe the like labour of good M. Thomas Blundeuil,
without due commendation : whofe painefull, and
fkillfull bookes of Horfemanfhip, deferue alfo to
be regiftred in the Catalogue of Xenophontian
woorkes. What fhould I fpeake of the two braue
Knightes, Mufidorus, and Pyrocles, combined in
one excellent knight, Sir Philip Sidney; at the
remembrance of whofe woorthy, and fweete
Vertues, my hart melteth? Will you needes haue

a written Pallace of Pleafure, or rather a printed
Court of Honour?   Read   the   Counteffe   of
Pembrookes Arcadia, a gallant Legendary, full
of pleafurable accidents, and proffitable difcourfes ;
for three thinges efpecially, very notable ; for
amorous Courting, (he was young in yeeres ;) for
fage counfelling, (he was ripe in iudgement ;) and
for valorous fighting, (his foueraine profeffion was
Armes :)   and   delightfull paftime by way of
Paftorall exercifes, may paffe for the fourth.   He
that will Looue, let him learne to looue of him,
that will teach him to Liue ; & furnifh him with
many pithy, and effectuall inftructions, delectably
interlaced by way of proper defcriptions of excel-
lent Perfonages, and common narrations of other
notable occurrences;   in the veine of Saluft, Liuy,
Cornelius Tacitus, Iuftine, Eutropius, Philip de
Comines, Guicciardine, and the moft fententious
Hiftorians, that haue powdred their ftile with the
falt of difcretion, and feafoned their iudgement with
the leauen / of experience.   There want not fome
futtle Stratagems of importance, and fome politique
Secretes of priuitie : and he that would fkillfully,
and brauely manage his weapon with a cunning
Fury, may finde liuely Precepts in the gallant
Examples of his valianteft Duellifts ; efpecially of
Palladius, and Daiphantus; Zelmane. and Am-
phialus ; Phalantus, and Amphialus : but chiefly

of Argalus, and Amphialus ; Pyrocles, and Anaxius;
Mufidorus, and Amphialus, whofe lufty combats,
may feeme Heroicall Monomachies. And that
the valour of fuch redoubted men, may appeere
the more confpicuous, and admirable, by compari-
fon, and interview of their contraries ; fmile at
the ridiculous encounters of Dametas, & Dorus;
of Dametas, and Clinias ; and euer when you
thinke vpon Dametas, remember the Confuting
Champion, more furquidrous then Anaxius, and
more abfurd then Dametas: and if I fhould al-
wayes hereafter call him Dametas, I fhould fitt him
with a name, as naturally proper vnto him, as his
owne. Gallant Gentlemen, you that honor Vertue,
and would enkindle a noble courage in your
mindes to euery excellent purpofe ; if Homer
be not at hand, (whome I haue often tearmed
the Prince of Poets, and the Poet of Princes)
you may read his furious Iliads, & cunning
Odyffes in the braue aduentures of Pyrocles, and
Mufidorus: where Pyrocles playeth the dowty
fighter, like Hector, or Achilles ; Mufidorus, the
valiant Captaine, like Pandarus, or Diomedes;
both, the famous errant Knightes, like Æneas, or
Vlyffes. Lord, what would himfelfe haue prooued
in fine, that was the gentleman of Curtefy, the
Efquier of Induftry, and the Knight of Valour at
thofe yeeres ? Liue euer fweete Booke; the filuer

Image of his gentle witt, and the golden Pillar of his noble courage: and euer notify vnto / the worlde, that thy Writer, was the Secretary of Eloquence; the breath of the Mufes ; the hooney-bee of the dayntieft flowers of Witt, and Arte; the Pith of morall, & intellectuall Vertues; the arme of Bellona in the field ; the toung of Suada in the chãber; the fpirite of Practife in effe; and the Paragon of Excellency in Print.   And now whiles I confider, what a Trompet of Honour, Homer hath bene to fturre-vp many woorthy Princes; I cannot forget the woorthy Prince, that is a Homer to himfelfe, a Golden fpurre to Nobility, a Scepter to Vertue, a Verdùre to the Spring, a Sunne to the day; and hath not onely tranflated the two diuine Poems of Saluftius du Bartas, his heauenly Vrany, and his hellifh Furies : but hath readd a moft valorous Martial Lecture vnto himfelfe in his owne victorious Lepanto, a fhort, but heroicall worke, in meeter, but royal meeter, fitt for a Dauids harpe.   Lepanto, firft the glory of Chriften-dome againft the Turke ; and now the garland of a foueraine crowne.   When young Kings haue fuch a care of their flourifhing Prime; and like Cato, are ready to render an accompt of their vacant howers ; as if Aprill were their Iuly, and May their Auguft : how fhould gentlemen of yeeres, employ the golden talent of their Induftry, and trauaile?

with what feruency ; with what vigour ; with
what zeale, with what inceffant, and indefatigable
endeuour ? Phy vpon fooleries : there be honour-
able woorkes to doe ; and notable workes to read.
The afore-named Bartas, (whome elfewhere I haue
ftiled the Treafurer of Humanity, and the Ieweller
of Diuinity) for the highneffe of his fubiect, and
the maiefty of his verfe, nothing inferiour vnto
Dante, (whome fome Italians preferre before Virgil,
or Homer,) a right infpired and enrauifhed Poet ;
full of chofen, graue, profound, venerable, and
ftately matter ; euen / in the next Degree to the
facred, and reuerend ftile of heauenly Diuinity it
felfe. In a manner the onely Poet, whom Vrany
hath voutfafed to Laureate with her owne heauenly
hand : and worthy to bee alleadged of Diuines,
and Counfellours, as Homer is quoted of Philofo-
phers, & Oratours. Many of his folemne verfes,
are oracles : & one Bartas, that is, one French
Salomō, more weighty in ftern, and mighty
counfell, then the Seauen Sages of Greece. Neuer
more beauty in vulgar Languages : but his ftile
addeth fauour, and grace to beauty ; and in a
goodly Boddy reprefenteth a puiffant Soule. How
few verfes carry fuch a perfonage. of ftate ? or how
few argumentes, fuch a fpirite of maiefty ? Or
where is the diuine inftincte, that can fufficiently
commend fuch a volume of celeftiall infpiration ?

What a iudgement hath the noble youth, the harueſt of the Spring, the ſapp of Apollos tree, the diademe of the Muſes, that leaueth the enticingeſt flowers of delite, to reape the matureſt fruites of wiſedome? Happy plants, that ſpeedily ſhewfoorth their generous nature : and a ſoueraigne good poſſeſſeth thoſe worthy mindes, that ſuffer not their affections to be inueigled, or entangled with any vnworthy thought. Great Exerciſes become great perſonages : as the Magnes approoueth his Nobility in commaunding Iron, and taming the Sea : baſer, or meaner paſtimes belong vnto meaner Perſons ; as Iett diſcouereth his gentry, in drawing chaffe, haires, and ſuch trifles. A meete qualitie for Iett, or a pretty feate for Amber, to iuggle chaffe, feſtues, or the like weighty burdens : but excellent mindes are employed, like the noble Magnes, and euer conuerſant either in effecting, or in peruſing, or in penning excellent workes. It were an impoſſible attempte, to do right vnto the great Captaine, Monſieur de la Noë, and the / braue ſoldiour, the French King himſelfe, two terrible thunderboltes of warre, and two impetuous whirlewinds of the Field : whoſe writinges are like their actions, reſolute, effectuall, valiant, politique, vigorous, full of aëry, & fiery ſpirite, honourable, renowned whereſoeuer Valour hath a mouth, or Vertue a pen. Could the Warlie

Horfe fpeake, as he can runne, and fight, he would tell them, they are hoat Knightes: and could the bluddy Sword write, as it can fheare, it would dedicate a volume of Fury vnto the one, and a monument of Victory vnto the other. Albeit men fhould be malitious, or forgetfull, (Spite is malitious, and Ingratitude forgetfull) yet Proweffe hath a Clouen Tounge ; and teacheth Admiration in a fiery language to pleade the glorious honour of emproued valiancy.

Some accufe their deftiny ; but bleffed Key, that openeth fuch lockes : and lucky, moft lucky fortune, that yeeldeth fuch vertue. Braue Chiualry, a continuall witneffe of their valour and terribility in warre : and gallant Induftry the dayly bread of their life, in peace, or truce. Report fhining Sunne, the dayes-worke of the King : and burning Candle, relate his Nightes-ftuddy : and both ridd me of an endleffe labour. For who euer prayfed the wonders of Heauen ?

And what an infinite courfe were it, to runne-thorough the particular commendations of the famous redoubted actours, or the notable pregnant writers of this age, euen in the moft-puiffant Heroicall, and Argonauticall kinde?

Nimble Entelechy hath beene a ftraunger in fome Countries : albeit a renowned Citifen of Greece ; and a free Denifen of Italy, Spaine, Fraunce, and

Germany : but wellcome the moft-naturall inhabit-
ant of the world ; the faile of the fhip, the flight
of the bowe, the fhott of the gunne, the / wing
of the Eagle, the quinteffence of the minde, the
courfe of the funne, the motion of the heauens,
the influence of the ftarres, the heate of the fire,
the lightneffe of the Ayer, the fwiftneffe of the
winde, the ftreame of the water, the frutefulneffe
of the Earth, the fingularitie of this age : and
thanke thy moft-vigorous felfe for fo many
precious workes of diuine furie, and powerable
confequence ; refpectiuely comparable with the
richeft Treafuries, and braueft armories of Anti-
quitie.   Thrife-happie, or rather a thoufand times-
happie Creature, that with moft aduantage of all
honorable opportunities, & with the extremeft
poffibilitie of his whole powers, inward, or out-
ward, emploieth the moft-excellent excellencie of
humane, or diuine Nature.   Other Secretes of
Nature, and Arte, deferue an high reputation in
their feuerall degrees, and may challenge a fouerain
interteinement in their fpeciall kinds : but Ente-
lechy is the myfterie of myfteries vnder heauen,
and the head-fpring of the powerfulleft Vertues,
that diuinitie infufeth, humanitie imbraceth, Philo-
fophie admireth, wifedome practifeth, Induftrie
emproueth, valour extendeth ; or he conceiued,
that conceiuing the wonderfull faculties of the

mind, & aftonifhed with the incredible force of a
rauifhed, & enthufiafticall fpirite ; in a profound
contemplation of that eleuate, and tranfcendent
capacitie, (as it were in a deepe ecftafie, or Sera-
phicall vifion,) moft-pathetically cryed-out ; *ô*
magnum miraculum Homo. No maruel, ô great
miracle, & ô moft powerful Entelechy, though
thou feemift A Pilgrim to Dametas, that art the
Familiar Spirite of Mufidorus: & what wõder,
though he empeach thy eftimation, that defpifeth
the graces of God, flowteth the conftellations of
heauē, frumpeth the operations of nature, mocketh
the effectualleft & auayllableft Arts, difdayneth / the
name of Induftrie, or Honefty, fcorneth whatfoeuer
may appeare Vertuous, fawneth onely ' vpon his
owne conceits, claweth only his owne fauorits, and
quippeth, bourdeth, girdeth, affeth the excellēteft
writers of whatfoeuer note, that tickle not his
wãton fenfe. Nothing memorable, or remarkable
with him, that feafteth not the riotous appetite of
the ribald, or the humorous conceit of the phãtaft.
It is his S. Fame, to be the infamy of learning :
his reformatiõ, to be the corruption of his reader :
his felicitie, to be the miferie of youth : his health,
to be the fcurfe of the Citie, the fcabbe of the
Vniuerfitie, the bile of the Realme : his faluation,
to be the damnation of whatfoeuer is termed good,
or accounted honeft. Sweet Gentlemen, and florifh-

ing youthes, euer aime at the right line of Arte
and Vertue, of the one for knowledge, of the other
for valour: and let the crooked rectifie itſelfe.
Reſolution wandreth not, like an ignorant Traueller,
but in euery enterpriſe, in euery affaire, in euery
ſtuddie, in euery cogitation leuelleth at ſome cer-
taintie ; and alwayes hath an eye to Vſe, an eare
to good report, a regard to worth, a reſpect to
aſſurance, and a reference to the end. He that
erreth, erreth againſt Truth, and himſelfe: and he
that ſinneth, ſinneth againſt God, and himſelfe:
he is none of my charge: it ſuffiſeth me to be the
Curate of myne owne actions, the maſter of mine
owne paſſions, the frend of my frends, the pittyer
of my enemies, the loouer of good witts, and
honeſt mindes, the affectionate ſeruant of Artes,
& Vertues, the humble Oratour of noble Valour,
the Commender of the foreſaid honorable writinges,
or any commendable workes. Reaſon is no mans
tyrant : & Dutie euery mans vaſſall, that deſerueth
well. Would this pen were worthy to be the ſlaue
of the worthieſt actours, or the bondman of the /
aboue mentioned, and the-like important Autours.

Such Mercuriall, and Martiall Diſcourſes, in the
actiue, and chiualrous veine, pleade their owne
eternall honour: and write euerlaſting ſhame in
the forhead of a thouſand friuolous, & ten
thouſand phantaſticall Pamflets. I would to Chriſt,

fome of them were but idle toyes, or vayne trifles :
but impuritie neuer prefumed fomuch of impunitie :
and licentious follie by priuiledge, lewd ribaldrie
by permiffion, and rank villanie by conniuance,
are become famous Autours : not in a popular
ftate, or a petty-principalitie, but in a fouerain
Monarchie, that tendereth politique gouernment,
& is to fortifie itfelfe againft forein hoftilitie. If
Wifedome fay not, Phie for fhame ; & Autoritie
take not other order in conuenient time : who can
tell, what generall plague may enfue of a fpeciall
infection? or when the kinges-euill is paft cure,
who can fay, we will now heale it? The baddeft
weed groweth fafteft : and no Gangrene fo preg-
nantly difpreddeth itfelfe, as riott. And what riott
fo peftiferous, as that, which in fugred baites
prefenteth moft poifonous hookes? Sir Skelton,
and Mafter Scoggin, were but Innocents to Signior
Capricio, and Monfieur Madneffe : whofe peftilent
canker fcorneth all the Medicine of Earth, or
heauen.

My writing, is but a priuate note for the publique
aduertifemēt of fome fewe : whofe youth afketh
inftruction, & whofe frailtie needeth admonition.
In the cure of a canker, it is a generall rule with
Surgeōs : It neuer perfectly healeth, vnleffe the
rootes and all be vtterly extirped ; and the flefhe
regenerate. But the foundeft Principle is : *Prin-*

cipijs obſta : & it goeth beſt with them, that neuer knewe, what a canker, or leper meant.

I ſtill hoped for ſome graffes of better fruite : but this graund / Confuter of my Letters, and all honeſtie, ſtill proceedeth from worſe to worſe, from the wilding-tree to the withie, from the dogge to the goate, from the catt to the ſwine, from Prime-roſe hill to Colman hedge : and is ſo rooted in deepe Vanitie, that there is no ende of his profound follie. Which deſerueth a more famous Encomi-aſticall Oration, then Eraſmus renowned Follie : and more gloriouſly diſdaineth any cure, then the Goute. I may anſwer his hoat rauing in cold termes : and conuince him of what notorious falſe-hood, or villanie I can : but ſee the fräke ſpirite of a full ſtomack : & who euer was ſo parlouſly matched ? Were not my ſimplicitie, or his omni-ſuficiencie exceeding great ; I had neuer bene thus terriblie ouer-challēged. *Gabriel, if there be any witt, or induſtrie in thee, now I will dare it to the vttermoſt : write of what thou wilt, in what language thou wilt, and I will confute it, and anſwere it. Take Truthes part, & I will prooue truth to be no truth, marching out of thy doung-voiding mouth :* & ſo forth in the brauing tenour of the ſame redoubt-able ſtile. Good Gentlemen, you ſee the ſweet diſpoſitiō of the man ; & neede no other window into the cloſet of his cōſcience, but his owne Gloſſe

vpon his owne Text. Whatfoeuer poore I fay, in
any matter, or in any language, albeit Truth auerr
and iuftifie the fame, he will flatly denie, and
confute, euen bicaufe I fay it; & onely bicaufe
in a frolick and dowtie iollitie, he will haue the
laft word of me. His Grammer, is his Catechifme ;
Si ais, nego : his ftomack, his Dictionarie in any
language : and his quarrell, his Logique in any
argument : *Lucian, Iulian, Aretin, I proteft were
you ought elfe but abhominable Atheifts, that I
would obftinatly defende you, onely bicaufe Laureate
Gabriel articles againft you.* Were there not other-
wife a maruelous oddes, and incomprehenfible
difference betwixt our habi / lities, he would neuer
dare me, like a bold Pandare, with fuch ftout
challenges, and glorious proteftations : but fingular
wittes haue a great aduantage of fimple men : and
cunning Falfehood is a mightie confuter of plaine
Truth. No fuch champion, as he that fighteth
obftinatly with the target of Confidence, and the
long-fword of Impudence. If any thing extra-
ordinarily emprooueth valour, it is Confidence :
and if any thing miraculoufly fingularizeth witt,
it is Impudence. Diftruft, is a naturall foole :
and Modeftie, an artificiall foole : he that will
exploit wõdermentes, and karrie all before him,
like a fweepe-ftake, muft haue a hart of Iron, a
forhead of Braffe, and a toung of Adamant.

Pelting circumftances, marre braue executions :
looke into the proceedinges of the greateft doers;
and what haue they more then other men, but
Audacitie, and Fortune?

*Audendum eft aliquid, Vinclis, & carcere dignum,
Si vis effe aliquid.*   Simplicitie may haue a geffe
at the Principles of the world : and Nafhe affecteth
to feeme a compound of fuch Elementes; as bold,
as æger, and as æger, as a madd dogge.   He will
confute me, bicaufe he will : and he can conquer
me, bicaufe he can.   If I come vpon him with a
gentle reply, he will welcome me with a fierce
reioynder : for any my briefe Triplication, he will
prouide a Quadruplication at-large : & fo forth
in *infinitā*, with an vndauntable courage : for he
fweareth, *he will neuer leaue me as long as he is
hable to lift a penne.*   Twentie fuch famous depo-
fitions proclaime his dowtie refolution, and inde-
fatigable hand at a pight fielde.   Were I to begin
agayne, or cold I handfomely deuife to giue him
the cleanly flipp, I would neuer deale with a fprite
of Coleman hedge, or a May-Lord of Primerofe
hill ; that hath all humours / in his liuerie, & can
put confcience in a Vices coate.   Na, hee will
atchieue impoffibilities ; and in contempt of my
fimplicitie, prooue Truth a counterfaict, and him-
felfe a true witneffe of falfeft lyes.   But Lord, that
fo inuincible a Gentleman fhould make fo folemne

account, of confuting, and reconfuting a perfon of
fo litle worth in his valuation? Sweet man, what
fhould you thinke of troubling your-felfe with fo
tedious a courfe, when you might fo blithly haue
taken a quicker order, and may yet proceede more
compendioufly? It had bene a worthy exploit,
and befeeming a witt of fupererogation, to haue
dipped a fopp in a goblet of *rennifh wine*; and
naming it Gabriel, (for you are now growne into
great familiaritie with that name) to haue de-
uoured him vpp at one bit: or taking a *pickle
herring* by the throte, and chriftening it Richard
(for you cã chriften him at your pleafure) to haue
fwallowed him downe with a ftomack. Did you
neuer heare of deteftable Iewes, that made a picture
of Chrift; and then buffetted, cuggelled, fcourged,
crucified, ftabbed, pierced, and mangled the-fame
moft vnmercifully? Now you haue a patterne, I
doubt not but you can with a dexteritie, chopp-of
the head of a dead hoony bee, and boaft you haue
ftricken Iohn, as dead as a doore-nayle. Other
fpoyle, or victorie (by the leaue of the forefaid
redoubted daring) will prooue a bufie peece of
worke for the fonne of a mule, a rawe Gram-
marian, a brabling Sophifter, a counterfaict cranke,
a ftale rakehell, a piperly rymer, a ftump-worne
railer, a dodkin autor: whofe two fwordes, are
like the hornes of an hodmandod; whofe courage,

like the furie of a gad-bee; and whofe furmount-
ing brauerie, like the wings of a butterfly. I take
no pleafure to call thee an Affe; but thou prooueft
thi-felfe a Haddock: and although I fay not, /
Thou art a foole, yet thou wilt needs bewray thy
diet, and difgorge thy ftomack of the Lobfter, and
coddefhed, wherewith thou didft englutt thifelfe,
fince thy notorious furfett of pikle herring, and
dogfifh. Thou art neither *Dorbell, nor Duns, nor
Thomas of Aquine:* they were three fharp-edged,
and quickfented fchoolemen, full of nimble witt,
and intricate quiddities in their arguing kinde,
efpecially *Duns, and Thomas:* but by fome of thy
cauilling *Ergos,* thou fhouldft feeme to be the
fpawne of Iauell, or Tartaret: & as very a crab-
fifh at an *Ergo,* as euer crawled-ouer Carters
Logique, or the *Pofteriorums of Iohannes de
Lapide.* When I looke vpõ thy firft page (as
I daily behold that terrible Emprefe for a recrea-
tion) ftill methinkes there fhould come flufhing-
out the great Atlas of Logique, and Aftronomie,
that fupported the orbes of the heauens by Art:
or the mightie Hercules of Rhetorique and Poetrie,
that with certaine maruelous fine, and delicate
chaines, drewe after him the vaffals of [the] world
by the eares. But examin his futtellieft *Ergos,* &
taft his nappieft Inuention, or daintieft Elocution,
(he that hath nothing elfe to do, may hold him-

felfe occupied) : and Art will foone finde the huge
Behemoth of Conceit, to be the fprat of a pickle
herring; and the hideous Leuiathan of Vainglorie,
to be a fhrimpe in Witt, a periwinkle in Art, a
dandiprat in Induftrie, a dodkin in Valu; and
fuch a toy of toyes, as euery right Schollar hiffeth
at in iudgement, and euery fine Gentleman maketh
the Obiect of his fcorne. He can raile: (what
mad Bedlam cannot raile?) but the fauour of his
railing, is grofely fell, and fmelleth noyfomly of
the pumpe, or a naftier thing. His gayeft
flooriſhes, are but Gafcoignes weedes, or Tarletons
trickes, or Greenes crankes, or Marlowes brauados:
his ieftes, but the dregges of cõmon fcurrilitie, the /
fhreds of the theater, or the of-fcouring of new
Pamflets : his frefheft nippitatie, but the froth of
ftale inuentiõs, long-fince lothfome to quick taftes :
his fhrouing ware, but lenten ftuff, like the old
pickle herring : his luftieft verdure, but ranke
ordure, not to be named in Ciuilitie, or Rhetorique:
his only Art, & the vengeable drift of his whole
cunning, to mangle my fentences, hack my argu-
ments, chopp and change my phrafes, wrinch my
wordes, and hale euery fillable moft extremely ;
euen to the difioynting, and maiming of my
whole meaning. O times: ô paftimes: ô mõftrous
knauerie. The refidue whatfoeuer, hath nothing
more in it, then is vfuallie in euery ruffianly

Copefmate, that hath bene a Grãmar fchollar,
readeth riotous bookes, hanteth roifterly companie,
delighteth in rude fcoffing, & karrieth a defperate
minde. Let him be thorowly perufed by any
indifferent reader whomfoeuer, that can iudicioufly
difcerne, what is what ; and will vprightly cenfure
him according to his fkill, without partialitie *pro*,
or *contra* : and I dare vndertake, he will affirme
no leffe, vpon the credit of his iudgement; but
will definitiuely pronounce him, the very Baggage
of new writers. I could nominate the perfon, that
vnder his hand-writing hath ftiled him, The cockifh
challenger, the lewd fcribler, the offal of corrupteft
mouthes, the draff of filthieft pennes, the bag-
pudding of fooles, & the very pudding-pittes of
the wife, or honeft. He might haue read of foure
notable thinges, which many a iollie man weeneth
he hath at will, when he hath nothing leffe : much
knowledge ; found wifedome ; great power ; &
many frends. And he might haue heard of other
foure fpeciall thinges, that worke the deftruction,
or confufion of the forwardeft practitioners : a
headlong defire to know much haftily; a greedie
thirft to haue much fud / dainly ; an ouerweening
conceit of themfelues; and a furly contempt of
other. I could peraduẽture arread him his fortune
in a fatall booke, as verifiable, as peremptorie : but
I looue not to infult vpõ miferie : & Deftinie is a

Iudge, whofe fentence needeth no other execution,
but itfelfe. No preuention, but deepe repentance ;
an impoffible remedy, where deepe Obftinacie is
grounded, and high Prefumption afpireth aboue
the Moone. Hawtie minds may flie aloft, and
haften their owne ouer-throw ; but it is not the
wainfcott forhead of a Rudhuddibras, that can
arreare fuch an huge opinion, as himfelfe in a
ftrong conceit of a mighty conception, feemeth to
trauaill withall : as it were with a flying Bladude,
attempting wonderments in the Ayre, or a Simon
Magus, experimenting impoffibilities, from the top
of the Capitoll. He muft either accomplifh fome
greater worke of Supererogation, with actual at-
chieuement, (that is now a principall point): or
immortalize himfelfe the prowdeft Vaine fott, that
euer abufed the world with foppifh oftentation ;
not in one, or two pages, but in the firft, the laft,
& euery leafe of his Strange Newes. For the end
is like the beginning ; the midft like both ; and
euery part like the whole. Railing, railing, railing :
bragging, bragging, bragging : and nothing elfe,
but fowle railing vpon railing, and vayne bragging
vpon bragging ; as rudely, grofely, odioufly, filthily,
beaftly, as euer fhamed Print. Vnleffe he meant
to fett-vpp a Railing fchoole, and to read a pub-
like Lecture of bragging, as the onely regall
profeffour of that, and that facultie, now other

ſhiftes begin to fayle. I wonder, his owne mouth can abide it without a phah. You haue heard ſome worthie Premiſſes : behold a braue concluſion :

Awaite the world, the Tragedy of Wrath :
What | next I paint, ſhall tread no common Path :

with an other doubble *Aut,* for a gallant Embleme, or a glorious Farewell; *Aut nunquam tentes, aut perfice.* Subſcribed with his owne hande; *Thomas Naſh.* Not expect, or attend, but *a wait* : not ſome few, or the Citty, or the Vniuerſity, or this Land, or Europe, *but the World* : not a Comedy, or a Declamation, or an Inuectiue, or a Satire, or any like Elencticall diſcourſe : but a *Tragedy,* and the very *Tragedy of Wrath*; that ſhall daſh the direfulleſt Tragedies of Seneca, Euripides, or Sophocles, out of Conceit. *The next peece,* not of his Rhetorique, or Poetry, but of his *Painture,* ſhall *not treade* the way to Poules, or Weſtminſter, or the Royall Exchange ; but at leaſt ſhall perfect the Venus face of Apelles, or ſett the world an euerlaſting Sample of inimitable artificiality. Other mens writing in proſe, or verſe, may plodd-on, as before ; but *his Painting* will now tread *A rare Path*; and by the way beſtow A new Leſſon vppon Rhetorique, how to continue a metaphor, or vphold an Allegory with aduauntage. *The tread-*

ing of that rare Path, by that exquifite *Painting,*
(his woórkes are miracles ; and his *Painting,* can
treade, like his dauncing, or frifking, *no common
but a proper Path*) who expecteth not with an
attentiue, a feruiceable, a coouetous, a longing
expectation ? *A wait world :* and Apelles tender
thy moft affectionate deuotion, to learne a wonder-
full peece of curious workemanfhip, when it fhall
pleafe his next *Painting* to *tread the path* of his moft
fingular fingularity. Meanewhile it hath pleafed
foome fweete wittes of my acquaintaunce, (whome
Heauen hath baptized the Spirites of harmony, and
the Mufes haue enterteyned for their Paramours)
to reacquite Sonnets with Sonnets, and to fnibb the
Thrafonicall rimefter with Angelical meeter, that
may haply / appeare in fitt place : and finely
difcouer young Apuleius in his ramping roabe ;
the fourth Furie in his Tragicall Pageant; the
new Sprite in his proper haunt, or buttry ; and
the confuting Diuell in the horologe. One She,
& two He's haue vowed, they will pumpe *his
Railing Inkhorne* as dry, as euer was Holborne
Conduit : and fquife *his Craking Quill* to as emptie
a fpunge, as any in Hofier Lane. Which of you,
gallat Gentlemé, hath not ftripped *his ftale Ieftes*
into their thredbare ragges ; or fo feldome as an
hundred times pittied his creaft-falne ftile, & his
focket-worne inuention ? Who would haue thought,

or could haue imagined, to haue found the witt
of Pierce, fo ftarued and clunged: the conceit of
an aduerfarie, fo weather-beaten, and tired: the
learning of a fchollar, fo pore-blind, and lame: the
elocutiō of the Diuels Oratour, fo lanke, fo wan,
fo meager, fo blunt, fo dull, fo fordead, fo gaftly,
where the mafculine Furie meant to play his
griflieft, and horribleft part? Welfare a good
vifage in a bad caufe: or farwell Hope, the
kindeft coofener of forlorne harts. The defperate
minde, that affayeth impoffibilities in nature, or
vndertaketh incredibilities in Art, muft be cōtent
to fpeed thereafter. When euery attempt faileth
in performance, and euery extremitie foileth the
enterprifer, at-laft euen Impudencie it felfe muft
be faine to giue-ouer in the plaine fielde: and
neuer yeeld credit to the word of that moft
credible Gentlewoman, if the very brafen buckler
prooue not finally a notorious Dafh-Nafh. He
fummed all in a briefe, but materiall Summe; that
called *the old Affe,* the great A, and the eft Amen
of the *new Supererogation.* And were I here
cōpelled to difpatch abruptly, (as I am prefently
called to a more commodious exercife) fhould I
not fufficiētly haue difcharged my tafke; and
plentifully haue cōmended / *that famous crea-
ture,* whofe prayfe the Title of this Pamflet pro-
feffeth? He that would honor Alexander, may

crowne him the great A. of puiffance : but Pyrrhus, Hanniball, Scipio, Pompey, Cæfar, diuers other mightie Conquerours, & euē fom moderne Worthies would difdaine, to haue him fceptred the eft-Amen of Valour. What a braue, and incomparable Alexander, is that great A that is alfo the eft-Amen of Supererogatiō; a more miraculous and impoffible peece of worke, thē the dowtieft puisfance, or worthieft valour in the old, or new world? Shall I fay, bleffed, or peereleffe young Apuleius, that from the fwathing bandes of his infancie in Print, was fuckled of the fweeteft nurfes, lulled of the deereft groomes, cockered of the fineft miniōs, cowled of the daintieft paramours, hugged of the enticingeft darlinges, and more then tenderly tendered of the moft delitious Mufes, the moft-amiable Graces, and the moft-powerfull Vertues of the faid vnmatchable great A. the graund founder of Supererogatiō, and fole Patron of fuch meritorious clients. As for other remarkable Particulars in the Straunge Newes ; Ink is fo like Ink, fpite fo like fpite, impudencie fo like impudencie, brocage fo like brocage, and Tom-Penniles now, fo like Papp-hatchet, when the time was ; that I neede but ouerrun an old cenfure of the One, by way of new application to the Other. The notes of Martinifme appertaine vnto thofe, whom they concerne. Pierce would laugh, to be charged with

Martinifme, or any Religion : though Martin
himfelfe for a challenging, rufling, and railing ftile,
not fuch a Martin.   Two contraries ; but two
fuch contraries, as can teach Extremities to play
the contraries, and to confound themfelues.

Papp-hatchet, defirous for his benefit, to currie
fauour with / a noble Earle ; and in defecte of
other meanes of Commendatiō, labouring to in-
finuate himfelfe by fmooth glofing, & coūterfait
fuggeftiōs, (it is a Courtly feate, to fnatch the leaft
occafionet of aduantage, with a nimble dexteritie);
fome yeares fince prouoked me, to make the
beft of it, inconfideratly ; to fpeake like a frend,
vnfrendly ; to fay, as it was, intolerably ; without
priuate caufe, or any reafon in the world: (for in
truth I looued him, in hope prayfed him ; many
wayes fauored him, and neuer any way offended
him) : and notwithftanding that fpitefull prouoca-
tiō, and euen that odious threatening of ten .yeares
prouifion, he had euer paffed vntouched with any
fillable of reuenge in Print, had not Greene, and
this dog-fifh, abhominably mifufed the verbe paf-
fiue ; as fhould appeare, by his procurement, or
encouragement, affuredly moft vndeferued, and
moft iniurious.   For what other quarrel, could
Greene, or this dogge-fifh euer picke with me :
whom I neuer fo much as twitched by the fleeue,
before I founde mifelfe, and my deareft frendes,

vnfufferably quipped in moft contumelious, and
opprobrious termes.   But nowe there is no
remedie, haue amongeft you, blind Harpers of
the Printing houfe : for I feare not fix hundred
Crowders, were all your wittes affembled in one
capp of Vanitie, or all your galles vnited in one
bladder of choler.   I haue loft more labour, then
the tranfcripting of this Cenfure : which I dedicate
neither to Lord, nor Lady, but to Truth, and
Æquitie; on whofe fouerain Patronage I relye.

An | *Aduertiſement for* Papp-hatchett, *and Martin Mar-prelate.*

App-hatchett (for the name of thy good nature is pittyfully growen out-of re-queſt) thy olde acquaintance in the Sauoy, when young Euphues hatched the egges, that his elder freendes laide, (ſurely Euphues was ſomeway a pretty fellow: would God Lilly had alwaies bene Euphues, and neuer Pap-hatchet;) that old acquaintance, now ſome-what ſtraungely ſaluted with a new remembrance, is neither lubbabied with thy ſweete Papp, nor ſcarre-crowed with thy ſower hatchet. And al-though in ſelfe-conceit thou knoweſt not thy ſelfe, yet in experience, thou mighteſt haue knowen him, that can Vnbutton thy vanity, and Vnlaſe thy folly: but in pitty ſpareth thy childiſh ſimplicity, that in iudgement ſcorneth thy roiſterly brauery; and neuer thought ſo baſely of thee, as ſince thou began'ſt to diſguiſe thy witt, and diſgrace thy arte with ruffianly foolery. He winneth not moſt

abroad that weeneth moſt at-home : and in my
poore fancy, it were not greatly amiſſe, euen for
the perteſt, and gayeſt companions, (notwithſtand-
ing whatſoeuer courtly holly-water, or plauſible
hopes of preferment) to deigne their olde familiars
the continuance of their former courteſies, without
contempt of the barraineſt giftes, or empeachment
of the meaneſt perſons. The ſimpliſt man in a
pariſh, is a ſhrewd / foole; and Humanity an
Image of Diuinity ; that pulleth-downe the hawty,
and ſetteth-vp the meeke. Euphues, it is good to
bee merry : and Lilly, it is good to bee wiſe: and
Papp-hatchet, it is better to looſe a new ieſt, then
an old frend ; that can cramme the capon with his
owne Papp, and hew-downe the woodcocke with
his owne hatchet. Bolde men, and marchant
Venturers haue ſometime good lucke: but happ-
hazard hath oftentimes good leaue to beſhrow his
owne pate ; and to imbarke the hardy foole in the
famous Shipp of wiſemen. I cannot ſtand noſing
of Candleſtickes, or euphuing of Similes, *alla
Sauoica* : it might happly be done with a trice :
but euery man hath not the guift of *Albertus
Magnus* : rare birds are dainty ; and they are
queint creatures, that are priuiledged to create new
creatures. When I haue a mint of precious ſtones;
& ſtraunge Foules, beaſtes, and fiſhes of mine owne
coyning, (I could name the party, that in com-

parifon of his owne naturall Inuentions, tearmed
Pliny a barraine woombe ;) I may peraduenture
bleffe you with your owne croffes, & pay you
with the vfury of your owne coyne.   In the meane
while beare with a plaine man, as plaine as old
Accurfius, or Barthol de Saxo ferrato ; that wil
make his Cenfure good vpon the carrion of thy
vnfauory, and ftincking Pamflett; a fitt booke to
be ioyned with Scoggins woorkes, or the French
Mirrour of Madneffe.   The very Title dis-
couereth the wifedome of the young-man : as
an olde Fox not long fince bewrayed himfelfe
by a flap of his taile; and a Lion, they fay, is
foone defcried by his pawe ; a Cocke by his
combe ; a Goat by his bearde; an Affe by his
eare; a wife-man by his tale ; an artift by his
tearmes.

Papp with an hatchet: aliàs, a Figg for my God-fonne
  or, Cracke me this nutt : or, a Country Cuffe,
  that | is, A found boxe of the eare, & cetera.
  Written by one, that dares call a Dog a Dog.
Imprinted by Iohn Anoke, and Iohn Aftile, for the Baily
  of Withernam, Cum priuilegio perennitatis :
And are to be fold at the figne of the Crabbtree Cudgell
  in Thwack-coate Lane.

What deuife of Martin, or what inuention of
any other, could haue fett a fairer Orientall Starre

vpon the forhead of that foule libell? Now you
fee the brande, and know the Blackamore by his
face, turne ouer the leafe ; and by the wittineffe
of his firft fentence, aime at the reft. Milke is
like milke: hoony like hoony: Papp like papp:
and hee like himfelfe ; in the whole, a notable
ruffler, and in euery part a dowty braggard.
Roome for a roifter: fo thats well faid: itch a
little further for a good fellow : now haue at you
all, my gaffers of the rayling religion : tis I, that
muft take you a pegg lower. Ile make fuch a fplinter
runne into your wittes : and fo foorth in the fame
lufty tenour. A very artificiall beginning, to
mooue attention, or to procure good-liking in
the reader : vnleffe he wrote onely to roifter-
doifters, & hackfters, or at-leaft to iefters and
vices. Oh, but in his Preamble to the indifferent
reader, he approueth himfelfe a maruellous difcreet,
and modeft man of the fobereft fort, were he not
prouoked in confcience, to aunfweare contrary to
his nature, and manner. You may fee, how graue
men may be made light, to defend the Church.
I perceiue, they were wife, that at riotous times,
when youth was wantonneft, and knauery luftieft,
as in Chriftmas, at Shrofetide, in May, at the
ende of Harueft, and by fuch wild fittes, created
a certaine extraordinary Officer, called a Lord of
Mifrule, as a needefull gouernour, or Dictatour,

to fet thinges in order, and to rule vnruly people ;
with whome otherwife / there were no Ho.   So,
when Reuell-rout beginneth to be a current Autour ;
or Hurly-burly a bufy Promotour : *roome for a
roifter,* that will bore them thorough the nofes
with a cufhion ; that will bung-vp their mouthes
with a Collyrium of all the ftale ieftes in a country ;
that will fuffer none to play the Rex, but himfelfe.
For that is the very depth of his plot : and who
euer began with more roifterly tearmes; or pro-
ceeded with more ruffianly fcoffes ; or concluded
with more haire brain'd trickes ; or tired himfelfe
with more weather-beaten franckes? Whatfcholler,
or gentleman, can reade fuch alehoufe and tinkerly
ftuffe without blufhing ?   They were much deceiued
in him, at Oxford, and in the Sauoy, when Mafter
Abfolon liued ; that tooke him onely for a dapper
& deft companion, or a pert-conceited youth, that
had gathered-togither a fewe prettie fentences,
and could handfomly helpe young Euphues to
an old *Simile :* & neuer thought him any fuch
mighty doer at the fharpe. But *Ile, Ile, Ile,* is a
parlous fellow at *a hatchett : hefe like Death : hele
fpare none : hele fhowe them an Irifh tricke : hele
make them weepe Irifh : hefe good at the fticking
blow : his Pofie, what care I? Vie ftabbes,* good
Ecclefiafticall learning in his Apologie ; and good
Chriftian charitie in his Homilie.   Mufter his

arrant braueries togither : and where fuch a terrible killcowe, or fuch a vengeable bull-beggar to deal withall ? O dreadfull dubble V. that carrieft the dubble ftoccado in thy penne, what a dubble ftabber woldeft thou be, were thy hand as tall a fellow, as thy hart, or thy witt as luftie a ladd, as thy minde ? Other good fellowes may tell Tales of Gawin : thou art Sir Gawin reuiued, or rather Terrour in perfon. Yet fhall I putt a beane into Gawins ratling fcull : and tell thee, where thy flafhing / Long-fword commeth fhort ? Thou profeffeft Railing ; and emprooueft thifelfe in very deede an egregious Railer, as difdaining to yeelde vnto any He, or She Scolde of this age : but what faith my particular Analyfis ? Dubble V. is old-excellent at his *Cornu copiæ* ; and I warrant you, neuer to feeke in his Horne-booke : but debarre thoffame horefon Tales of a tubb ; and put him befide his Horning, Gaming, Fooling, and Knauing : and he is no boddy, but a fewe pilfred *Similes* ; a little Pedanticall Latin ; and the higheft pitch of his witt, Bulles motion, *alias* the hangmans apron. His Ryme, foreftalled by Elderton, that hath Ballats lying a fteepe in ale : his Reafon, by a Cambrige wagg, a twigging Sophifter, that will *Ergo* Martin into an ague, and concludeth peremptorily, Therfore Tiburne muft be furr'd with Martins : nothing left for the Third difputer,

but Railing thorough all the moodes, and figures
of knauerie, as they come frefh, and frefh to his
hand. All three iumpe *in eodem tertio* : nothing
but a certaine exercife, termed hanging, will ferue
their turne : (if it be his deftinie, what remedie?)
they muft draw cuttes, who fhall play the Hange-
man : and that is the argument of the Tragedie,
and the very papp of the hatchet. Thefe are yet
all the common-places of his great Paper-boke, &
the whole Inuentarie of his witt : though in time
he may haply learne to play at ninehole-nidgets ;
or to canuas a liuerie flowt thorough all the
Predicaments of the fower, & twentie orders.
When I firft tooke a glancing vewe of *Ile,* Ile, Ile,
& durft fcarfely, be fo hardy, to looke the hatchet
in the face; methought his Imagination, was
hedded like a Saracen ; his ftomack bellyed, like
the great Globe of Orontius ; & his breath, like
the blaft of Boreas in the great Mapp of Mer-
cator. But when we began to renue our old
acquain / tance, and to fhake the handes of dis-
continued familiaritie, alas good Gentleman ; his
mandillion was ouer-cropped ; his witt paunched,
like his wiues fpindle ; his art fhanked, like a lath ;
his conceit as lank, as a fhotten herring ; and that
fame bluftering eloquence, as bleake, and wan, as
the Picture of a forlorne Loouer. Nothing, but
pure Mammaday, and a fewe morfels of fly-blowne

Euphuifme, fomewhat nicely minced for puling
ftomackes. But there be Painters enough, though
I goe roundly to worke: and it is my onely
purpofe, to fpeake to the purpofe. I long fithence
founde by experience, how Dranting of Verfes,
and Euphuing of fentences did edifie. But had I
confulted with the Prognoftication of Iohn Securis,
I might peraduenture haue faued fome loofe endes
for after clapps. Now his nephew Hatchet muft
be content to accept of fuch fpare intertainement,
as he findeth.

It was Martins folly, to begin that cutting
vaine: fome others ouerfight, to continue it: and
doubble V⁵ triumph, to fet it agogg. If the world
fhould applaude to fuch roifterdoifterly Vanity,
(as Impudency hath beene prettily fuffered to
fett-vpp the creaft of his vaineglory:) what good
could grow out of it, but to make euery man
madbrayned, and defperate; but a generall con-
tempt of all good order, in Saying, or Dooing
but an Vniuerfall Topfy-tur[v]y? He were a
very fimple Oratour, a more fimple politician, and
a moft-fimple Deuine, that fhould fauour Martin-
izing: but had I bene Martin, (as for a time I
was vainely fufpected by fuch madd Copefmates,
that can furmize any thing for their purpofe,
howfoeuer vnlikely, or monftrous:) I would haue
beene fo farre from being mooued by fuch a fan-

tafticall Confuter, that it fhould haue beene one
of my May-games, or Auguft triumphes, to haue
driuen /Officials, Commiffaries, Archdeacons, Deanes,
Chauncellors, Suffraganes, Bifhops, and Archbifhops,
(fo Martin would haue florifhed at the leaft) to
entertaine fuch an odd, light-headded fellow for
their defence ; a profeffed iefter, a Hick-fcorner,
a fcoff-maifter, a playmunger, an Interluder ; once
the foile of Oxford, now the ftale of London, and
euer the Apefclogg of the preffe, *Cum Priuilegio
perennitatis.* Had it not bene a better courfe, to
haue followed Ariftotles doctrine : and to haue
confuted leuity with grauity, vanity with difcre-
tion, rafhnes with aduife, madneffe with fobriety,
fier with water, ridiculous Martin with reuerend
Cooper ? Efpecially in Ecclefiafticall caufes : where
it goeth hard, when Scoggin, the Iouiall foole, or
Skelton, the Malancholy foole, or Elderton, the
bibbing foole, or Will Sommer the chollericke
foole, muft play the feate ; and Church-matters
cannot bee difcuffed without rancke fcurrility,
and as it were a Synode of Diapafon fooles.
Some few haue a ciuill pleafant vaine, and a
dainety fplene without fcandale : fome fuch per-
cafe might haue repayed the Marr-prelate home
to good purpofe : other obfcenity, or vanity con-
futeth itfelfe, and impeacheth the caufe. As good
forbeare an irregular foole, as beare a foole hetero-

clitall : and better abide a comparitiue knaue, that
pretendeth religion, then fuffer a knaue fuperlatiue,
that fetteth cocke on hoope. Serious matters
would be handeled ferioufly, not vpon fimplicity,
but vppon choice; not to flefh, or animate, but
to difgrace, and fhame Leuity. A glicking *Pro*,
and a frumping *Contra*, fhall haue much-adoe to
fhake handes in the *Ergo*. There is no ende of
girdes, & bobbes: it is found Argumentes, and
grounded Authorities, that muft ftrike the defini-
tiue ftroke, and decide the controuerfy, with
mutuall fatisfaction. Martin bee wife, though /
Browne were a foole : and Papp-hatchet be
honeft, though Barrow be a knaue: it is not
your heauing, or hoifing coile, that buildeth-vpp
the walles of the Temple. Alas poore miferable
defolate moft-woefull Church, had it no other
builders, but fuch architects of their owne fan-
tafies, and fuch maifons of infinite contradiction.
Time, informed by fecrete intelligence, or refolued
by curious difcouery, fpareth no coft, or trauaile,
to preuent Mifchiefe : but employeth her two
woorthy Generals, Knowledge, & Induftry, to
cleere the coaft of vagarant errours in Doctrine ;
and to fcoure the fea of rouing corruptions in
Difcipline. Roome was not reared-vpp in one
day ; nor cannot be pulled downe in one day.
A perfect Ecclefiafticall Difcipline, or autentique

Pollicy of the Church, (that may auowe, I haue
neither more, nor leffe, then enough ; but iuſt
the nomber, weight, and meaſure of exact gouerne-
ment) is not the worke of One man whoſoeuer,
or of one age whatſoeuer : it requireth an in-
credible-great iudgement : exceeding-much reading
in Eccleſiaſticall hiſtories, Councels, Decrees, Lawes :
long, and ripe practiſe in Church-cauſes. Plat-
formes offer themſelues to euery working conceit ;
and a few Tables, or Abridgements are ſoone
diſpatched : but, whatſoeuer pretext may coulerably
bee alledged, vndoubtedly they attempt, they know
not what, and enterpriſe aboue the poſſibility of
their reach, that imagine they can in a Pamflet, or
two, contriue ſuch an omniſufficient, and incorrup-
tible Method of Eccleſiaſticall gouernement, as
could not by any priuate meditation, or publike
occaſion be found-out, with the ſtuddy, or practiſe
of fifteene hundred yeeres. I am not to diſpute,
as a profeſſed Deuine ; or to determine, as a
ſeuere Cenſour : but a ſcholler may deliuer his
opinion with reaſon : and a frend may lend / his
aduiſe at occaſion : eſpecially when hee is vrged
to ſpeake, or ſuſpected for ſilence. They muſt
licence mee to diſſent from them, that autoriſe
thēſelues to diſagree from ſo many notable, and
woorthy men, in the common reputation of ſo
long a ſpace. They condemne ſuperſtitious, &

credulous fimplicity: it were a fond fimplicity
to defende it, where it fwarueth from the Trueth,
or ftrayeth out-of the way: but difcretion can as
little commend opiniotiue and preiudicate affer-
tions, that ftriue for a needeleffe, and daungerous
Innouation. It is neither the Exceffe, nor the
Defect, but the Meane, that edifyeth. Plato com-
paring Ariftotle, and Xenocrates togither; Xeno-
crates, quoth he, needeth a fpurre: Ariftotle a
Bridle. And if Princes, or Parlaments want a
goade, may not Subiects, or Admonitions want
a fnaffle? Is there pretence, for Libertie to
aduife the wifeft, or for Zeale to pricke-forward
the higheft: and no reafon for Prudence to curbe
Rafhneffe, or for Autoritie to reane Licentious-
neffe? May Iudgement be whoodwinked with
friuolous traditions: and cannot Phantafie be en-
ueigled with newfangled conceites? Superftition,
and Credulitie, are fimple Creatures: but what are
Contempt, and Tumult? What is the principall
caufe of this whole Numantine Warre, but affecta-
tion of Nouelty, without ground? If all without
exception, from the very fchollers of the Primitiue,
and heroical fchoole, wanted knowledge, or zeale:
how rare, and fingular are their bleffinges, that haue
both, in fo plentifull, and incomparable meafure?
Affuredly there were many excellent witts, illumi-
nate minds, and deuout foules before them: if

nothing matchable with them, what greater
Maruell in this age? Or if they were not rightly
difciplined, that liued fo Vertuoufly, and Chriftianly
togither ; what an ineftimable treafure is founde,
& what a cleere fountaine of holy life? Where
are godly minds become, that they embrace not
that facred focietie? What aile Religious handes
that they ftay from building-vpp the Cittie of
God? Can Platos Republique, and Mores Vtopia
winne hartes : and cannot the heauenly Hierufalem
conquer foules? Can there be a greater impietie,
then to hinder the rearing-vp of thofe celeftiall
walles? why forgetteth the grofe Church, that it
ought to be the pure kingdome of heauen? To
zeale, euen fpeede is delay ; / and a yeare, an age.
But how maturely, and iudicioufly fome bufie
motions haue bene confidered-vpon, by their hoat
follicitours, it would not paffe vnexamined. A
ftrong Difcipline ftandeth not vpon feeble feete :
and a weake foundation will neuer beare the
weight of a mightie Hierufalem. The great
fhoulders of Atlas oftentimes fhrinke and faint
vnder the great burden of heauen. The Taber-
nacle of Mofes ; the Temple of Salomon ; the
Golden Age of the Primitiue Church ; and the
filuer regiment of Conftantine, would be looked-
into, with a fharper, and cleerer eye. The
difference of Commonwealthes, or regiments, re-

quireth a difference of lawes, and orders: and
thofe lawes, and orders are moft fouerain, that
are moft agreable to the regiment, and beft
proportioned to the Commonwealth. The matter
of Elections, and offices, is a principall matter in
queftion: and how many not onely ignorant, or
curious, but learned, and confiderate wits, haue
loft themfelues, and founde errour, in the difcourfe
of that fubiect? But how compendioufly might
it be concluded, that is fo infinitly argued; or how
quietly decided, that is fo tumultuoufly debated?
I relye not vpon the vncertaintie of difputable
rules; or the fubtilitie of intricate arguments; or
the ambiguitie of doubtfull allegations; or the
cafualtie of fallible experiments: but grounde my
refolution vpon the affurance of fuch politique,
and Ecclefiafticall Principles, as in my opinion can
neither be deceiued grofely, nor deceiue danger-
oufly. Popular Elections, and offices, afwell in
Churches, as in Commonwealthes, are for popular
ftates: Monarchies, and Ariftocraties, are to cele-
brate their elections, and offices, according to their
forme of gouernement, and the beft correfpondence
of their ftates, Ciuill, and Ecclefiafticall: and may
iuftifie their / good proceeding by good diuinitie.
As they grauely, and religioufly prooued, that in
the florifhing propagation, and mightie encreafe
of the Catholique Church vnder Princes, before,

in, and after the Empire of Conſtãtine, were driuen
to varie from ſome primitiue Exãples : not by
vnlawfull corruptiõ, as is ignorãtly ſurmiſed ; but
by lawfull prouiſiõ, according to the exigence of
occaſions, & neceſſitie of alteration in thoſe ouer-
ruling caſes: as appeareth by pregnant euidence
of Eccleſiaſticall hiſtories, and Canons ; wherewith
they are to conſult, that affect a deepe inſight in
the deciſiõ of ſuch controuerſies; & not to leape at
all aduentures, before they haue looked about thẽ,
aſwell backward, as forward, & aſwell of the
one ſide, as of the other.   Conſideration is a good
Counſellour : & Reading, no badd Remẽbrancer;
eſpecially, in the moſt eſſentiall Common-places
of Doctrine, and the moſt important matters of
Gouernement.   Ignorance may ſome way be the
father of Zeale, as it was wont to be termed the
moother of Deuotion: but blind men ſwallow-downe
many flyes; and none more, then many of them,
that imagin they know all, and conceit an abſolute
omniſufficiencie in their owne platformes, with an
vniuerſall contempt of whatſoeuer contradiction,
ſpeciall, or generall, moderne, or auncient: when
vndoubtedly they are to ſeeke in a thouſand points
of requiſite, and neceſſarie conſideration.   Lord,
that men ſhould ſo pleaſe, and flatter themſelues in
their owne deuiſes : as if none had eyes, but they.
God neuer beſtowed his diuine giftes in vayne :

they are not fo lightly to be reiected, that fo grauely
demeaned themfelues, inftructed their brethren,
reclaimed infidels, conquered countryes, planted
Churches, confounded Heretiques, and inceffantly
trauailed in Gods caufes, with the whole deuotion
of / their foules: howfoeuer fome can be content to
thinke, that fince the Apoftles, none euer had the
fpirit of Vnderftanding, or the mindes of fincerity,
but themfelues. Pardon me, pure intelligences, and
incorruptible mindes. The auncient Fathers, and
Doctors of the Church, wanted neither learning,
nor iudgement, nor confcience, nor zeale: as fome
of their Greeke, and Latin woorkes very notably
declare : (if they were blinde, happy men that
fee :) and what wifer Senates, or hollyer Congrega-
tions, or any way more reuerent affemblies, then
fome Generall, and fome Prouinciall Councels?
Where they to a fuperficiall opinion, feeme to fett-
vpp a Gloffe, againft, or befide the Text; it would
bee confidered, what their confiderations were;
and whether it can appeare, that they directly, or
indirectly proceeded without a refpectiue regard
of the Commōwealth, or a tender care of the
Church, or a reuerend examination of that Text.
For I pray God, we loue the Text no worfe, from
the bottome of our hartes, then fome of them did.
They are not the fimpleft, or diffoluteft men, that
thinke, Difcretion might haue leaue to cutt his

coate according to his cloth; and commend their
humility, patience, wifdome, and whole conformity,
that were ready to accept any requifite order not
vnlawfull, and to admitt any decent, or feemely
rites of indifferent nature.   Put the cafe, iuft as
it was then, and in thofe countries ; and what if
fome fuppofe, that euen M. Caluin, M. Beza,
M. Meluin, or M. Cartwright, (notwithftanding
their new defeignementes) being in the fame eftate,
wherein they were then, and in thofe countries,
would haue refolued no otherwife in effeᨧ, then
they determined.   Or if they did not fo perfeᨧly
well, I pray God we may.   Howbeit none fo fitt
to reconcile contradiᨧions, or to accord differ-
ences, as hee that / diftinguifheth Times, Places,
Occafions, and other fwaying Circumftances ; high
pointes in gouernement, either Ciuill, or Ecclefiafti-
call.   As in the doubtfull Paragraphs, and Canons
of the Law of man; fo in the myfticall oracles of
the Law of God ; *Qui benè diftinguit, benè docet* :
in the one, when hee vfeth no diftinᨧion but of
the Law, or fome reafon equipollent to the Law :
in the other, when he interpreteth the Scripture
by the Scripture, either exprefly by conference of
Text with Text, or colleᨧiuely by the rule of
Analogy.   In cafes indifferent, or arbitrary, what
fo equall in generall, as Indifferency : or fo requifite
in fpeciall, as conformity to the pofitiue Lawe, to

the cuftome of the Countrey, or to the prefent
occafion? To be peruerfe, or obftinate without
neceffary caufe, is a peeuifh folly : when by fuch
a duetyfull, and iuftifiable order of proceeding,
as by a facred League, fo infinite Variances, and
contentions may be compounded. To the cleane,
all thinges are cleane. S. Paule, that layed his
foundation like a wife architeft, and was a fin-
gular frame of diuinity, (omnifufficiently furnifhed
to be a Doctour of the Nations, & a Conuertour
of People) became all vnto all, and as it were a
Chriftian Mercury, to winne fome. Oh, that his
Knowledge, or Zeale were as rife, as his Name:
and I would to God, fome could learne to behaue
themfelues toward Princes, and Magiftrates, as
Paul demeaned himfelfe, not onely before the
King Agrippa, but alfo before the twoo Romane
Procuratours of that Prouince, Felix, and Feftus :
whome he entreated in honourable termes, albeit
ethnicke gouernours. Were none more fcrupu-
lous, then S. Paul, how eafily, and gratioufly might
diuers Confutations bee reconciled, that now rage,
like Ciuill Warres? The chiefeft matter in ques-
tion, is no article of beliefe, but a point of pollicy, /
or gouernement : wherin a Iudiciall Equity being
duely obferued, what letteth but the particular
Lawes, Ordinances, Iniunctions, and whole manner
of Iurifdiction, may reft in the difpofition of Soue-

raine Autoritie? Whofe immediate, or 'mediate
actes, are to be reuerenced with Obedience, not
countermaunded with fedition, or controled with
contention. He is a bold fubiect, that attempteth
to binde the handes of facred Maiefty : and they
loue controuerfies well, I trow, that call their Princes
proceedinges into Controuerfie. Altercations, and
Paradoxes, afwell in Difcipline, as in Doctrine, were
neuer fo curioufly curious, or fo infinitely infinite :
but when all is done, and when Innouation hath
fett the beft countenance of proofe, or perfuafion,
vpon the matter ; Kingdomes will ftand, and Free-
Citties muft be content. Their Courts, are no
Prefidents for Royall Courts : their Councels, no
inftructions for the Councels of Kings, or Queenes:
their Confiftories, that would mafter Princes, no
informations for the Confiftories vnder Princes :
their Difcipline, no Canon, or platforme for foue-
raine gouernement, either in Caufes Temporall or
Spirituall. And can you blame them, that maruell,
how of all other Tribunals, or benches, that Iewifh
Synedrion, or Pontificall Confiftory fhould fo
exceedingly grow in requeft, that put Chrift him-
felfe to death, and was a whipp for his deereft
Apoftles ? I am loth to enter the liftes of argu-
mentation, or difcourfe, with any obftinate minde,
or violent witt, that weeneth his owne Conceit, a
cleere Sunne without Eclipfe, or a full Moone

without wanes: but fith Importunacy will neuer linne molefting Parliaments, and Princes, with Admonitions, Aduertifements, Motions, Petitions, Repetitions, Sollicitations, Declamations, Difcourfes, Methods, Flatteries, Menaces, and / all poffible inftant meanes of enforcing, and extorting the prefent Practife of their incorruptible Theorie; it would be fom-bodies tafke, to holde them a little occupied, till a greater Refolution begin to fub-fcribe, & a furer Prouifion to execute. May it therefore pleafe the bufieft of thofe, that debarre Ecclefiafticall perfons of all Ciuill iurifdiction, or temporall function, to confider; how euery pettie *Parifh*, in England, to the number of about 5200. more, or leffe, may be made a Ierufalem, or Metropolitan Sea, like the nobleft Cittie of the Orient, (for fo Pliny calleth Ierufalem): how euery *Minifter* of the fayd Parifhes, may be promoted to be an high Prieft, and to haue a Pontificall Confiftorie: how euery *Affiftant* of that Confiftorie, may emprooue himfelfe an honorable, or worfhip-full Senior, according to his reuerend calling: (for not onely the Princes of Families, or the Princes of Tribes, but the Princes of Citties, or Iudges, the Decurions, the Quinquagenarians, the Centurians, the Chiliarkes, were inferiour Officiers to the Seniors): how a *Princely and Capitall Court*, and euen the high Councell of Parlament, or

fupreme Tribunall of a Royall Cittie, (for there
was no Seniorie in Iudæa, but at Ierufalem ; fauing
when the Proconful Gabinius, in a Romane Pollicy
deuided that nation into fiue parts, and appointed
foure other Confiftories), how fuch a Princely, and
ftately Court, fhould be the patterne of a *Prefbitery
in a poore Parifh* : how the Principalitie or *Pôti-
ficalitie of* a *Minifter* according to the degenerate
Sanedrim, fhould be fett-vpp, when the *Lordfhip
of a Bifhop*, or Archbifhop, according to their
pofition, is to be pulled-downe : finally how the
fupremacie ouer Kings, and Emperours fhould be
taken from the higheft Prieft, or *Pope*, to be
beftowed vpon an *ordinarie Minifter*, or Curate :
and how / that Minifter fhould difpenfe with
Ariftotles *Law of inftrumēts*, ἔνκρος ἕν : or be-
come more mighty then Hercules, that could not
encounter *two charges att once :* or at leaft how
that Ciuil Court, that *meere Ciuill Court*, for fo it
was ; before it declined frō the firft inftitutiō ;
euen as meerly ciuill, as the Romane Senate)
fhould be transformed into a Court *meerly
Ecclefiafticall.* When thefe points are confidered ;
if withall it be determined by euidēt demōftration,
as cleere as the Sunne, and as inuincible as
Gods-word, that whatfoeuer the Apoftles did for
their time, is immutably perpetuall, and neceffarie
for all times : and that nothing by way of fpeciall

refpect, or prefent occafiō, is left to the ordinaunce,
difpofitiō, or prouifiō of the Church, but the ftrict
and precife practife of their Primitiue Difcipline,
according to fome Precepts in S. Paules Epiftles,
and a few Examples in the Actes of the Apoftles :
So be it, muft be the fuffrage of vs, that haue no
Voyce in the Sanedrim. All is concluded in a
fewe pregnant propofitions : we fhall not neede to
trouble, or entangle our wittes with many Articles,
Iniunctions, Statutes, or other ordinances : the
Generall, Prouinciall, and Epifcopall Councels, loft
much good labour in their Canons, Decrees, and
whatfoeuer Ecclefiafticall Conftitutions : the workes
of the fathers, and Doctours, howfoeuer auncient,
learned, or Orthodoxall, are little, or nothing
worth: infinite ftuddies, writings, commentaries,
treatifes, conferences, confultations, difputations,
diftinctions, conclufions of the moft-notable Schol-
lers in Chriftendome, altogither fuperfluous. Well-
worth a fewe refolute Aphorifmes; that difpatch
more in a word, then could be boulted-out in
fiften hundred yeares ; and roundly determine all
with an *Vpfy-downe.* No reformation without an
Vpfy-downe. In deede that is one of Ma/chiauels
Pofitions: and feeing it is prooued a peece of
found doctrine, it muft not be gain-fayd. Euery
head, that hath a hand, pull-downe the pride of
Bifhops, and fet vp the humilitie of Minifters.

Diogenes treade vpon Platos pompe. An vniuer-
fall reformation be proclaimed with the founde of
a Iewes-trumpe : let the Pontificall Confiftorie be
erected in euery Parifh : let the high Prieft, or
Archbifhop of euery Parifh, be enftalled in Mofes
Chaier, (it was Mofes, not Aarons Chayer, that
they challenge in their Senate : & he muft be
greater then Hercules, that can fulfill both) : let
the Minifterie be a Royall Priefthood; and the
dominiõ of his Segniorie, raigne like a Prefbiter
Iohn : let it euerlaftingly be recorded for a foue-
rain Rule, as deare as a Iewes eye, that Iofephus
alledgeth out-of the Law ; *Nihil agat Rex, fine
Pontificis, & Seniorum fententia.* Onely let the
fayd Pontife beware, he prooue not a great Pope
in a little Roome; or difcouer not the humour of
afpiring Stukely, that would rather be the king of
a moulhill, then the fecond in Ireland, or England.
Some Stoiques, and melancholie perfons haue a
fpice of ambition by themfelues : and euen *Iunius
Brutus* the firft, was fomway a kinde of *Tar-
quinius Superbus* : and *Iunius Brutus* the fecond,
is not altogither a mortified Creature, but be-
wrayeth as it were fome reliques of flefhe, and
bloud, afwell as his inwardeft frend *Eufebius
Philadelphus.* I dare come no neerer : yet Green-
wood, and Barrow begin already to complaine of
ſurly, and folemne brethren : and God knoweth

how that Pontificall chayer of eftate, might worke
in man, as he is man.   Mercurie fublimed, is
fomewhat a coy, and ftout fellow : and I beleeue,
thofe high, and mighty Peeres, would not fticke,
to looke for a low, and humble legge.   Euery /
man muft haue his due in his place : and honour
aliably belongeth to redoubted Seniours.   That is
their proper title at Geneua.   Now if it feeme as
cleere a cafe in Pollicie, as in Diuinitie ; that one,
and the fame Difcipline may ferue diuers, and con-
trarie formes of regiment, and be as fitt for the
head of England, as for the foote of Geneua : The
worft is, Ariftotles Politiques muft be burned for
heretiques.   But how happie is the age, that in
ftead of a thoufand Pofitiue Lawes, and Lefbian
Canons, hath founde one ftanding Canon of Poly-
cletus, an immutable Law of facred gouernement?
And what a bliffefull deftinie had the Common-
wealth, that muft be the Modell of all other
Commonwealthes, and the very Center of the
Chriftian world?   Let it be fo for euer, and
euer, if that *Pamflet of the Lawes, and Statutes
of Geneua,* afwell concerning the Ecclefiafticall
Difcipline, as Ciuill regiment ; deferue any fuch
fingular, or extraordinarie eftimation, either for
the one, or for the other.   If not ; are they not
bufie men, that will needes beare a rule, and ftrike
a maine ftroke, where they haue nothing to doe,

or are to be ruled? It were a good hearing in
my eare, that fome of them could gouerne them-
felues, but in reafonable wife fort, that are fo for-
ward to fwey kingdomes, and to fwing Churches
after their new fafhion; and can ftande vpon no
grounde, but their owne. If certaine of them be
godlyer, or learneder, then many other, (according
to their fauorableft reputation,) it is the better for
them : I would alfo, they were wifer, then fome of
them, whom they impugne. Surely I feare, they
will be founde more peremptorie in Cenfure, then
founde in Iudgement; and more fmart in reproofe,
then fharpe in proofe. And may it not be a pro-
bable doubt, how they haue compared togither the
Law of Gods people, *and the Gofpell* / of Chriftes
Church in the Bible : or how they haue ftuddied
Iofephus, Philo, & *Egefippus* of the Iewifh affaires;
or *Sigonius* of the Hebrue Commonwealth; or
Freigius his Mofaicus; or their owne *Bonauentura*
of the Iudaicall Pollicy; that fetch their Iuris-
diction from the *Sanedrim* corrupted; and ground
their Reformation vpon the Iewes *Thalmud,* the
next neighbour to the Turkes *Alcoran.* Had
Ramus Treatife of Difcipline come to light, they
would long-ere-this haue beene afhamed of their
Sanedrim, and haue blufhed to foift-in the Thal-
mud, in fteede of the Bible. God helpe poore
Difcipline, if the `water bee like the Conduit, the

Oile like the Lampe, and the Plant like the Tree.
Abraham was the beginning : Dauid the middeſt :
and Chriſt the ende of the Hebrue hiſtory : his
Goſpell, not his ennemies Thalmud, the pure
fountaine of reformation, and the onely cleere
reſplendiſhing Sunne, that giueth light to the
ſtarres of heauen, & earth; vnto which the
Church, his moſt deere and ſweete ſpouſe, is
more deepely, and more incomprehenſibly bounden,
then the day vnto the Sunne, that ſhineth from
his gliſtering chariot. It is not for a Pontificall
Seniory or a Mechanicall Elderſhip, to ſtopp the
courſe of any riuer, that ſucceſſiuely floweth from
that liquid fountaine : or to putt-out any Candle,
that was originally lighted at that inextinguible
Lampe. The Church hath ſmall cauſe, to dote
vppon the Cooſen-germane of Tyranny : and the
Commonwealth hath no great affeſtion to the
Sworn-brother of Anarchy. Certainely States
neede not long to interteine tumultuous, and
neuer-ſatisfied Innouation. And I hope he was
not greatly vnaduiſed, that being demaunded his
opinion of the Elderſhip in queſtion; anſwered,
he conceiued of the *Elderſhip*, (as it is intended,
and motioned in England) as he thought of the
Elder-tree, that whatſoeuer it appeared in ſhewe,
it would in triall prooue fruteleſſe, ſeedeleſſe, bitter,
fraile, troublous, and a friend to ſurging waues,

and tempestuous stormes.   And being further
pressed touching the forward Zeale of dowtie
Martin Seniour, liuely Martin Iuniour, pert Penry,
lusty Barrow, and some other bragge Reformistes:
(for that rowling stone of Innouation was neuer so
turled and tumbled, as since those busie limmes
began to rowse, and besturre them, more then
all the Pragmatiques in Europe): when young
Phaeton, quoth he, in a presumptuous resolution
would needes rule the Chariot of the Sunne,
as it might be the Temple of Apollo, or the
Church of S. Paule, or some greater Prouince
(for the greater Prouince, Commonwealth, or
Monarchy, the fitter for Phaetons reformation):
his suddaine ruine ministred matter of most
lamentable teares, to his deare mother, and louing
Sisters: in somuch, that they were pittifully
chaunged, as some write, into *Elder-trees*, as
some, into *Poplars*. *Sic fleuit Clymene: sic &*
Clymeneides altæ: as it might be the mourne-
full Church and her wailing members, wofully
transmewed into *Elders*, or *Poplars*. Good my
Masters, either make it an euident, and infallible
case, without sophisticall wrangling, or personall
brawling; that your vnexperienced Discipline, not
the order approoued, is the pure / well of that
diuine Spring, and the cleere light of that heauenly
Sunne: or I beseech you, pacifie yourselues, and

furceafe to endaunger kingdomes with vnneedefull
vprores. Crooked proceedings would be rectified
by a right, not a crooked line : and Abufes re-
formed, not by abufing the perfons, but by well-
vfing the things thēfelues. I fpare my auncients,
afwell at home as abroade : yet Beza might haue
bene good to fome Doctours of the Church ; and
better then he is, to *Ramus, Eraftus, Kemnitius,*
and fundry other excellent men of this age :
(neither can it fufficiently appeare, that the two
famous Lawyers, *Gribaldus,* and *Baldwinus,* were
fuch monftrous Apoftataes, or poyfonous Here-
tiques, as he reporteth) : and whither fome other,
neerer hand, haue not bene too-familiarly bold
with their Superiours, of approoued learning, and
wifedome, meete for their reuerend, and honorable
calling; my betters Iudge.

Modefty is a Ciuil Vertue, and Humility a
Chriftian quality : Surely Martin is too too-mala-
pert to be difcreet ; and Barrow too too-hoat, to
bee wife: if they be godly, God helpe Charity :
but in my opiniō they little wot, what a Chaos of
diforders, confufions, & abfurdities they breed, that
fweat to build a reformation in a monarchy, vpon
a popular foundation, or a mechanicall plott ; &
will needes be as fiery in execution, euen to
wring the Clubb out of Hercules hand, as they
were aëry in refolution. Alas, that wife men, and

reformers of ftates (I know not a weightier Pro-
uince) fhould once imagine, to finde it a matter of
as light confequence, to feniorife in a realme, ouer
the greateft Lordes, and euen ouer the highneffe
of Maieftie ; as in a towne, ouer a company of
meane marchantes, and meaner artificers. I will
not fticke, to make the beft of it. M. Caluin, /
the founder of the plott, (whome Beza ftileth the
great Caluin) had reafon to eftablifh his miniftery
againft Inconftancy, and to fortify himfelfe againft
Faction (as he could beft deuife, and compaffe
with the affiftance of his French party, and other
fauorites) by encroaching vpon a mechanicall,
and mutinous people, from whofe variable and
fickle mutability he could no otherwife affecure
himfelfe.   As he fenfibly found not onely by
dayly experiences of their giddy and factious
nature, but alfo by his owne expulfion, and
banifhment : whome after a little triall, (as it were
for a dainety nouelty, or fly experiment) they
could be content to vfe as kindly, and loyally,
as they had vfed the old Bifhopp, their lawfull
Prince.   Could M. Cartwright, or M. Trauerfe
feaze vpon fuch a Citty, or • any like popular
towne, Heluetian or other, where Democraty
ruleth the roft : they fhould haue fome-bodies
good leaue to prouide for their owne fecurity ;
and to take their beft aduauntage vppon tickle

Cantons. Some one peraduenture in time would canton them well-enough ; and giue a fhrewd pull at a Metropolitan Sea, as foueraine, as the old Bifhoprike of Geneua. It were not the firft time, that a Democraty by degrees hath prooued an Ariftocraty ; an Ariftocraty degenerated into an Oligarchy ; an Oligarchy amounted to a Tyranny, or Principality. No Rhetorique Climax fo artificiall, as that Politique Gradation. But in a iuft kingdome, where is other good affuraunce for Minifters, and meeter Councels for Princes, then fuch fwarmes of imperious Elderfhips ; it is not for fubiectes to vfurpe, as Commaunders may tirannife in a fmall territory. Vnleffe they meane to fett-vp a generall Deformation, in lieu of an Vniuerfall Reformation; and to bring-in an order, that would foone prooue a diluge of diforder ; an ouerflow of Anarchy ; / and an open Fludgate, to drowne Pollicy with licentioufnes, nobility with obfcurity, and the honour of realmes with the bafeneffe of Cantons. They that long for the bane, and plague of their Country, pray for that many-hedded, and Cantonifh reformation: in iffue good for none, but the high Iudges of the Confiftory, and their appropriate Creatures: as I will iuftify at large, in cafe I be euer particularly challenged. I am no pleader for the regiment of the feete ouer the head, or the gouernement of the

ftomacke over the hart : furely nothing can bee
more pernitious in practife, or more miferable
in conclufion, then a commaunding autority in
them, that are borne to obey, ordained to liue
in priuate condition, made to follow their occu-
pations, and bound to homage. You that be
fchollars, moderate your inuention with iudgement :
and you that be reafonable gentlemen, pacify
your felues with reafon. If it be an iniury, to
enclofe Commons ; what iuftice is it, to lay open
enclofures ? and if Monarchies muft fuffer popular
ftates to enioy their free liberties, and ampleft
fraunchifes, without the leaft infringment, or
abridgment : is there no congruence of reafon,
that popular ftates fhould giue Monarchies leaue,
to vfe their Pofitiue lawes, eftablifhed orders, and
Royall Prerogatiues, without difturbance, or con-
futation ?   Bicaufe meaner Minifters, then Lordes,
may become a popular Cittie, or territorie ; muft
it therefore be an abfurditie in the maiefty of a
kingdome, to haue fome Lordes fpirituall amongft
fo many temporall : afwell for the fitter corres-
pondence and combination of both degrees ; their
more reuerend priuate direction in matters of
confcience ; their weightier publique Counfell in
Parlaments and Synods ; the firmer affurance of
the Clergie in their caufes ; and the more honor-
able efti / mation of Religion in all refpectes ; as

for the folemnèr vifitation of their Dioces, & other
competent Iurifdiction. It is Tyrannie, or vain-
glorie, not reuerend Lordfhip, that the Scripture
condemneth. There were Bifhops, or as fome
will haue them termed, Superintendents, with
Epifcopall fuperioritie, and iurifdiction ; in the
golden age of the Apoftles : *Timothie* of Ephefus ;
Titus of Crete ; *Marke* of Alexandria ; *Iames* of
Ierufalem ; *Philemon* of Gaza; the eloquent *Apollos*
of Cæfarea : *Euodius* of Antioche ; *Sofipater* of
Iconium, according to Dorotheus, of Theffalonica,
according to Origene ; *Tychicus* of Chalcedon ;
Ananias of Damafcus : and fo forth. Diuers of
the auncient Fathers, and Doctours, afwell of the
Orientall, as of the Occidentall Churches, were
Bifhops, reuerend Fathers in Chrift, and fpirituall
Lordes. The fame ftile, or title of reuerence, hath
fucceffiuely continued to this age, without any
empeachment of value, or contradiction of note ;
fauing that of the angrie Malcontent, and prowd
heretique Aërius, fcarfely worth the naming. What
cruell outrage hath it lately committed, or what
haynous indignitie hath it newly admitted, (more
then other aduauncementes of Vertue, or ftiles of
honour,) that it fhould now be cancelled, or aban-
doned in all haft ? Would God, fome were no
ftouter, or hawtier without the title, then fome are
with it ? Many temporall Lordes, Dukes, Princes,

Kinges, and Emperours, haue fhowen very-notable
effectuall examples of Chriftian humilitie : and
may not fpirituall Lordes carrie fpirituall mindes?
I hope, they do : I know, fome doe : I am fuer,
all may ; notwithftanding their ordinarie title, or
an hundred plaufible Epithits.   I would the Lord-
fhip, or pompe of Bifhops, were the greateft abufe
in Commonwealthes, or Churches.   I fear me, I
fhall neuer liue to / fee fo happie a world vpon
the Earth, that aduifed Reformation fhould haue
nothing worfe to complaine-off, then that Lordfhip,
or pompe.   What may be, or is amiffe, in any
degree ; I defend not : (the delict of fome one,
or two Prelates, were it manifeft, ought not to
redounde to the damage, or detriment of the
Church) : what may ftande with the honour of
the realme ; with the benefite of the Church ; with
the approbation of antiquitie, and with the Canon
of the Scripture, I haue no reafon to impugne, or
abridge.   I haue more caufe to fufpect that fome
earneft dealers might be perfuaded to difpenfe with
the name of Lordfhip in Bifhops, on condition,
themfelues might be the parties : that would not
fecularlie abufe the title to any priuate pompe, or
vanitie, but religiouflie applie it to the publique
adminiftration of the Churche, according to the
firft inftitution.   Were dalliance fafe in fuch cafes ;
I could wifhe the experiment in a perfon, or

two, in whofe complexions I haue fome infight.
Doctour Humfry of Oxford, and Doctour Fulke
of Cambridge, two of their ftandard-bearers a
long time, grew conformable in the end, as they
grew riper in experience, and fager in iudgement :
and why may not fuch, and fuch, in the like, or
weightier refpectes, condefcend to a like toleration
of matters Adiaphorall ? Sith it will be no other-
wife (maugre all Admonitions, or whatfoeuer
zealous Motiues) better relent with fauour, then
refift in vayne. Were any fayre offer of prefermēt,
handfomely tendered vnto fome, that gape not
greedily after promotion, nor can-away with this-
fame feruile waiting, or plaufible courting for
liuing : I doubt not but wife men would fee
what were good for themfelues, commodious for
their frendes, and conuenient for the Church. If
they fhould obftinatly refufe / Deaneryes, and
Bifhoprickes ; I fhould verely beleeue, they are
mooued with ftronger arguments, and pregnanter
autorities, then any, they haue yet publifhed in
Print, or vttered in difputation : and I would be
very glad to conferre with them, for my inftruc-
tion. Sound reafons, & autenticall quotations
may preuayle much : & no fuch inuincible de-
fence, as the armour of Proofe. In the mean time,
the caufe may be remembred, that incenfed the
forefayd factious malcontent, Aërius, to maintaine

the equalitie of Bifhops, and other Prieftes, when
himfelfe failed in his ambitious fuite for a Bifhop-
ricke: and all refteth vpon a cafe of confcience,
as nice and fqueamifh a fcruple with fome zealous
Marr-prelates, as whither the Fox in fome good
refpe#ts, might be woon to eate grapes. They
that would pregnantly try Conclufions, might
peraduenture finde fuch a temptation, the material-
left and learnedeft Confutation, that hath yet bene
Imprinted. Melancholie is deepely wife; and
Choler refolutely ftout: they muft perfuade them
effentially, and feelingly, that will mooue them
effe#tually. Were they entreated to yeelde, other
arguments would fubfcribe of their owne gentle
accord; and ingenuoufly confeffe, that Opinion
is not to preiudice the Truth, or Fa#tion to dero-
gate from Autoritie. Poffeffion was euer a ftrong
defendant: and a iuft title maketh a puiffant
aduerfarie. Bifhops will goouerne with reputa-
tation, when Marr-Prelats muft obey with
reuerence, or refift with contumacie. Errours
in do#trine; corruptions in manners; and abufes
in offices, would be reformed: but degrees of
fuperioritie, and orders of obedience are needefull
in all eftates: and efpecially in the Clergie as
neceffarie, as the Sunne in the day, or the Moone
in the night: or Cock-on-hoope, with a hundred /
thoufand Curates in the world, would prooue a

mad Difcipline. Let Order be the golden rule
of proportion ; & I am as forward an Admoni-
tioner, as any Precifian in Ingland. If diforder
muft be the Difcipline, and confufion the Refor-
matiō, (as without difference of degrees, it muft
needes) I craue pardon. *Anarchie*, was neuer yet
a good States-man : and *Ataxie*, will euer be a
badd Church-man. That fame luftie Downefall,
is too-hoat a Pollicie for my learning. They were
beft, to be content to let Bifhopricks ftande, that
would be loth to fee Religion fall, or the Clergie
troden vnder foote. He conceiueth little, that
perceiueth not, what bondes hold the world in
order, and what tenures maintaine an affurance
in eftates. Were Minifters Stipendiaries, or
Penfionars, (which hath alfo bene a wife motion)
and all without diftinction, alike efteemed, that
is, all without regard, alike contemned, & abiected,
(which would be the iffue of vnequal Equallity) ;
woe to the poore Miniftery : and the cunningeft
practife of the confiftorie, fhould haue much-adoe,
to ftopp thofe gapps, and recure thofe fores.
Neuer a more fuccourleffe Orphan ; or a more
defolate widdow ; or a more diftreffed Pilgrim ;
then fuch a Miniftery: vntill in a thirfty, &
hungry zeale, it fhould eftfoones retire to former
prouifions, & recoouer that aunciēt Oeconomy
Ecclefiafticall. The fureft reuenue, & honorableft

falary of that coate; much-better iwis, thē the
fouldiours pay, or the Seruing-mās wages. Equality,
in things equall, is a iuſt Law : but a refpeċtiue
valuation of perſons, is the rule of Equity : &
they little know, into what incōgruities, & ab-
furdities they runne headlong, that are weary of
Geometricall proportion, or diſtributiue Iuſtice, in
the collation of publique funċtions, offices, or
promotions, ciuile, or ſpirituall.   God beſtoweth
his bleſſings with difference; / and teacheth his
Lieutenant the Prince, to eſtimate, and preferre
his fubieċtes accordingly.   When better Autors
are alledged for equalitie in perſons Vnequall ; 1
will liue, and dye in defence of that equalitie ;
and honour *Arithmeticall Proportion*, as the onely
ballance of Iuſtice, and fole ſtandard of gouerne-
ment.   Meane-while, they that will-be wifer, then
God, and their Prince, may continue a peeuiſh
fcrupulofitie in fubfcribing to their ordinances ;
and nurriſh a rebellious Contumacie, in refuſing
their orders.   I wiſh vnto my frendes, as vnto
mifelfe : and recommende Learning to difcretion,
conceit to iudgment, zeale to knowledge, dutie
to obedience, confuſion to order, Vncertaintie
to aſſurance, and Vnlawfull noueltie to lawfull
Vniformitie : the fweeteſt repofe, that the Com-
mon-wealth, or Church can enioy.   *Regnum
diuiſum*, a fouerain Text ;   and what notabler

Gloſſe vpon a thouſand Texts? Or what more cordiall reſtoratiue of Boddy, or Soule, then, *Ecce quàm bonum, & quàm iucundum*? Sweet my maſters, be ſweet: and without the leaſt bitterneſſe of vnneceſſarie ſtrife, tender your affectionateſt deuotiõs of Zeale, and Honour, to the beſt contentment of your frends, your Patrons, your Prince, the Cõmonwealth, the Church, the Almightie : which ſo dearely looue, ſo bountifully maintaine, ſo mightily protect, ſo gratiouſly fauour, and ſo indulgentially tender you. Confounde not yourſelues : and what people this day more bleſſed, or what nation more flooriſhing? Some feruent, and many counterfait loouers, adore their miſtreſſes ; and commit Idolatrie to the leaſt of their bewties : oh, that we knew what a Sacrifice, Obedience were ; and what a Iewell of Iewells he offereth, that preſenteth Charitie. Without which, we may talke of Doctrine, and diſcourſe of Diſcipline : but Doctrine is a Parrat; / Diſcipline an Eccho ; Reformation a ſhaddow ; Sanctification a dreame without Charitie : in whoſe ſweet booſome Reconciliation harboureth; the deareſt frend of the Church, and the only Eſt Amen of ſo infinite Controuerſies. That Reconciliation ſettle itſelfe to examine matters barely, without their veales, or habiliments, according to the counſell of Marcus Aurelius : and to define

thinges fimply, without any colours, or embel-
lifhments, according to the preceptes of Ariftotle,
and the examples of Ramus: and the moft-
endleffe altercations; being generally rather
Verbal, then reall, and more circumftantiall,
then fubftantiall: will foone grow to an ende.
Which end humanitie haften, if there be any
fpice of humanitie; diuinitie difpatch, if there be
any remnant of diuinitie; heauen accomplifh, if
the graces of heauen be not locked-vpp; and
Earth embrace, if reconciliation hath not forfaken
the Earth. If Falfhood be weake, as it is weake,
why fhould it longer hold-vpp head: and if Truth
be truth, that is, great and mightie, why fhould
it not preuayle? Moft-excellent Truth, fhow
thifelfe in thy victorious Maieftie; and mauger
whatfoeuer encounter of witt, learning, or furie,
preuayle puiffantly.

Thefe Notes, if they happen to fee light, are
efpecially intended to the particular Vfe of a fewe,
whom in affectionate good-will I would wifh to
ftay their wifedomes. Did I not entirely pittie
their cafe, and extraordinarily fauour fome com-
mendable partes in them, they fhould not eafely
haue coft me halfe thus many lines; euery one
worfe beftowed, then other, if conftancie in errour,
be a creddit; in difobedience, a bonde; in vice, a
vertue; in miferie, a felicitie. He that writt the

premiſſes, affecteth Truth, as preciſely, as any
Preciſian in Cambrige, or Oxford; and hateth /
euen Looue itſelfe, in compariſon of Truth, which
he is euer to tender with a curious deuotion : but
a man may be as blinde in ouerſeeing, as in ſeeing
nothing : and he may ſhoote farther from the
marke, that ouerſhooteth, then he that ſhooteth
ſhort, or wide : as alwayes ſome moteſpying
heades haue ſo ſcrupulouſly ordered the matter,
Vt intelligendo nihil intelligerent. I would be
loth to fall into the handes of any ſuch captious,
and mutinous witts : but if it be my fortune, to
light vpon hard interteinement, what remedie? I
haue had ſome little tampering with a kinde of
Extortioners, and barratours in my time : and
feare not greatly any bugges, but in charitie, or
in dutie. Wrong him not, that would gladly be
well-taken, where he meaneth-well; and once for
all proteſteth, he looueth humanitie with his hart,
and reuerenceth diuinitie with his ſoule : as he
would rather declare indeede, then profeſſe in
worde. If he erreth, it is for want of know-
ledge, not for want of Zeale. Howbeit for his
fuller contentment, he hath alſo done his endeuour,
to know ſomething on both ſides; and laying-aſide
Partialitie to the perſons, hath priuately made the
moſt equall & ſincere Analyſis of their ſeuerall
allegations, and proofes, that his Logique, and

diuinitie could fett-downe.   For other Analyfes
he ouer-paffed, as impertinent, or not fpecially
materiall.   After fuch examination of their auto-
rities, and argumentes, not with a rigorous Cenfure
of either, but with a fauorable Conftruction of
both : Pardon him, though he prefume to deliuer
fome part of his animaduerfions in fuch termes, as
the inftant occafion prefenteth : not for any con-
tentious, or finifter purpofe (the world is too-full
of litigious, and barratous pennes) but for the
fatisfaction of thofe, that defire them, & the
aduertifement of thofe, that regard them.   Who /
according to any indifferent, or reafonable Analyfis,
fhall finde the fharpeft Inuentions, & weightieft
Iudgementes of their leaders, nothing fo autenticall,
or current, as was preiudicatly expected.   It is no
peece of my intention, to inftruct, where I may
learne : or to controwle any fuperiour of qualitie,
that in confcience may affect, or in Pollicie feeme
to countenance that fide.   With Martin, and his
applauders; Browne, and his adherents; Barrow,
and his complices; Kett, and his fectaries; or
whatfoeuer Commotioners of like difpofition, (for
neuer fuch a flufh of fcifmatique heads, or here-
tique witts), that like the notorious H. N. or the
prefumptuous Dauid Gorge, or that execrable
Seruetus, or other turbulent rebells in Religion,
would be Turkefing, and innouating they wott

not what; I hope it may become me, to be
allmoſt as bold; as they haue bene with Iudges,
Biſhops, Archbiſhops, Princes, and with whom
not? howſoeuer learned, wiſe, vertuous, reuerend,
honorable, or ſouerain. Or if my coole dealing
with them, be inſupportable: I beleeue their hoat
practiſing with Lordes, and Princes, was not
greatly tolerable. Be, as it may : that is done
on both ſides, cannot be vndone : and if they
weene, they may offende outragiouſly without in-
iurie ; other are ſuer, they may defend moderately
with iuſtice. When that ſeuen-fold Sheild faileth,
my plea is at an ende; albeit my making, or
marring were the Client. Whiles the ſeuen-fold
Sheild holdeth-out, he can doe little, that cannot
hold it vpp. A ſtrong Apologie, enhableth a
weake hand ; and a good cauſe is the beſt
Aduocate. Some ſleepe not to all : and I watch
not to euery-one. If I be vnderſtood with effect,
where I wiſh at-leaſt a demurrer with ſtayed
aduiſement, & conſultation; I haue my deſier,
& wil not tediouſly importune other. I doubt
not of many / cõtrary inſtigatiõs, & ſome bold
examples of turbulẽt ſpirits : but heat is not
the meeteſt Iudge on the bench, or the ſoundeſt
Diuine in diſputation : & in matters of gouern-
ment, but eſpeciálly in motions of altercatiõ, that
runne their heads againſt a ſtrong wall; Take

heede is a fayre thing. Were there no other
Confiderations; the Place, and the Time, are
two weightie, and mightie Circumftances. It is
a very-nimble feather, that will needes out-runne
the wing of the Time; and leaue the fayles of
regiment behinde. Men are men, and euer had,
and euer will haue their imperfections : Paradife
tafted of imperfections : the golden age, when-
foeuer it was moft golden, had fome droffe of
imperfectiōs : the Patriarkes fealt fome fits of
imperfections : Mofes tabernacle was made ac-
quainted with imperfectiōs; Salomōs Temple could
not cleere itfelfe frō imperfections : the Primitiue
Church wanted not imperfections : Conftantines
deuotion founde imperfections : what Reformatiō
could euer fay? I haue no imperfectiōs : or will
they, that dubb themfelues the little flocke, and
the onely remnant of Ifrael; fay? we haue no
imperfectios. Had they none, as none haue more,
then fome of thofe Luciferian fpirits; it is an
vnkinde Birde, that defileth his kinde neaft; and
a prowd hufband-man, that can abide no tares
amōgft wheate, or vpbraideth the Corne with the
Cockle. There is a God aboue, that heareth
prayers : a Prince beneath, that tendereth fuppli-
cations : Lordes on both fides, that Patronife good
caufes : learned men, that defire Conference : time,
to confider vpon effentiall pointes : Knowledge,

that loueth zeale, as zeale muſt reuerence know-
ledge : Trueth, that diſplayeth, & inueſteth itſelfe :
Conſcience, that is a thouſand witneſſes, euen againſt
it ſelfe. When the queſtion is *de Re* ; to diſpute
de Homine is ſophiſticall : / or when the matter
dependeth in controuerſie, to cauill at the forme
is captious : the abuſe of the one, were it proued,
aboliſheth not the vſe of the other : what ſhould
impertinent ſecrecies be reuealed ; or needles
quarrels picked ; or euery propoſition wrinched
to the harſheſt ſenſe? What ſhould honeſt
mindes, and excellent wittes, be taunted, and
bourded, without rime, or reaſon? What ſhould
inſolent, and monſtrous Phantaſticality extoll, and
glorify itſelfe aboue the cloudes, without cauſe,
or effect? When, where, and how ſhould Mar-
tin Iunior be purified ; Martin Senior ſaintified ;
Browne Euangeliſtified ; Barrow Apoſtolified ; Kett
Angelified ; or the Patriarke of the loouely Fami-
liſtes, H. N. deified, more then all the world
beſide? Were it poſſible, that this age ſhould
affoord a diuine and miraculous Elias : yet, when
Elias himſelfe deemed himſelfe moſt deſolate, and
complained hee was left all-alone ; there remained
thouſandes liuing, that neuer bowed their knees
vnto Baal. But Faction, is as ſure a Keeper of
Counſell, as a ſiue : Spite, as cloſe a Secretary, as
a ſkummer : Innouation, at the leaſt a bright

Angell from heauen: & the forefaid abftractes
of pure diuinity, will needes know, why Iunius
Brutus, or Eufebius Philadelphus fhould rather
be Pafquils incarnate, then they. If there be one
Abraham in Vr; one Lot in Sodome; one Daniell
in Babilon ; one Ionas in Niniue ; one Iob in Huz;
or if there bee one Dauid in the Court of Saule;
one Obadia in the Court of Achab; one Ieremy in
the Court of Zedechias ; one Zorobabel in the
Court of Nabuchodonofor; one Nehemias in the
Court of Artaxerxes; or any fingular bleffed One
in any good, or bad Court, Citty, State, Kingdome,
or Nation; it muft be one of them: all other of
whatfoeuer dignity, or defert, what but reprobates,
apoftataes, monfters, tyrants, / pharifes, hypocrites,
falfe prophets, belly-gods, worldlinges, rauenous
wooluves, crafty foxes, dogs to their vomite, a
generation of vipers, limmes of Sathan, Diuels
incarnate, or fuch like. For Erafmus poore
Copia Verborum, and Omphalius fory furniture
of inuectiue and declamatory phrafes muft come-
fhorte in this comparifon of the rayling faculty.
I know no remedy, but the prayer of Charitie,
and the order of Autority: whome it concerneth
to deale with libels, as with thornes; with
phanfies, as with weedes ; and with herefies, or
fcifmes, as with Hydras heads. It hath bene
alwayes one of my obferuations, but efpecially

of later yeares, fince thefe Numantine fkir-
mifhes : The better fchollar indeede, the colder
fcifmatique ; & the hotter fcifmatique, the worfe
fchollar. What an hideous and incredible opinion
did Dauid Gorge conceiue of himfelf ? H. N.
was not affraide to infult ouer al the Fathers,
Doctors, fchoolemē, & new-writers, euer fince the
Euāgelifts, & Apoftles : Browne challēged all the
Doctours, & other notableft graduats of Cambridge,
and Oxford : Kett, though fomething in Aftrology,
and Phyficke, yet a rawe Deuine, how obftinate,
and vntractable in his fantafticke affertions?
Barrow taketh vpon him, not onely aboue Luther,
Zuinglius, Oecolampadius, Brentius, and all the
vehementeft Germane Proteftants ; but alfo aboue
Caluin, Viret, Beza, Marlorat, Knox, Meluin,
Cartwright, Trauerfe, Fenner, Penry, and all our
importunateft follicitours of reformation ; howfo-
euer qualified with giftes, or reputed amongft their
fauorits. Illuminate Vnderftanding, is the rare
byrd of the Church; and graund intendimentes
come by a certaine extraordinarie, and fuper-
naturall reuelation. One Vnlearned Singularift
hath more in him, then ten learned Precifians :
giue me the braue fellow, that can carrie / a
Dragons tayle after him. Tufh, Vniuerfitie-learn-
ing is a Dunfe : and Schoole-diuinitie a Sorbonift.
It is not Art, or Modefty, that maketh a Rabi

Alphes, or a ringleader of multitudes. Dauid Gorge the Archprophet of the world: H. N. the Archeuangelift of Chrift: and Barrow the Archapoftle of the Church. Superhappy Creatures, that haue illuminate vnderftanding, and graund intendiments at the beft hand. Miraculous Barrow, that fo hugely exceedeth his auncients in the pure arte of Reformation. But vndoubtedly his Kingdome cannot flourifh long: as he hath bleffed his Seniors, fo he muft be annointed of his Iuniors: me thinkes I fee an other, and an other headd, fuddainely ftarting-vpp vpon Hydras fhouldiers: farewell H. N. and welcome Barrow: adieu Barrow, and All-haile thou Angelicall fpirite of the Gofpell, whofe face I fee in a Chriftall, more pure, then Purity it felfe: the depreffion of one, the exaltation of another: the corruption of one, the generation of an other: no feede fo fértile, or rancke, as the feede of fcifme, and the fperme of herefy. Chrift aide his affaulted fort; and bliffe the feede of Abraham: and in honor of excellent Arts, and worthy Profeffions, be it euer faide; The beftlearned, are beft-aduifed. Euen Cardinall Sadolet, Cardinall Poole, and Omphalius, commended the milde, and difcreete difpofition of Melancthon, Bucer, and Sturmius, when they firft ftirred in Germany: the Queene Moother of Fraunce, and the Cardinall of Lorraine prayfed Ramus, albeit

hee was knowen to fauourife the Prince of Condy:
Iouius prayfed Reuclin, and Camerarius, as Peucer
prayfed Iouius, and Bembus: Oforius prayfed
Afcham, as Afcham prayfed Watfon: and who
prayfed not Sir Iohn Cheeke ; how exceedingly
did Cardan praife him? Sir Thomas Smith, her /
Maiefties Ambaffadour in France, in the raignes
of Henry the Second, Francis the Second, and
Charles the Ninth ; was honored of none more,
then of fome French, and Italian Cardinals, and
Bifhops: the Kinges fonnes fauored his fonne,
afwell after, as before their Coronation. Neander
in his late Chronicle, and later Geographie, praifeth
here, & there certaine Papiftes: and did not
Agrippa, Erafmus, Duarene, and Bodine occafion-
ally prayfe as many Proteftants? It was a fweet,
and diuine Vertue, that ftirred-vp looue, & admira-
tion in fuch aduerfaries : & doubtleffe they carried
an honeft, & honorable mynde, that forgot them-
felues, and their frendes, to doe their enemies
reafon, and Vertue right. A vertue, that I often
feeke, feldome finde ; wifh-for in many, hope-for
in fome, looke-for in few; reuerence in a Superiour,
honour in an inferiour ; admire in a frend, looue
in a foe ; ioy, to fee, or heare, in one, or other.
Peruerfe natures are forward to difguife themfelues,
and to condemne not onely Curtefie, or humanitie,
but euen humilitie, & charitie it felfe, with a nick-

name of Newtralitie, or Ambidexteritie : terme it,
what you lift, and mifcall it at your pleafure :
certes it is an excellent and fouerain qualitie, that
in a firme refolution neuer to abandon Vertue, or
to betray the Truth, ftealeth interteinement from
difpleafure, fauour from offence, looue from
enmitie, grace from indignation ; and not like
Homers Syren, but like Homers Minerua, traineth
Partialitie to a liking of the aduerfe Partie; diffen-
fion to a commendation of his Contrarie; errour
to an embracement of truth ; and euen Corruption
himfelfe to an aduauncement of valour; of defert,
of integretie, of that morall, and intellectuall good,
that fo gratioufly infinuateth, and fo forciblie
emprooueth itfelfe.   Oh, that learning were euer
married to fuch / difcretion; witt to fuch wifedome ;
Zeale to fuch vertue ; contention to fuch moralitie :
and oh, that fuch priuate gouernement might appeare
in thofe, that pleade moft-importunatly for publique
gouernement.   Oh, that Plato could teach Xeno-
crates ;   Ariftotle, Callifthenes ;   Theophraftus,
Ariftotle ; Eunapius, Iamblicus ; to facrifice to the
fweet Graces of Mercurie.   What fhould I vayle,
or fhadow a good purpofe?   Oh a thoufand times,
that Melanct[h]on could traine Iunius Brutus ;
Sturmius, Philadelphus ;   Ramus, Beza ; Iewell,
Cartwright ; Deering, Martin ; Baro, Barrow ; to
embrace the heauenly Graces of Chrift, and to

kiſſe the hand of that diuine Creature, that paſſeth all Vnderſtanding.   What a felicitie were it, to ſee ſuch heades as pregnant, as Hydras heades; or Hydras heades as rare as ſuch heades?

It is not my meaning, to deface, or preiudice any, that Vnfainedly meaneth well: if Percaſe I happen to touch ſome painted walles, and godly hypocrites (Godlineſſe is become a ſtrange Creature, ſhould they be truly godly) let them keepe their owne Counſel, and ceaſe to affect new reputation by old hereſies.   The Iewes had their holly-holly-holly *Eſſæans*: their ſeperate, / and preciſe *Phariſes*: their daily regenerate, & Puritane *Hemerobaptiſtes*: their feruent, and illuminate Zelotiſtes : onely in ſhape men, in conuerſation Sainīts, in inſinuation Angels, in profeſſion Demi-gods ; as deſcended from heauen, to bleſſe the Earth, and to make the Citie a Paradiſe, that waſhed their feete.   Ieſus bleſſe good mindes from the blacke enemy, when he attireth himſelfe like an Angell of light.   Iudas the Gaulonite, in the reigne of Herode the Great, was an hoat toſt, and a maruelous Zelotiſt ; when the Emperour Octauian taxing the world, and aſſeſſing Iudea, like other nations, who but he, / in the abundance of his mightie Zeale, was the man, that ſett it downe for a Canonicall Doctrine: That the people of God, was to acknowledge no other Lord, but God: and that it was a ſlauiſh

bondage, to pay any such exaction, or imposition
to Auguftus : and hauing giuen-out that principle,
for an infallible rule, or rather a facred law, very
vehemently follicited and importuned the people
(as the manner is) to liue, and dye in the caufe of
their God, and their libertie.   But fweet Chrift
was of a milder & meeker fpirite ; & both payed
tribute himfelfe to auoyde offence ;   and fet it
downe for an eternal Maxime in his Gofpell ; Giue
vnto Cæfar, that belongeth vnto Cæfar, and vnto
God, that belongeth vnto God.   Zealous Iudas
the Gaulonite, and feruent Simon the Galilean,
two fingular reformers of the Iudaicall Synagòge,
pretended fayre for a pure Type, or exquifite
platforme of the foundeft, exacteft, and precifeft
Hebraicall Difcipline : but what prophane Idolatrie
fo plagued that diuine Common-wealth, as that
fame fcrupulous Zeale? or what made that bleffed
ftate, vtterly miferable, but that fame vnruly, and
tumultuous Zeale ; that would not be content
with reafon, vntill it was too-late?   For a time,
they fuppofed themfelues, the worthieft, & rareft
Creatures in Iudea, or rather the onely men of
that ftate ; and in a deepe conceit of a neat &
vndefiled puritie, diuorced, or fequeftred them-
felues frō the corrupt focietie of other : but alas,
that any purified mindes, fhould pay fo dearely,
and fmartly for their fine Phanfies; which coft

them no leffe, then the moft lamentable ouerthrow of their whole Common-wealth. You that haue Languages, and Arts, more than diuers others of good qualitie, and can Vfe them with Methode, and a certaine plaufible opinion of great learning, be as excellent, and fin / gular, as you poffiblie can for your liues, in a direct courfe : but be not peeuifh ; or odd in a crooked balke, that leadeth out-of the Kinges high-way, and Chriftes owne path, into a maze of confufion, and a wildernesse of defolation : the finall ende of thefe endlesse Contentions, if they be not otherwife calmed by priuate difcretion, or cutt-fhort by publique order. The firft example of diuifion, was perillous : and what rankes, or fwarmes of infatiable fcifme, in-continently followed? It is a mad world, when euery crew of conceited Punyes, puffed-vp with a prefumptuous, or phantafticall imagination, muft haue their feuerall complot, or faction, as it were a certaine Punicall warre : whofe victorie wilbe like that of Carthage againft Roome, if it be not the fooner quieted. Remember Iudas the Gaul-onite ; and forgett not yourfelues : inordinate Zeale is a pernitious Reformer : and Deftruc-tion, a deare purchafe of Plotts in Moone-fhine. S. Paule, the heroicall Apoftle, could not finde a more excellent way, then Charitie, the moft-fouerain way of Faith, and Hope : any other

defeigne of puritie, or fingularitie, buildeth not
vp, but pulleth-downe ; and of more then a
Million in hope, prooueth leffe then a cipher in
effect. What the faluation of Dauid Gorge? a
nullitie ; what the deification of H. N.? a nullitie:
what the glorification of Kett? a nullitie : what
the fanctification of Browne? a nullitie : what the
cõmunitie of Barrow? a nullitie: what the plaufi-
bilitie of Martin? a nullitie : what a thoufand
fuch popular motiues, allectiues, incenfiues, aggra-
uations of the leaft corruptiõ, amplificatiõs of
the higheft felicitie, new landes of promife, ouer-
flowing with milke, and honny, fooles Paradifes,
glorious innouations ; but prefent fhame, wretched
confufion, vtter ruine, euerlafting infamie, horrible
damnation, & a moft hideous / nullity? Euẽ the
great hurly-burly of the Church, the imagined-
heauenly Difcipline ; and the very topfy-turuy
of the ftate, the pretended-diuine Reformation ;
of two mightie Giants, what can they poffiblie
emprooue themfelues, but filly Pigmyes, and a
moft pittifull nullitie? Sweet Charitie, enfweeten
thefe bitter garboiles : and feing they fo inftantly,
and importunatly affect a perfect Platforme, giue
them a moft-curious, and exquifite Table of pure
Reformation, euen the true Picture of Thifelf.
Surer Preuention of mifchiefe, and ruine, I know,
none.

I had here bidden Martin in the Vintry farwell, and taken my leaue of this tedious Difcourfe ; (for no man taketh leffe delight in Inuectiues) ; were I not newly certified of certaine frefh, & frantique practifes for the erection of the Synedrion in all haft : whofe complotters are weary of melancholy Proiects, and begin to refolue on a cholerique courfe. Hoat arguments are fiercely threatened, in cafe the Difcipline be not the fooner enterteined: but methinks that warme courfe fhould fcarfely be the ftile of pure Mortification : and haply fofter fier would make fweeter mault. A little aduifement, doth not much amiffe in capitall, or daungerous attemptes. It were well, the blowing bellowes might be entreated to keepe their winde for a fitter opportunitie : or if fier boilyng in the ftomacke, muft needes breake-out at the mouth ; the beft comfort is, the Country affordeth fufficient prouifiõ of water, to encounter, the terribleft Vulcanift, that brandifheth a burning fword, or a fierie toung. Howbeit fome lookers-on, that feare not greatly the flame, cannot but maruell at the fmoake ; and had rather fee them, breathing-out the fume of diuine Tobacco, thē of furious rage. I haue read of Politique Iewes, that for their commoditie haue become Chriftiãs : / whom in Spaine, & Italy they terme *Retaliados* : but that Politique Chriftiãs for any benefit, promotiõ, or

other regard whatfoeuer, fhould practife to become
Iews, in doctrine, or in difcipline, in earneft, or in
deuife, in whole, or in part, it were ftrange, &
almoft incredible : if the world were not growen
a môftrous *Retaliado* for his aduantage ; & the
voyce of Iacob prooued a more gaynfull Strata-
geme for the hands of Efau, then euer the hands
of Efau were for the voyce of Iacob. I charge
not any, that are cleere ; (would there were no
more Iewifh Pharifes, then Hebrue Worthies) ;
but let not them accufe me for fpeaking, that
condemne themfelues for doing ; or fhew them-
felues Saincts in the Premiffes, that will fcantly
prooue honeft men in the Conclufion. All are
not ledd with the fame refpectes, that hang on the
fame ftring : fome are carried with one confidera-
tion, fome with an other : fome tender diuinity,
as their foule : fome looue Religion, as their
boddy ; fome fauour the Gofpell, as their fortune :
I doubt not, but fome defier Difcipline for Con-
fcience ; and do none coouet Reformation for
gayne ; or were it impoffible, to point-out a
Retaliado Conuert, in the whotteft throng of thofe
frefh Profelites. If there be no *Retaliados* in
Chriftendome, I am glad I haue fayd nothing : if
there be, they may fo long mocke other in wordes,
that at-laft they will moft deceiue themfelues in
deedes. I am beholding to the old Iurie ; but

haue no great phanfie to a new, either in London,
or elfewhere; when amongft diuers other hiftories
of Iewifh enormities, I remember how an auncient
Archbifhop of Canterbury, one Iohn Peckam, was
fayne to take order with the Bifhop of London
then being, for the diffolutiō, and deftruction of
all the Synagoges in his Dioces. The leffe neede
of any fuch order at this inftant, all the better. I /
will not difpute, whether a Synedrion prefuppofe a
Synagoge ; or whether it be not as infupportable a
yoke for any King, or mightie ftate, as it was for
King Herode, or the Romanes, that found it in-
tolerable : (me thinkes the wifeft Sanedrift of a
thoufand, fhould hardly perfuad me, that he is a
frend of Princes, or no enemie of Monarchies) :
but I know fomuch by fome, none of the meaneft
Schollers, or obfcureft men in Europe, touching
their opinion of the old, and new Teftament, of
the Thalmud, of the Alcoran, of the Hebrue,
Chriftian, and Turkifh Hiftories; that I deeme
anything fufpicious, and perillous, that anyway
inclineth to Iudaifme; as fell an aduerfarie to
Chriftianitie, as the Wolfe to the Lambe, or the
Gofhawk to the Dooue. Graunt them an inche;
they will foone take an ell with the aduantage :
and were any part of their Difcipline one foote,
could the boddy of their Doctrine want an head?
or might not the Parifhe prooue a diforderly Con-

gregation, as bad as a Synagoge, where the Iudiciall
bench were a Synedrion? The Iewes are a futtle,
and mifcheeuous people: and haue cunningly in-
uegled fome ftudents of the holly toung, with their
miraculous Cabala from Mofes, their omnifcious
Cofmologie from Salomon, their Caldæan Sapience
from Daniell, and other profound Secrets of great
pretence: but their liberall gifts bite like their
Vfurie; and they are finally founde to interteine
them beft, that fhutt them quite out-of doores,
with their Sanedrim, and all. They can tell a
precious tale of their diuine Senate; and of their
Venerable Meokekim, reuerenced like liuing
Lawes: but were all iudgements actually drawen
to the diuine Senate, and all lawes folemnely to be
fetched from the Venerable Meokekim, as from
fpeaking Oracles; might not thefe, and their other
Metaphyficall myfteries, be / enregiftered in the
fame Thalmud; or might it not prooue a pinching
Reformation for Chriftendome? I haue tafted of
their Verball miracles; and cannot greatly com-
mend their perfonall vertues: but their reall
Vfurie is knowen through-out the Chriftian world,
to be an vnmercifull Tyrant, & I feare me, their
Confiftoriall Iurifdictiō would growe a Cruell
griper; efpecially being fo Vniuerfally extended
in euery Parifh, as is intended by the promoters
thereof, and powerably armed with that fupreme,

& Vncontrowlable authoritie, which they affect in caufes Ecclefiafticall. A braue fpirituall motion, and worthie not onely of thefe pidling fturres, but euen of a Troian warre. Yet their Precedent, the Mofaicall Synedrion, was a Ciuil Court, (as is afore mentioned, & would be reconfidered) *cum mero imperio* : and when it became mixt, it was not meerly Ecclefiafticall; & when it became meerly Ecclefiafticall, of a Pōtifical Confiftory, it foone prooued a Tyrannicall Court; and by your good leaue, was as nimble to encroach vpon Ciuill caufes, being an Ecclefiafticall Court, as euer it was to intermeddle with Ecclefiafticall caufes, being a Ciuill Court. The fineft Methodifts, according to Ariftotles golden rule of artificiall Boundes, condemne Geometricall preceptes in Arithmetique, or Arithmeticall preceptes in Geometrie, as irregular, and abufiue : but neuer Artift fo licentioufly heterogenifed, or fo extrauagantly exceeded his prefcribed limits, as Ambition, or Coouetice. Euery Miller is ready to conuey the water to his owne mill : and neither the high Prieftes of Ierufalem, nor the Popes of Roome, nor the Patriarckes of Conftantinople, nor the Paftors of Geneua, were euer haftie to binde their owne handes. They that refearch Antiquities, and inquier into the priuities of Practifes, fhall finde an Act of *Præmunire* / is a neceffarie Bridle in fome

cafes. The firft Bifhops of Roome, were vn-
doubtedly vertuous men, and godly Paftors: from
Bifhops they grew to be Popes: what more reue-
rend, then fome of thofe Bifhops; or what more
Tyrannicall, then fome of thofe Popes? Aaron,
and the high-Prieftes of Ierufalem, and of other
ceremoniall nations, were their glorious Mirrours;
and they deemed nothing too-magnificall, or pom-
pous, to breede an Vniuerfall reuerence of their
facred autoritie, and Hierarchie. We are fo farre
alienated from imitating, or allowing them, that
we cannot abide our owne Bifhops; yet withall
would haue euery Minifter a Bifhop, and would
alfo be fetching a new patterne from old Ierufalem,
the moother-fea of the high-Priefthood. So the
world (as the manner is) will needes runne-about
in a Circle: pull-downe Bifhops; fet vp the
Minifter; make him Bifhop of his Parifh, and
head of the Confiftorie, (call him, how you lift,
that muft be his place): what will become of him
within a fewe generations, but a high Prieft in a
low Ierufalem, or a great Pope in a fmall Roome?
And then, where is the difference betweene him,
and a Bifhop, or rather betweene him, and a Pope?
not fo much in the qualitie of his Iurifdiction,
when in effect he may be his owne Iudge, as in
the quantitie of his Dioces, or temporalties. Or
in cafe he be Politique; as fome Popes haue bene

glad for their aduantage, to tyrannife Popularly, fo
he may chaunce be content for his aduauncement,
to popularife, tyrannically : and fhall not be the
firft of the Clergie, that hath cunningly done it
with a comely grace. Something there muft be of
a Monarchie in free ftates : and fomething there
will be of free ftates, in a Monarchie. The dis-
creeter, and Vprighter the Curate is, the more
circumfpectly he will walke, and degenerate the
leffe. / Yet what generation without degeneration :
or what reuolution without irregularitie? One
inconuenience begetteth an other : enormities grow
like euill weedes : take heede of a mifchiefe : and
where then will be the corruptions? Or how
fhall defection, (acknowledging no primacie, or
fuperioritie in any perfon, or Court) retire to his
firft inftitution : if percafe there fhould growe a
Confpiracie in fellowfhip ; one Confiftorie iuftifie
another for aduantage ; and their whole Synods
fall-out in confequence, to be like their Parts?
Men may erre : and frailtie will flipp. What
fhould I alledge Hiftoryes, or autorities? It is
no newes for infirmitie to fall, when it fhould
ftand ; or for appetite to rebell, when it fhould
obey. Euery fonne of Adam, a reed fhaken with
the wind of paffion, a weake Veffell, a Schollar of
imperfection, a Mafter of ignorance, a Doctour of
errour, a Paftour of concupifcence, a Superintendent

of auarice, a Lord of ambition, a Prince of finne, a flaue of mortalitie. Flefh is flefh; and Blud a Wanton, a chaungeling, a compound of contrary elementes, a reuoulting and retrog[r]ade Planet, a Sophifter, an hypocrite, an impoftour, an Apoftata, an heretique; as conuertible as Mercury, as variable as the weather-cock, as lunatique as the Moone; a generation of corruption, a Whore of Babylon, a limme of the world, and an impe of the Diuell. It is their owne argument in other mens cafe: and why fhould it not be other mens argument in their cafe, Vnleffe they can fhew a perfonall Priuiledge *ad imprimendum folum*? They may fpeake, as they lift: termes of fanctification, and mortificatiõ, are free for them, that will vfe them: but the Common opinion is, euen of the forwardeft fkirmifhers at this day, they doe like other men; and liue like the children of the world, and the brethren of themfelues. Some of them haue / their neighbours good leaue, to be their owne Proctors, or Aduocats, if they pleafe. Yet how probable is it, they are now at their very beft, and euen in the neateft and pureft plight of their incorruption, whiles their mindes are ab-ftracted from worldly thoughts, to a high medita-tion of their fuppofed-heauenly Reformation: and whiles it neceffarily behooueth them, to ftand charily and nicely vpon the credit of their in-

tegritie, finceritie, precifeneffe, godlineffe, Zeale,
and other vertues? When fuch refpects are ouer,
and their purpofe compaffed according to their
harts defier; who can tell how they, or their
fucceffours may vfe the Keyes; or how they
will befturr them with the Sworde? If Flefh
prooue not a Pope Ioane; and Bloud a Pope
Hildebrand, good enough. Accidents, that haue
happened, may happen agayne; and all thinges
vnder the Sunne, are fubiect to cafualtie, muta-
bilitie, and corruption. At all aduentures, it is a
braue Pofition, to maintaine a Souerain, and
fupreme autoritie in euery Confiftorie; and to
exempt the Minifter from fuperiour Cenfure;
like the high Prieft, or greateft Pontiffe, whom
Dionyfius Halycarnaffeus calleth ἀνυμέννον. He
had neede to be a wife, and Confcionable man,
that fhould be a Parlamēt, or a Chauncerie vnto
himfelfe: and what a furniture of diuine perfec-
tions were requifite in the Church, where fo many
Minifters, fo many fpirituall high Iuftices of
Oier, and Terminer: and euery one a fupreme
Tribunall, a Synode, a Generall Councell, a Canon
Law, a heauenly Law, and Gofpel vnto himfelfe?
If no Serpent can come within his Paradife, fafe
enough. Or were it poffible, that the Paftor,
(although a man, yet a diuine man) fhould as it
were by inheritance, or fucceffion, continue a Sainct

from generation to generation : is it alſo neceſſary, that the whole company of the redoubted / Seniors, ſhould wage euerlaſting warre with the fleſh, the world, and the Diuell; and eternally remaine an incorruptible Areopage, without wound, or ſcarre? Neuer ſuch a Colledge, or fraternitie vpon Earth, if that be their inuiolable order. But God helpe Conceit, that buildeth Churches in the Ayer, and platformeth Diſciplines without ſtayne, or ſpott.

They complaine of corruptions ; and worthily, where Corruptions encroche, (I am no Patron of corruptions) : but what a ſurging ſea of corruptiō would ouerflow within few yeares, in caſe the ſword of ſo great and ample autoritie, as that at Ieruſalem moſt capitall, or this at Geneua moſt redoubted, were putt into the hand of ſo little capacitie in gouernement, ſo little diſcretion in Diſcipline, ſo little iudgement in cauſes, ſo little moderation in liuing, ſo little conſtancie in ſaying, or dooing, ſo little grauitie in behauiour, or ſo little whatſoeuer ſhould procure reuerence in a Magiſtrate, or eſtabliſh good order in a Cōmonwealth. Trauaile thorough ten thouſand Pariſhes in England ; and when you haue taken a fauourable vew of their ſubſtantialleſt, and ſufficienteſt Aldermen, tell me in good ſooth, what a comely ſhowe they would make in a Conſiſtorie ; or with how ſolemne a preſence they would furniſh a

Councell Table. I beleeue, *Grimaldus* did little
thinke of any fuch Senatours, whē he writt *de
Optimo Senatore* : or did Doctour *Bartholmew
Philip*, in his Perfect Counfellour, euer dreame of
any fuch Coūfellours? Petty Principalities, petty
Tyrants ; & fuch Senats, fuch Senatours. Witt
might deuife a pleafurable Dialogue betwixt the
Leather Pilch, and the Veluet Coate : and helpe
to perfuade the better, to deale neighbourly with
the other ; the other to cōtēt himfelfe with his
owne calling. I deny not, but the fhort apron
may / be as honeft a man, or as good a Chriftian,
as the long gowne : but methinkes he fhould
fcantly be fo good a Iudge, or Affiftant in doubt-
full caufes: and I fuppofe, *Ne futor vltrà crepidam*
is as fitt a Prouerbe now, as euer it was, fince
that excellent Painter rebuked that fawcie Cobler.
Euery fubiect is not borne to be a Magiftrate, or
Officer: and who knoweth not, whofe creature
Superiour Power is? They are very-wife, that
are wifer then he, by whofe diuine permiffion,
euery one is that he is. The *Laconicall Ephory*
hath lately borne a great fwing, in fome refolute
Difcourfes of Princes, and Magiftrates; that
thought they faued the world from the abhomina-
tion of defolatiō, when they found-out a bridle,
or yoke for Princes : but old Ariftotle was a
deepe Politician *in diebus illis*: and his Reafons

againſt that Ephorie (for Ariſtotle confuted the
Ephorie with founder arguments, then euer it was
confirmed to this day) would not yet perhaps be
altogither contemned : That ſo great iudiciall
cauſes were committed to men, indued with ſo
little, or no Vertue : That the poore Plebians
for very penurie were eaſely bribed, and cor-
rupted : That there enſued an alteration of the
ſtate, the good Kinges being fayne to currie
fauour with their great Maſters, and to become
Popular. Whither this would be the end, and
may be the marke of thoſe, or our Populars, I
offer it to their conſideration, that are moſt inter-
eſſed in ſuch motions of Ephoryes, and Senioryes.
The world is beholding to braue and heroicall
myndes, that like Hercules, would praċtiſe meanes
to pull-downe Tyranny, ſmal, or great : and
reforme whole Empires, and Churches, like the
three viċtorious Emperours, ſurnamed *Magni*, Con-
ſtantine, Theodoſius, and Charles. Thankes, were
an vnſufficient recompenſe for ſo noble intentions.
It muſt / be a guerdon of value, that ſhould
counteruaile their deſert, that pretend ſo fatherly,
and Patronly a care of reedifying Commonwealthes,
and Churches. Some voluntarie Counſellours doe
well in a State : and men of extraordinary voca-
tion, ſingularly qualified for the purpoſe, are
worth their double weight in gold. When other

fleepe, they watch : when other play, they worke :
when other feaft, they faft : when other laugh,
they figh : whiles other are content to be lulled
in fecuritie, and nufled in abufe, they occupie
themfelues in deuifing pregnant bondes of affur-
ance, and exquifite models of Reformation. Which
muft prefently be aduaunced without farther con-
fultatiõ : or they haue courage, and will vfe it in
mainetenaunce of fo diuine abftractes. Melancholie
is peremptorie in refolution : and Choler an ægar
Executioner. Were it not for thofe two inuincible
arguments, there might ftill be order taken with
other reafons, and autorities whatfoeuer. They
do well to prefuppofe the beft of their owne
defeignes, and to giue out Cardes of Fortunate
Ilandes, artificially drawen : but as I neuer read,
or heard of any people, that committed fwordes
into fuch hands, but bought their experience with
loffe, and had a hard penyworth of their foft
cufhion : fo in my fimple confideration, I cannot
conceiue, how Ignoraunce fhould become a meeter
Officer, then Knowledge ; Affection a more in-
corrupt Magiftrate, then Reafon ; headlong Rafh-
neffe, or wilfull Stubberneffe, a more vpright
Iudge, then mature Deliberation; bafe Occupations
enact, and eftablifh better orders, then liberall
Sciences, or honourable Profeffions; (any traffique,
howfoeuer current, or aduantageous, hath bene

iudged vndecent for a Senatour); tagg, & ragg
adminifter all things ˏ abfolutely-well, with due
prouifion againft whatfoeuer poffible / inconueni-
ences, where fo many faults are found with perfons
of better qualitie; that incomparablie haue more
fkil in the adminiftration of publique affaires; more
knowledge, and experience in caufes; more refpect
in proceeding ; more regard of their credit ; more
fenfe of daungerous enormities, or contagious
abufes ; more care of the floorifhing and durable
eftate of the Prince, the Commonwealth, and the
Church. Na, I can fee no reafon, according to the
beft groundes of Pollicie, that euer I read, but for
euery Ciuill tyranny or Pettie mifdemeanour that
can poffiblie happen now, the gouernemēt ftanding
as it doth ; there muft needes Vpftart a hundred,
and a hundred barbarous tyrannies, and huge
outrages, were the new platformes, Actes of Par-
lament ; and the Complotters, fuch high Com-
miffioners, as are defcribed in their owne proiects,
the floorifhes of Vnexperienced wittes. When they
haue nothing elfe to alledge, that fhould make
them fuperiour, or equall to the prefent Officers ;
Confcience muft be their Text, their Gloffe, their
Sanctuarie, their Tenure, and their ftrong hold.
Indeede Confcience, grounded vpon Science, is a
double Ancher; that neither deceiueth, nor is
deceiued : and no better rule, then a regular, or

publique Confcience; in diuinitie ruled by Diuinitie,
in law, by Law, in art by Art, in reafon by
Reafon, in experience by Experience. Other
irregular, or priuate Confcience, in Publique
funƈtions, will fall-out to be but a lawleffe Church;
a fhip-mans hofe; a iugglers fticke ; a phantafticall
freehold, and a conceited Tenure *in Capite* : as
interchaungeable as the Moone, and as fallible
as the winde. How barratous, and mutinous at
euery puffe of Suggeftion, lett the world iudge. I
would there lacked a prefent Example, as hoat, as
frefh : but hoat looue, foone cold, and the fittes
of / youth like the fhowers of Aprill. There
goeth a prettie Fable of the Moone, that on a time
fhe earneftly befought her moother, to prouide her a
comely garment, fitt and handfome for her boddy:
How can that be, fweet daughter, (quoth the
moother) fith your boddy neuer keepeth at one cer-
taine ftate, but changeth euery day in the moneth?
That priuate Confcience, the fweet daughter of
Phanfie, be the Morall: and the affurance of the
Common People, where there wanteth a curbe, the
application. What Chameleon fo chaungeth his
colour, as Affeƈtion? or what Polypus fo variable,
as *Populus, chorus, fluuius*? Doƈtour Kelke, when
he was Vicechauncelour in Cambridge, would often
tell the Aduocats, and Proƈtors in the Confiftorie
there, that he had a knacke of Confcience, for

their knacke of Law.   Truly the man, as he was
knowen to be learned, and religious, fo feemed to
carrie a right-honeſt and harmeleſſe minde, and
would many times be pleaſantly difpofed after his
blunt manner : but in very deede his Confcience
(be it ſpoken without appeachmēt of his good
memorie) other-whiles prooued a knacke, and
admitted more inconueniences (ſome would haue
ſayd, committed more abſurdities) then became
the grauitie, and reputation of that iudicious
Confiſtorie.   Yet were this new-plotted Confiſtorie
erected, according to the map of their owne imagi-
nation, euen vpon the topp of the preſumed mount
Sion : by the fauour of that goodly profpect I dare
vndertake, amongſt ſo many thouſand Miniſters,
with Epifcopall, or more then Epifcopall autoritie,
there muſt be but a fewe hundred Iudges, like
Doctour Kelke ; and a very great dearth of ſuch
Affiſtants, or Seniours, as that flooriſhing Vniuer-
ſitie affourdeth.   Alas, many thouſands of them,
Vnworthy to carrie the Beadles ſtaffe before the
one, / or their bookes after the other : how meete
for ſupreme, or free Iurifdiction, I report me vnto
you.   It is notably ſayd of Ariſtotle in his Poli-
tiques : He that would haue the Lawe to rule,
would haue a God to rule : but he that commit-
teth the rule to a man, committeth the rule to a
beaſt.   The Lawe, is a mynde without appetite ;

a foule without a boddy ; a Iudge without flefhe
and bloud ; a ballance without Partialitie; a
meane without extreames. Where Confcience is
fuch a Law, I am for Confcience, let vs profeffe
no other law ; let vs build vs Confiftories, and
tabernacles vpon that hill of Equitie : let vs dwell
in thofe Elifian fieldes of Integritie : let vs honour
that incorruptible fcepter of Sinceritie : let vs fet
the Imperiall crowne vpon the head of that Pol-
licie ; and let that Difcipline weare the Pōtificall
miter. The world wrongeth itfelfe infinitly, if
it runneth not to the gaze of that bewtifull
Bel-uedere ; or refufeth any order frō that facred
Oracle. Otherwife, if men be men, & that Cōfis-
tory, no quire of Angels, or Tribunall of Sainꞔts,
but a meeting of neighbours, fome of them rude,
and grofe enough, after the homelyeft guife, (for
without miraculous illumination, it muft neceffarily
be fo in moft Parifhes) : now I befeech you, hath
not Confideration fome reafon, to feare the Delphi-
call Sword? And the conuented partie, that was
nothing affrayde of the Deane, or the Canons ;
they, quoth he, are good Gentlemen, and my
fauourable frendes, but the Chapter is the Diuell ;
would peraduenture go nigh-hand to fay afmuch
for the new Confiftorie, as for the old Chapter.
Our Minifter is a Zealous Preacher : and fuch,
and fuch my honeft neighbours : but God bleffe

me from the curft Confiftorie. They that fkill
of Popular humours, and know the courfe of
mechanicall dealinges, or artifan gouernements,
or / what you pleafe ; can hardlie hope for any
fuch Paradife, or All-hallowes in hoony-lane, as
is plaufiblie pourtrayed in fome late drawghts of
Reformatiō ; fweeter in difcourfe, then in practife.
I will not prophecie of Contingēts in fpeculation :
but were their Complot a matter *in effe*, it is pos-
fible that euen the Platformers themfelues, fhould
haue no fuch exceeding caufe, to ioye in their
redoubted Seniours. Some Poteftats are queint
men, and will by fittes beare a braine, maugre
the beft reafon or Pureft Confcience in a Con-
fiftorie. And God knoweth, how the People
would digeft it, (efpecially after fome little triall
of their inexorable rigour, and other furly dealing)
that their neighbour Whatchicalt, fometime no
wifer then his fellowes, and fuch, and fuch a
Free-holder of this, and that homely occupation,
(fomewhat bafe for a Senatour) fhould fo iollily
perke on the bench, amongft the Fathers Con-
fcript, when fome, that haue a ftate of inheritance,
or maintaine themfelues vpon ciuiler trades, muft
humbly wait at the barre, and yeeld themfelues
obedient to the fterne commandements of thofe
fage benchers. Iwis, the penny is a ftrong argu-
ment with fuch natures : and he that carrieth

the heauieft purfe, how vnmeete foeuer he may
feeme for a Confiftorie, thinketh himfelfe mightily
wronged, Vnleffe he be taken for the beft, or
one of the beft in the Parifh: and if for his
countenaunce, or other charitable refpect, he will
not fticke fometime to pleafure a good fellow, or
a poore neighbour, (fome good fellowes are kill-
cowes, and fome poore neighbours all-hart) he
may perhaps get fom hardy partakers, & bare
himfelfe for as mighty a man in the borrowgh,
or village, as fome of the forefaid redoubted
Poteftats. How that would be allowed in Con-
fiftorie, or how a thoufand fuites, quarrels, vprores,
& hurliburlyes might be pacified, / yet vn-prouided-
for, or vnthought-vpon by the compendious Sum-
mifts; it would be confidered in time, whiles there
is leyfure from Practife. For after the Confiftorie
is once vp; in fuch a fweating harueft of moft-bufie
bufineffe, a fimple Pragmatique may eafely Prog-
nofticate, how fmall a remnant of leyfure will
remaine for confideration. There was much adooe,
& otherwhiles little helpe, firft at Ierufalem, with
one Synedrion ; and then at Geneua with one
Seniorie, the two onely exemplary Prefbiteryes :
(for other Primitiue Elderfhips will not fit the
turne: what a wonderfull fturre would one, and
fome 52000. Confiftories make in England? Were
not our Reformation likely to prooue a greater

Sweat, or a mightier Drowt, then any in Graftons,
Stowes, or Holinſheads Chronicle? Martin, vnder
correction of your high Court of Conſcience, giue
me leaue to bethinke me attonce, vpon the fier-
worke of your Diſcipline, and Phaetons regiment,
in the hoat Countryes of the Orient. When his
braue deſeigne came to the Execution; *ſolitaque*
iugum grauitate carebat; a light beginning, a
heauie ending.

Nec ſcit, quâ ſit iter; nec ſi ſciat, imperet illis:
and ſo forth : (it is not conceit, or courage, but
ſkill, and authoritie, that manageth gouernement
with honour): what was the iſſue of that yonkerly
& preſumptuous enterpriſe, but a Diluge of fier,
as ruthfull, and horrible, as Deucalions Diluge of
water.

> *Magnæ pereunt cum mœnibus Vrbes:*
> *Cumq. ; ſuis totas populis incendia Gentes*
> *In cinerem vertunt.* You can beſt tranſlate

it yourſelfe : and I leaue the warm application to
the hoat Interpreter : with addition of that ſhort,
but weightie, and moſt remarkable aduertiſe-
ment; *Poenam | Phaeton, pro munere poſcis.*
Phaeton thou deſireſt thy ruine for thy aduaunce-
ment : and Martin, thou affecteſt, thou wotteſt
not what: a Diſcipline? a confuſion? a Refor-
mation? a deformation : a Salue? a plague: a
Bliſſe? a curſe : a Commonwealth? a Common-

wo: a Happy, and Heauenly Church? a wretched,
and hellifh Synagogue. Amount in imagination
as high, as the hawtieft conceit can afpire ; and
plat-forme the moft-exquifite defeignes of pure
Perfection, that the niceft curiofitie can deuife :
were not the wifeft on your fide, moft fimplie-
fimple in weying the Confequents of fuch ante-
cedents, they would neuer fo inconfideratly labour
their owne fhame, the miferie of their brethren,
the defolatiõ of the Miniftery, & the deftructiõ
of the Church. Good Martin, be good to the
Church, to the Miniftery, to the ftate, to thy
country, to thy patrons, to thy frends, to thy
brethren, to thifelfe : and as thou looueft thifelfe,
take heede of old Puritanifme, new Anabaptifme,
& finall Barbarifme. Thou art young in yeares,
I fuppofe : but younger in enterprife, I am affured.
Thy age in fome fort pleadeth thy pardon : and
couldeft thou with any reafonable temperance aduife
thifelfe in time, as it is high time to affuage thy
ftomachous and ouerlafhing outrage ; there be
fewe wife men of qualite, but would pittie thy
rafh proceeding, and impute thy wanton fcurrilous
Veine to want of Experience, and Iudgement,
which is feldome ripe in the Spring. I will not
ftand to examine the Spirite, that fpeaketh, or
endighteth in fuch a phrafe : but if that were the
tenour of a godly, or zealous ftile, methinkes fome

other Sainct, or godly man, fhould fome way haue
vfed the like elocution before : vnleffe you meant
to be as fingular in your forme of writing, as in
your manner of cenfuring ; & to publifh as graue
an Innouation in wordes, as / in other matters.
Some fpirituall motion it was, that caufed you fo
fenfiblie to applie your rufling fpeach, and whole
method, to the feeding and tickling of that humour,
that is none of the greateft ftudentes of Diuinitie,
vnleffe it be your Diuinitie ; nor any of the
likelyeft creatures to aduance Reformation, vnleffe
it be your Reformation. But whatfoeuer your
motion were, or howfoeuer you perfuaded your-
felfe, that a plaufible and roifterly courfe would
winne the harts of good fellowes, and make
ruffians become Precifians, in hope to mount higher
then Highgate, by the fall of Bifhopfgate ; fome
of your well-willers hold a certaine charitable
opiniō, that to reforme yourfelfe, were your beft
Reformatiō. Good Difcipline would doe many
good ; and doe Martin no harme ; had he leyfure
from trainyng of other, to trayne himfelfe, and as
one termed it, to trimme his owne beard. How-
beit in my Method, Knowledge would go before
Practife, and Doctrine before Difcipline. I chal-
lenge fewe, or none for learning, which I rather
looue as my Frēd, or honour as my Patron then
profeffe as my Facultie : but fome approoued good

Schollars of both Vniuerſities, and ſome honorable wiſemen of a higher Vniuerſitie, take Martin to be none of the greateſt Clarkes in England ; and maruell, how he ſhould preſume to be a Doctour of Diſcipline, that hath much-a-doe to ſhewe him-ſelfe a Maſter of Doctrine. For mine owne part, I hope he is a better Doctriniſt, then Diſcipliniſt : or elſe I muſt needes conclude ; Pride is a buſie man, and a deeper Counſellour of ſtates, then of himſelfe. Publique Proiectes become publique perſons ; and may doe well in ſome other, being well employed : but priuate perſons, and the common crewes of Platformers, might haue moſt vſe of priuate deſignements, appropriat to their owne Voca / tion, Profeſſion, or qualitie. When I finde Martin as neat a reformer of his owne life, as of other mens actiõs ; it ſhal go hard, but I wil in ſom meaſure proportion my cõmendation to the ſingularite of his deſert ; which I would be glad to crowne with a garland of preſent, and a diademe of future prayſe. For I long to ſee a Larke without a creaſt ; and would trauaile farre, to diſcoouer a Reformer without a fault ; or onely with ſuch a fault, as for the rareneſſe ſhould deſerue, or for the ſtrangeneſſe might challenge, to be Chronicled, like the Eclipſe of the Sunne. The State Demonſtratiue, not ouerlaboured at this inſtant, would fayne be employed in blaſoning a

creature of fuch perfections: and the very foule of
Charitie thirfteth to drinke of that cleere *Aqua
Vitæ*. It is not the firft time, that I haue pre-
ferred a Gentleman of deedes, before a Lord of
wordes: and what if I once by way of familiar
difcourfe fayd? I was a Proteftant in the Ante-
cedent, but a Papift in the Confequent: for I liked
Faith in the Premiffes, but wifhed works in the
Conclufion: as S. Paul beginneth with Iuftifica-
tion, but endeth with Sanctification: & the
Schoole-men reconcile many Confutations in
one diftinction; We are iuftified by Faith ap-
prehenfiuely; by Workes declaratiuely; by the
bloud of Chrift effectiuely. I hope, it is no euill
figne, for the flower to floorifh, for the tree to
fructifie, for the fier to warme, for the Sunne to
fhine, for Truth to embrace Vertue, for the
Intellectuall good to practife the Morall good, for
the caufe to effect. He meant honeftly, that faid
merrily; He tooke S. Auftins, and S. Gregories
by Pauls, to be the good frendes of S. Faithes
vnder Paules. What needeth more? If your
Reformation be fuch a reftoratiue, as you pretende;
what letteth, but that the world fhould prefently
behold a Vifible difference betweene the fruites of
the / pure and the corrupt diet? Why ceafeth the
heauenly Difcipline, to penne her owne Apologie,
not in one or two fcribled Pamflets of counterfait

Complements, but in a thoufand liuing Volumes
of heauenly Vertues? Diuine Caufes were euer
wont to fortifie themfelues, and weaken their
aduerfaries, with diuine Effectes, as confpicuous,
as the brighteft Sunne-fhine. The Apoftles, and
Primitiue founders of Churches were no railers,
or fcoffers : but painfull trauailers, but Zelous
Preachers, but holly liuers, but fayre-fpoken, mild,
and loouing men, euen like Mofes, like Dauid,
like the fonne of Dauid; the three gentleft perfons,
that euer walked vpon Earth. Where foeuer they
became, it appeared by the whole manner of their
meeke, and fweet proceding that they had bene
the feruants of a meeke Lord, and the Difciples of
a fweet Mafter : in fo much, that many nations,
which knew not God, interteined them, as the
Ambaffadours, or Oratours of fome God; and
were mightily perfuaded, to conceiue a diuine
opinion of him, whom they fo diuinely Preached ;
& euen to beleeue, that he could be no leffe, then
the fonne of the great God. Their miracles got the
harts of numbers: but their Sermons, and Orations,
were greater wonders, then their miracles, and woon
more rauifhed foules to heauen. Their Doctrine
was full of power: their Difcipline full of Charitie:
their Eloquence celeftiall : their Zeale inuincible :
their Life inuiolable : their Conuerfation loouing :
their Profeffion, Humilitie ; their Practife, Humili-

tie ; their Conqueft, Humilitie.   Read the fweet
Ecclefiafticall Hyftories, replenifhed with many
cordiall narrations of their fouerain Vertues : and
perufe the moft rigorous Cenfures of their pro-
feffed enemies, Plinie, Suetonius, Tacitus, Anto-
ninus, Symachus ; Lucian, Libanius, / Philoftratus,
Eunapius, or any like, Latinift, or Grecian, (I
except not Porphyrie, Hierocles, or Iulian him-
felfe) : and what Chriftian, or heathen iudgement,
with any indifferencie can denie, but they alwayes
demeaned themfelues, like well-affected, faire-
conditioned, innocent, and kinde perfons ; many
wayes gratious, and fomewayes admirable?   Peace
was their warre: Vnitie their multiplication: good
wordes, and good deedes, their edifying inftru-
ments : a generall humanitie toward all, where-
foeuer they trauailed ; and a fpeciall beneficence
toward euery one, with whom they conuerfed, one
of their Souerain meanes, for the Propagation of
Chriftianitie.   They knew his mercifull, and God-
full meaning, that in an infinite and incomprehen-
fible looue, defcended from heauen to faue all
vpon Earth, and remembred how gratioufly his
diuine Selfe voutfaued, to conuerfe with Publicans,
and other finners: what a fweet and peerleffe
Example of humbleft Humilitie he gaue his
Difciples, when with his owne immaculate handes
he wafhed their feete: how appliably he framed

himſelfe to the proper diſpoſition of euery Nation
in drawing vnto him the Magicians of the
Eaſt, with the wondrous ſight of a new Starre ;
in moouing the Iewes with miracles, and Parables ;
in ſhewing himſelfe a Prophet, & the very Meſſias,
to the Samaritans ; in ſending eloquent Paule to
the eloquent Grecians, Zealous Peter to the deuout
Hebrues, and vertuous Romans, his brother An-
drew to the ſtout Scythians, incredulous Thomas
to the infidell Parthians, and ſo forth : what a
loouing, and precious deare Teſtament he left
behinde him, and with how vnſpeakable fauour
he bequeathed and diſpoſed the rich hereditaments,
and ineſtimable gooddes of his kingdome : how
neerly it concerned the members of one boddy, /
without the leaſt inteſtine diſagreement, or faction,
to tender and cherriſh one another with mutuall
indulgence : how frutefully the militant Church
had already encreaſed by Concord, like a Plant
of the triumphant Church, whoſe bliſſefull conſort
incomparably paſſeth the ſweeteſt harmonie. The
effect of ſuch diuine motions was heauenly : and
whiles that celeſtiall courſe continued, with an
inuiolable conſent of Vnited mindes, euen in ſome
diſſenſion of opinions, (for there was euer ſome
difference of opinions) the Goſpell reigned, and
the Church flooriſhed miraculouſly. It would
make the hart of Pietie, to weepe for ioyfull

compaſſion, to remember how the Bloud of thoſe, and thoſe moſt-patient, but more glorious Martyrs, that might be ſlaine, but not vanquiſhed, was the Seede of the Church. The Church, that grew victorious, and mightie, by the beheading of Paule, and Iames ; by the crucifying of Peter, Andrew, Philip, and Simon ; by the ſtoning of Stephen ; by the burning of Marke, and Barnabas ; by the flaying of Bartholmew ; by the murdering of Thomas with a dart, of Mathew with a ſword, of Matthias with an axe, of Iames Alphæus with a club ; of how many renowned Martyrs with how many cruell and tyrannicall torments ; immortall monuments of their inuincible Faith, and moſt honorable Conſtancie. When Aſperitie, and Diſcorde, degenerating from that Primitiue order ; tooke an other courſe, and began to proceede, more like Furies of hell, then Sainćts of the Church, or honeſt neighbours of the world ; alas, what followed ? And vnleſſe we retire to our principles, although miſchief vpon miſchief be bad enough, yet ruine vpon ruine will be worſe. It is not a ruffianly ſtile, or a tumultuous plot, that will amend the matter : ſome Apoſtolicall vertues would doe well ; and that-ſame / Euangelicall humilitie were much-worth. In the meane ſeaſon, ſuerly reuerend Biſhops, and learned Doćtours, albeit corruptible men, ſhould be

meeter to adminifter or gouerne Churches, then
luftie Cutters, or infufficient Plotters, albeit re-
formed creatures. Sweet Martin, afwell Iunior,
as Senior, (for Iuniours, and Seniours are all one,
as old Mafter Raye fayd in his maioraltie) and
you fweet whirlewinds, that fo fiercely befturr
you at this inftant; now agayne, and agayne I
befeech you, either be content to take a fweeter
courfe; or take all for me. My intereft in thefe
caufes is fmall: and howfoeuer fome bufie heades
looue to fet themfelues aworke, when they might
be otherwife occupied, yet by their fauours, there
is a certaine thing, that paffeth all Vnderftanding;
which I commend Vniuerfally vnto all, efpecially
vnto my frends, and fingularly vnto mifelfe.
Nulla falus bello: pacem te pofcimus omnes. No
Law to the Feciall Law; nor any Conqueft to
Pacification. Would Chrift, Reformation could
be entreated to begin at itfelfe; and Difcipline
would be fo good, as to fhew by example of
her owne houfe, wher fhe inhabiteth, and con-
forteth, what a Precious, and heauenly thing it
were for a whole kingdome, to liue in fuch
a celeftiall harmony of Pure Vertues, and all
perfections. Theoricks, and Idees are quickly
imagined in an afpiring phantafie: but an inuiolable
Practife of a diuine excellencie in humane frailtie,
without excefle, defect, or abufe, doubtleffe were

a Chriſtall worth the ſeeing, and a glorious
Mirrour of eternall Imitation. When Contem-
plation hath a little more experience, it ſhall
finde, that Action is ſcantly ſo ſmooth, and nimble
a creature, as Speculation : two notable Preſidēts
in Concreto, more rare, then twentie ſingular Types
in abſtracto : they that ſhoote beyond the marke,
in / imagination, come ſhort in tryall : good,
intētions were neuer too-rife, & the beſt intentiōs
haue gone aſtray. All men are not of one
mould : there is as great difference of Miniſters
and Aldermen, as of other perſons : euen where
the ſpirite is ſtrong, the fleſh is ſometime founde
weake enough ; and the world, is a world of
temptations, murmurings, offences, quarrels, tres-
paſſes, crimes, and continuall troubles in one ſort
or other.

If the preciſeſt, and moſt ſcrupulous Treatiſes
haue much-adooe to vphold the credit of any
perfection, or eſtimation, with their owne aſſociats ;
(how many heads, ſo many plottes) what may
Reaſon conceiue of the aſſurance, or maturitie of
their iudiciall or other Morall Proceedings *in Eſſe?*
When His, and His Scripture, after ſome prettie
pauſing, is become Apocryphall with his, and his
owne adherents, whoſe writing was Scripture with
many of them ; how can any of them aſcertaine,
or reſolue themſelues of the Canonicall incorrup-

tion, or autenticall omnifufficiencie of his, or his
actuall gouernement? When euen He, that within
thefe fewe yeares was alledged for Text, hath fo
emprooued his autoritie with a number of his
feruenteft brethren, that he will now be fcantly
allowed for a current Gloffe ; why fhould defeated
Affection any longer delude itfelfe with a pre-
iudicate & vayne imagination of an Alchimifticall
Difcipline, not fo fweet in conceit, as fower in
proofe ; and as defectiue in needfull prouifion, as
exceffiue in vnneedfull prefumption? If Second
cogitations be riper, and founder, then the firft ;
may not a Third, or Fourth confultations take
more & more aduifement? If Bifhops-gate be
infected, is it vnpoffible for Alders-gate to be
attainted? and if neither can be long cleere in
an Vniuerfall plague of Corruption, what reafon /
hath Zeale to fly from Gods bleffing into a warme
Sunne : What a wifedome were it, to chaunge
for the worfe? or what a notorious follie were it,
to innouate, without infallible affurance of the
better? What Politique ftate, or confiderate
people, euer laboured any Alteration, Ciuill, or
Ecclefiafticall, without Pregnant euidence of fome
fingular, or notable Good, as certaine in con-
fequence, as important in eftimation? To be
fhort, (for I haue already bene ouer-long, and
fhall hardlie qualifie thofe headdie younkers with

any Difcourfe) had Martin his luft, or Penry
his wifh, or Vdal his mynde, or Browne his
will, or Ket his phanfie, or Barrow his pleafure, or
Greenwood his harts-defire, or the frefheft Practi-
tioners their longing, (euen to be Iudges of the
Confiftorie, or Fathers Confcript of Senate, or
Domine fac totum, or themfelues wott not what) ;
there might fall-out fiue hundred practicable cafes,
and a thoufand difputable queftions in a yeare,
(the world muft be reframed· anew, or fuch
points decided) wherewith they neuer difquieted
their braynes, and wherein the learnedeft of them
could not fay A. to the Arches, or B. to a
Battledore. If the grauer motioners of Difcipline
(who no doubt are learneder men, and might be
wifer : but M. Trauers, M. Cartwright, Doctour
Chapman, and all the grayer heads begin to be
ftale with thefe Noouellifts) haue bethought them-
felues vpon all cafes, and cautels in Practife, of
whatfoeuer nature, and haue thorowly prouided
againft all poffible mifchieffs, inconueniences, and
irregularities, afwell future, as prefent ; I am
glad they come fo well prepared : fuerly fome
of the earnefteft and egreft follicitours, are not yet
fo furnifhed. Wordes are good fellowes, and
merry men : but in my poore opinion, it were
not amiffe for fome fweating, and fierce / dooers
at this inftant, that would downe with Clement,

and vp with Hildebrand, either to know more
at home, or to fturr leffe abroad. It is no trifling
matter in a Monarchie, to hoife-vp a new
Autoritie, like that of the Iewifh Confiftorie
aboue Kinges, or that of the Lacedemonian
Ephorie aboue Tyrants, or that of the Romane
Senate aboue Emperours. Howbeit if there be
no remedie, but M. Fier muft be the Paftour,
M. Aier the Doctour, goodman Water the
Deacon, and goodman Earth the Alderman of
the Church ; let the young Calfe, and the old
Affe draw Cuttes, whither of their heads fhall
weare the garland. And thus much in generalitie
touching Martinizing, being vrged to defend it,
if I durft : but for feare of indignation I durft
not. The feuerall particularities, and more
gingerly nicityes of rites, fignes, termes, and
what not? I referre to the difcuffion of pro-
feffed Deuines : or referue for more leyfure and
fitter occafion.

As for that new-created Spirite, whom double
V. like an other Doctour Fauftus, threateneth to
coniure-vpp at leyfure, (for I muft returne to the
terrible creature, that fubfcribeth himfelfe Martins
Double V. and will needes alfo be my Tittle-
tittle) were that Spirite difpofed to appeare in his
former likeneffe, and to put the Necromancer to
his purgation, he could peraduenture make the

coniuring wifard forfake the center of his Circle, and betake him to the circumference of his heeles. Simple Creature, iwis thou art too-young an Artift *to coniure him* vp, that can exorcife thee downe: or to *lamback him* with *ten yeares* preparation, that can lamfkin thee with a dayes warning. Out vpon thee for a cowardly lambacker, that ftealeft-in at the back doore ; and thinkeft to filch aduauntage on the back wing. / Knaues are backbiters; whores bellybiters ; and both fheepebiters. Pedomancie fitter for fuch Coniurers, then either Chiromancie, or Necromancie, or any Familiar Spirite, but contempt. It is fome-boddyes fortune, to be haunted with backfrendes : and I could report a ftraunge Dialogue betwixt the Clarke of Backchurch, and the Chaunter of Pancridge, that would make the better vifard of the two to blufh : but I fauour modeft eares ; and a thoufand honeft tongues will iuftifie it to thy face, Thou art as it were a grofe Idiot, and a very *Affe in prefenti,* to imagine that thou couldeft go fcotfree in this fawcy reckoning, although the partie coniured fhould fay nothing, but Mum. Honeftie goeth neuer Vnbacked : and Truth is a fufficient Patron to itfelfe : and I know One, that hath written a Pamflet, intituled *Cockalilly,* or *The white fon of the Black Art.* But he that can *maffacre Martins wit,* (thou remembreft thine owne phrafe) can rott Pap-hatchets braine :

and he that can *tickle Mar-prelate with taunts,* can
twitch double V. to the quicke : albeit he threaten
no leffe, then the fiege of Troye in his Note-
booke ; and his penne refounde, like the harneffed
woombe of the Troian horfe. I haue feene a
broad fword ftand at the doore, when a poinado
hath entered : and although I am neither Vlyffes,
nor Outis, yet perhaps I can tell, how, No-boddy
may doe, that fomeboddy cannot doe. Poly-
phemus was a mightie fellow, and coniured Vlyffes
companions into excrements : (few Giants euer fo
hideous, as Polyphemus) : but poore Outis was
euen with him, and No-boddy coniured his goggle
eye, as well. I prey-thee fweet Pap, infult not
ouer-much vpon quiet men : though my penne be
no-boddy at a hatchet, and my tongue leffe then
no-boddy at a beetle ; yet Patience looueth not to
be made a / cart of Croiden ; and no fuch libbard
for a liuely Ape, as for dead Silence. The merry
Gentleman deuifeth to difport himfelfe, and his
Copefmates, with a pleafurable conceit of *quaking
eares :* and *all my workes, at leaft fix fheetes in
quarto, called by mifelfe, The firft tome of my familiar
Epiftle :* two impudent lyes, and fo knowen noto-
rioufly. He might as truly forge any lewd, or
villanous report of any man in England ; and for
his labour challenge to be preferred to the Clark-
fhip of the whetftone : which he is hable to main-

taine fumptuoufly, with a mint of queint, and
Vncouth Similes, daintie monfters of Nature.   I
muft deale plainly with the Spawne of rãke
Calumnie : his knauifh, & foolifh malice palpably
bewrayeth it felf in moft-odious fictions ; meet to
garnifh the forefayd famous office of the whet-
ftone. But what fayth his owne couragious Penne,
of his owne aduenturous eares?   *If ripping-vp of
Liues make fport, haue with thee knuckle deepe : it
fhal neuer be fayd, that I dare not venter myne eares,
where Martin hazards his necke.*   Some men are
not fo prodigall of their eares, how lauifh foeuer
Martin may feeme of his necke ; & albeit euery
mã cannot compile fuch graund Volumes as
Euphues, or reare fuch mightie tomes, as Pap-
hatchet ; yet he might haue thought, other poore
men haue tongues, and pennes to fpeake fome-
thing yet, when they are prouoked vnreafonably.
But loofers may haue their wordes, and Comedians
their actes : fuch drie bobbers can luftely ftrike at
other, and cunningly rapp themfelues.   He hath
not played the Vicemafter of Poules, and the
Foolemafter of the Theater for naughtes ; him-
felfe a mad lad, as euer twanged, neuer troubled
with any fubftance of witt, or circumftance of
honeftie, fometime the fiddle-fticke of Oxford,
now the very bable of London ; would fayne
forfooth haue fome / other efteemed, as all men

value him. A workeman is eafely defcried by
his termes: euery man fpeaketh according to his
Art: I am threatened with a Bable, and Martin
menaced with a Comedie: a fit motion for a
Iefter, and a Player, to try what may be done by
employmēt of his facultie: Bables & Comedies
are parlous fellowes *to decipher, and difcourage
men,* (that is the Point) with their wittie flowtes,
and learned Ierkes; enough to lafh any man
out-of countenance. Na, if you fhake the painted
fcabbard at me, I haue done: and all you, that
tender the preferuation of your good names, were
beft to pleafe Pap-hatchet, and fee Euphues be-
times, for feare leffe he be mooued, or fome One
of his Apes hired, to make a Playe of you; and
then is your credit quite vn-done for euer, and
euer: Such is the publique reputation of their
Playes. He muft needes *be difcouraged,* whom
they *decipher.* Better, anger an hundred other,
then two fuch; that haue the Stage at com-
maundement, and can furnifh-out Vices, and
Diuels at their pleafure. Gentlemen, beware of
a *chafing-penne, that fweateth-out whole realmes of
Paper,* and whole Theaters of Ieftes: tis auenture,
if he dye not of the Paper-fweat, fhould he chaunce
to be neuer fo little ouerchafed. For the Ieft-dropfie
is not fo peremptorie. But no point of Cunning,
to the *Tale of the Tubb*: that is the profounde

myfterie, and the very Secret of Secrets. The fweet Sifters Anfwer, *that in her confcience thought Lecherie the Superficies of finne,* (a rare word with women, but by her aunfwer fhe fhould feeme to be learned): the true Tale of one of Martins godly fonnes, *that hauing the Companie of one of his fifters in the open fieldes, faid he would not fmoother-vp finne, and deale in hugger-mugger againft his confcience:* (the Hiftoriographer hath many priuie intelligences): the fober tale of / the *Eldeft Elder, that receiued fortie Angels at his Table, where he fat with no leffe then fortie good difhes of the greateft dainties, in more pompe, then a Pope:* (he was not of the ftarued Pythagorean, or Platonicall diet: but liberall exhibition may maintaine good hofpitalitie): the Zelous *Looue letter, or a Corinthian Epiftle to the widow, as honeft a woman, as euer burnt malt:* (the wooer, or the Regifter of Aretines Religion): *the holie Othe of the Martinift, that thinking to fweare by his confcience, fwore by his Concupifcence:* (did not he forget himfelfe, that exprefly affirmed? *Martin will not fweare: but with In deede, In footh, and In truth, hele cogg the dye of deceit:*) thefe, and the reft of thofe bawdie Inuentions, wherewith that brothellifh Pamflet floweth, fmell fomewhat ftrongly of the Pumpe; and fhewe the credibilitie of the Autor, that dareth alledge any impudent, prophane, or blafphemous fiction to ferue his turne. So he may foone make-vp the autenticall Legendary of his *Hundred merrie Tales* : as true peraduenture, as Lucians true narrations ; or the heroicall hiftoryes of Rabelais ; or the braue Legendes of Errant Knights ; or the egregious prankes of Howle-glaffe, Frier Rufh, Frier Tuck, and fuch like; or the renowned *Bugiale* of Poggius, Racellus, Lufcus, Cincius, and that whole Italian crew of merry Secretaryes in the time of Pope Martin the fift ; of whom our worfhipfull Clarkes of the whetftone, Doctour Clare, Doctour Bourne, M. Scoggin, M. Skelton, M. Wakefield, diuers late Hiftoriologers, and haply this new Tale-founder himfelfe, learned their moft-wonder-full facultie. *Committing of matrimonie ; carouſing the ſapp of the Church ; cutting at the bumme Carde of conſcience ; beſmearing of conſcience ; ſpelling of Our Father in a horne-booke ; the railing Religion ;* and a whole finke of fuch arrant phrafes, fauour whotly / of the fame Lucianicall breath, & difcoouer the minion Secre-tarie aloofe. Faith, quoth himfelfe, thou wilt be caught by thy ftile : Indeede what more eafie, then to finde the man by his humour, the Midas by his eares, the Calfe by his tongue, the goofe by his quill, the Play-maker by his ftile, the hatchet by the Pap? Albertus Secrets, Poggius Fables, Bebelius ieftes, Scoggins tales, Wakefields lyes, Parfon Darcyes knaueries, Tarletons trickes, Eldertons Ballats, Greenes Pamflets, Euphues Similes, double V^s phrafes, are too-well knowen, to go vnknowen. Where the Veine of Braggadocio is famous, the arterie of Pappadocio cannot be obfcure. Gentlemen, I haue giuē you a taft of his Sugerloafe, that weeneth Sidneyes daintyes, Afchams cōfites, Cheekes fuccats, Smithes cōferues, and Mores iunkets, nothing comparable to his pap. Some of you dreamed of Electuaryes of Gemmes, and other precious reftoratiues ; of the quinteffence of Amber, & Pearle diffolued, of I wott not what incredible delicacies : but his Gemmemint is not alwayes current ; and as bufie men, fo painted boxes, and gallipots muft haue a Vacation. Yet wellfare the fweet hart of Dia-pap, Dia-fig, and Dia-nut, three foueraine Defenfatiues of the Commonwealth, and three cordiall Comfortatiues of the Church. It is a good hearing, when good fellowes haue a care of the Commonwealth, and the Church : and a godly motion, when Interluders leaue penning their pleafurable Playes, to become Zealous Ecclefiafticall writers. *Bona fide,* fome haue written notablie againft Martinifme : (it were a bufie tafke for the credibleft Precifian, to empeach the credit of Doctour Bancroft, or Doctour Sutcliff) : but this Mammaday hath excellently knocked himfelfe on

the fconfe with his owne hatchet. I will caft away
no more inke vpon a Com / pounde of fimples.
The Pap is like the hatchet : the fig like the nut :
the Country-cuff like the hangmans apron : the
dog like the dog : John Anoke, and Iohn Aftile
like the baily of Withernam : the figne of the
Crabtre cudgell like twackcoate Lane : Martins
hanging like Pappadocios mowing : Huff, Ruff,
and Snuffe, the three tame ruffians of the Church,
like double V : neuer a laye in the barrell, better
herring : the beginning, the midft, and the end,
all in one pickle. Some rofes amongft prickes,
doe well : and fome lillyes amongft thornes, would
haue done no harme. But Enuie hath no fanfie
to the rofe of the garden : and what careth Malice
for the lilly of the Valley ? Would, fayre Names
were fpelles, and charmes againft fowle Affections :
and in fome refpectes I could wifh, that Diuinitie
would giue Humanitie leaue to conclude other-
wife, then I muft. I could in curtefie be content,
and in hope of Recōciliation defirous, to mitigate
the harfheft fentences, and mollifie the hardeft
termes. But can Truth lye : or Difcretion approoue
follie : or Iudgement allowe Vanitie : or Modeftie
abide Impudencie : or good manners footh bad
fpeaches ? He that penned the abooue-mentioned
Cock-alilly, faw reafon to difplay the Black Artift
in his collier coolours : and thought it moft vn-

reafonable, to fuffer fuch light and emptie veffels, to make fuch a lowde, and prowde rumbling in the ayre. Other had rather heare the learned Nightingale, then the Vnlearned Parrat ; or taft the wing of a Larke, then the legge of a Rauen. The fineft wittes preferre the loofeft period in M. Afcham, or Sir Philip Sidney, before the trickfieft page in Euphues, or Pap-hatchet. The Mufes, fhame to remember fome frefhe quaffers of Helicon : and which of the Graces, or Vertues blufheth not, to name fome luftie tofpots / of Rhetorique? The ftately Tragedie fcorneth the trifling Comedie : and the trifling Comedie flowt-eth the new Ruffianifme. Wantonneffe was neuer fuch a fwill-bowle of ribaldry : nor Idleneffe euer fuch a carowfer of knauerie. What honeft mynde, or Ciuill difpofition, is not accloied with thefe noifome, & nafty gargarifmes? Where is the polifhed and refined Eloquence, that was wont to bedeck, and embellifh Humanity? Why fhould learning be a niggard of his excellent gifts, when Impudencie is fo prodigall of his rafcall trifh-trafh? What daintie, or neat Iudgement begin-neth not to hate his old looue, and loath his auncient delight, the Preffe, the moft-honorable Preffe, the moft-villanous Preffe? Who fmileth not at thofe, and thofe trim-trammes of gawdie wittes, how floorifhing Wittes, how fading witts?

Who laugheth not at *Il'e, Il'e, Il'e* ; or gibeth not
at fome hundred Pibalde fooleryes, in that hare
braind Declamation? They whom it neerelyeft
pincheth, cannot filence their iuft difdaine : and I
am forcibly vrged to intimate my whole Cenfure,
though without hatred to the perfon, or deroga-
tion from any of his commendable gift, yet not
without fpeciall diflike of the bad matter, and
generall condemnation of the vile forme. The
whole Worke, a bald Toy, full of ftale, and
woodden Ieftes ; and one of the moft paltry
thinges, that euer was publifhed by graduate of
either Vniuerfitie : good for nothing but to ftop
muftard pottes, or rubbe gridirons, or feather
rattes neaftes, or fuch like homely vfe. For
Stationers are already too-full of fuch Realmes,
and Commonwealthes of Waft-paper, and finde
more gaine in the lillypot blanke, then in the
lillypot Euphued : a day, or two fine for fheetes,
and afterward good for grofers. *Vanitas vanita-*
tum, the fome of grudge, the froth of leuitie, the
/ fcum of corruption, and the very fcurfe of
rafcallitie : nothing, worthy of a Schollar, or a
Ciuill Gentleman : altogether phantafticall, and
fonde, without ryme, or reafon : fo odly hudled,
and bungled togither, in fo madbraine fort, and
with fo braineficke ftuffe, that in an Ouer flowe
of fo many friuolous, and ridiculous Pamflets, I

fcarfely know any One in all points, fo incompar-
ably vayne and abfurde, whereunto I may refemble
that moft toyifhe and piperly trifle, the fruite of
an addle, and lewd wit, long-fince dedicated to a
diffolute, and defperate Licentioufneffe. Oh what
a *Magnifico* would he be, were his purfe as heauie,
as his head is light, and his hart franke? Euen
that fame Very Mirrour of Madneffe, hangeth
togither with fome more coherence of reafon ;
and fmelleth not fo rankly of the Tauerne, the
Alehoufe, the Stewes, the Cuckingftoole, or other
fuch honeft places, as that drunkē, and fhameleffe
Declamation ; Vnbefeeming any, but an Oratour
of Bedlam, a Rhetorician of Bridewell, or a Dis-
courfer of Primerofe hill. And although that
fame Frēch Mirrour, be *ex Profeſſo* deuifed in a
mad garifh Veyne, and ftuffed with geere homely
enough, fit for a Libertine & frantique Theame :
yet doth it no[t] fo bafely borrow of the Ruffians
bagge, the Tapfters fpigot, the Pedlars pack, the
Tinkars bugget, the Knaues truffe, and the Roges
fardle : vnto all which, and other Autors of like
reputation, but chiefly to the Hangmans apron,
(that, that is the biggin of his wit), this worthy
Autour is deeply beholding for great part of his
fine conceits, and dainty learning ; precious ware
for Euphued creatures, and phantafticall colts :
whofe wild and madbraine humour nothing fitteth

fo iuft, as the ftaleft dudgen, or abfurdeft balduc-
tum, that they, or their mates can inuent, in odd
and awke fpeaches, difguifedly fhapen after / the
antick fafhion, & monftroufly fhorne, like old
Captaine Lifters fpānel. They that affect fuch
ruffianifh braueryes, and deuide their roifter-
doiftering Ieftes into Cuttes, flafhes, and foines,
may beftow the reading : for any other of what-
foeuer qualitie, or calling, it will do them afmuch
good, as dirt in their fhooes, or draffe in their
bellyes: and in good footh there is all the vfe, Ciuill
or Ecclefiafticall, that I can finde of this Babees
papp : whom for his fweet interteinement with papp,
figg, and nut, I officioufly recommende to the Ship
of Fooles, and the Galeaffe of knaues. When he
vfeth himfelfe with more modeftie, and his friendes
with more difcretion, I may alter my ftile : (let
him chaunge, and I am chaunged) : or if already
he be afhamed of that coniuring leafe, foifted in
like a Bumbarde, I haue fayd nothing. Till he
difclaimeth his iniurie, in Print; or confeffeth his
ouerfight, in writing; or fignifieth his Penitence,
in fpeach : the abufed partie, that had reafon to
fet-downe the Premiffes without fauour, hath caufe
to iuftifie his owne hand without feare ; and is
afwell in equitie to auowe Truth, as in charitie
to difauowe Malice. At Trinitie hall : this fift of
Nouember : 1589.

SO then of Pappadocio: whom neuer-theleffe I efteeme a hundred times learneder, and a thoufand times honefter, then this other Braggadocio; that hath more learning, then honeftie, and more money then learning, although he truly intitle himfelfe, Pierce Penniles, and be elfewhere ftiled the Gentle / man Raggamuffin. Nafh, the Ape of Greene, Greene the Ape of Euphues, Euphues, the Ape of Enuie, the three famous mammets of the preffe, and my three notorious feudifts, drawe all in a yoke: but fome Schollars excell their mafters; and fome luftie bloud will do more at a deadly pull, then two, or three of his yokefellowes. It muft go hard, but he wil emprooue himfelfe, the incomparable darling of immortall Vanitie. Howbeit his frendes could haue wifhed, he had not fhowen himfelfe to the world, fuch a ridiculous *Suffenus*, or *Shakerly* to himfelfe, by aduauncing the triumphall garland vpon his owne head, before the leaft fkermifh for the victorie: which if he euer obtaine by any valiancie, or brauure, (as he

weeneth himfelfe, the valianteft and braueft Actour,
that euer managed penne) I am his bondman in
fetters, and refufe not the humbleft vaffalage to
the fole of his boote.   Much may be done by
clofe confederacie, in all fortes of coofenage, and
legierdemane : *Monfieur Pontalais* in French, or
Meffer Vnico in Italian, neuer deuifed fuch a
nipping Comedie, as might be made in Englifh,
of fome leagers in the queint practiques of the
Crofbiting Art : but I haue feene many Bear-
wardes, and Butchers in my time ; and haue heard
of the one, what belongeth to Apes ; and haue
learned of the other, not to be affrayde of a
doofen horned beaftes : albeit fome one of them
fhould feeme as dreadfull, as the furious dun Cowe
of Dunfmore heath, the terribleft foman of Sir
Guy. Æfops Oxe, though he be a fuer plough-
man, is but a flowe workeman : and Greenes
Ape, though he be a nimble Iuggler, is no fuer
executioner.   Yet well-worth the Mafter-Ape,
and Captaine mammet, that had a hatchet,
afwell as Papp ; a Country cuffe afwell as a
figge ; a crabtree cudgell, afwell as a nutt ;
fomething of a mans- / face, with more of an
Apes-face. Had his pen bene muzzled at the
firft, as his mouth hath bene bunged fince, thefe
frefh Euphuiftes would neuer haue aduentured
vpon the whip, or the bobb : but Silence is a

flaue in a chaine; and Patience the common
Pack-horfe of the world. Euen this brat of an
Apefclogge, that can but mowgh with his mouth,
gnafh with his teeth, quauer with his ten bones,
and brandifh his' goofe-quill; prefuming of my
former fufferance, layeth about him with the faid
quill, as if it were poffeffed with the fprite of
Orlando Furiofo, or would teach the clubb of
Gargantua to fpeake Englifh. For the flaile of
Aiax diftrawght, or the clubb of Hercules enraged,
were but hedge-ftakes of the old world; and
vnworth the naming in an age of puiffance em-
prooued horriblie. The neweft Legendes of moft
hideous exploits, may learne a new Art to kill-
cow men with peremptorie termes, and bugges-
wordes of certaine death. Pore I muft needes
be plagued; plagued? na, brayed & fquifed to
nothing, that am matched with fuch a Gargãtuift,
as can deuoure me quicke in a fallat; and
thundreth more direfull threatnings againft me
that onely touched him; then huge Polyphemus
rored againft Vlyffes, that blinded him: *Genus*
irritabile Vatum. The generation of rauing Poets,
is a fwarme of gad-bees; and the anger of a
moodie rimefter, the furie of a Wafpe. A mad
Tiger, not like a mad Wafpe; and a chafed
Wildbore, not comparable to a chafed gad-bee.
Take heede of the man, whom Nature hath

marked with a gag-tooth; Art furnifhed with a
gag-tongue; and Exercife armed with a gag-
penne; as cruell and murdrous weapons, as euer
drewe bloud. The beft is, who hath time, hath
life. He meaneth not to come vpon me with
a cowardly ftratageme of Scarborough / warning :
he vfeth a certaine gallant Homericall Figure,
called *Hyfteron-proteron*, or the Cart before the
horfe ; & with a refolution menaceth the effect,
before the Caufes be begotten. When the iron
Cart is made, and the fierie horfes foled, they
fhall bring the mightie Battring-ram of termes, and
the great Ordinance of miracles, to towne : afke
not then, how he will plague me. In the meane
feafon, it is a woonder to fee, how courageoufly
he taketh-on with his hoftiffes needles, and his
botchers bodkins. Indeede a good Souldiour will
make a fhrewd fhift with any weapons : but it
is a maruelous hart, that threatneth Ruine, ruine,
ruine, with the dint of a bodkin, and the blade
of an awle. Where fuch an other Rodomont,
fo furious, fo valorous, fo redoubtable? There
is a peece of a good old Song, peraduenture as
auncient, as the noble Legende of Syr Beuis, or
Sir Launcelot du Lake :

Dubba-dubba-dubb, kill him with a clubb :
And he will not dye, kill him with a flye.

He that made that Ryme in ieft, little con-
fidered, what a gad-fly may doe in earneft. It
is fmall wifedome, to contemne the fmalleft
enemy ; the gad-fly is a little creature; but
fome little creatures be ftingers : neuer fauchon
better managed, then fome tiny penneknifes :
and what will he do, when he rufheth vpon me
with the tempeftuous Engins of his owne wit,
that keepeth fuch a horrible coile with his Schoole-
fellowes poinardo? An Ape is neuer to feeke
of a good face, to fet vpon the matter. Bleffed
Euphues, thou onely happy, that haft a traine
of fuch good countenances, in thy floorifhing
greene-motley liuery : miferable I, the vnhappieft
on earth, that am left defolate. Ah but that might
be endured : euery mã is not borne, to be the
leader of a bande : euery birde carrieth not Argus
eyes difplayed in her taile : Fame is not euery /
boddies Sainct : to be forfaken, is no great
matter ; to be vtterly vndone, is miferable. That,
and the Vnmercifulleft perfecution that may be
inuented, is cruelly proclaimed againft quiet him,
that was once thronged and peftred with followers :
but when he began to giue-ouer that greene haunt,
and betooke himfelfe to a riper Profeffion, Dio-
medes companions were changed into birdes.
Times alter : and as Fortune hath more fectaries,
then Virtue ; fo Pleafure hath more adherents,

then Proffit. I had no fooner fhaken of my yoũg troupe, whõ I could not affociate as before, but they were feftiually reinterteined by fome nimble wightes, that could take the aduantage of opportunitie (with good vifages you may be fuer), and had purpofely lyne in waite to climbe in Print, by the fall of their Seniours: like ambitious Planets, that enhaunfe their owne dignities, by the combuftion, or retrogradation of their fellow-Planettes. Much good may that aduauncement doe them; and many daintie webbs may I fee of thofe fine Spiders: but although I dote vpon curious workemanfhip, yet I looue not artificiall poyfon; and am almoft angrie with the trimmeft Spinners, when they extort venom out of flowers, and will needes defile their friends Libraries with thofe encroching cobwebbs. I wis it were purer Euphuifme, to winne hoony out-of the thiftle; to fweeten Alöe with fugar; to perfume the ftinking Sagapenum with mufke; and to mitigate the heat of Euforbium with the iuice of the lilly. Tufh, you are a filly humanitian of the old world: that was the fimplicitie of the age, that loued frendfhip, more then gold, & efteemed euery thing fine, that was neat, & holefom: all was pure, that was feafoned with a little falt; & all trimme, that was befprinkled with a fewe flowers: now the fierceſt Gunpouder, and the rankeſt pike ſawce, are / the braueſt figures of Rhetorique *in eſſe* ; and he the onely man at the Scriueners Piſtoll, that will *ſo inceſſantlie haunt the Ciuilian, and Deuine, that to auoide the hoat chaſe of his fierie quill, they ſhalbe conſtrained to enſconſe themſelues in an old Vrinall caſe.* Giue me ſuch a *Bonifacius.* Now well-worth ſome termes of *Aqua fortis* at a pinch : and wellcome Vrinall caſe, a fit ſconſe for ſuch valiant termes ; and a meet Bulwarke againſt that fierie quill. I haue already felt his pulſe : and cannot well caſt his water, without an Vrinall either old, or new : but an old Vrinall will not ſo handſomly ſerue the turne : it would be as new, as the Capcaſe of Straunge Newes : but *a pure mirrour* of an impure ſtale ; *neither groſe,* the clearer to repreſent a groſe ſubſtāce ; *nor green,* the liuelyer to expreſſe ſome greene colours, & other wanton accidents ; *nor any way a harlot,* the trulyer to diſcoouer the ſtate of a harlatrie. I haue ſeene as hoat an Agent made a tame Patient ; and gladd to enſconſe the dregges of his ſhame in an old Vrinall. It is a blabb : but not euery mans blabb, that caſteth a ſheepes-eye out of a Calues-head ; but a blabb with iudgement ; but a blabb, that can make excrements bluſh, and teach Chawcer to retell a Canterbury Tale. But ſuch great Iudicials requier ſome little

ftuddie : and S. Fame is difpofed to make it
Hallyday. She hath already put-on her wifpen
garland ouer her powting Crof-cloth : and behold
with what an Imperiall Maieftie fhe commeth
riding in the ducking-chariot of her Triumphe.
I was neuer fo ficke of the milt, but I could
laugh at him, that would feeme a merry man,
& cannot for his life keepe-in the breath of a
fumifh foole. Phy, long Megg of Weftminfter
would haue bene afhamed to difgrace her Sonday
bonet with her Satterday witt. She knew fome
rules of Decorum : and although fhe were a luftie
bounfing rampe, fome / what like Gallemella, or
maide Marian, yet was fhe not fuch a roinifh
rannell, or fuch a diffolute gillian-flurtes, as this
wainfcot-faced Tomboy; that will needes be
Danters Maulkin, and the onely hagge of the
Preffe. I was not wont to endight in this ftile :
but for terming his fellow Greene, as he was
notorioufly knowen, the Scriuener of Crofbiters;
the founder of vgly othes, the greene mafter of
the blacke art; the mocker of the fimple world,
et cætera : fee, how the daggletaild rampalion
buftleth for the frank-tenement of the dunghill.
I confeffe, I neuer knew my Inuectiue Principles,
or confuting termes before : and perhaps fome
better Schollars are nigh-hand as farre to feeke
in the kinde rudiments, and proper phrafes of

pure Naſherie. *Why, thou errant Butter whore,*
(quoth he, or rather ſhe) *thou Cotqueane and
ſcrattop of ſcolds, wilt thou neuer leaue afflicting
a dead carcaſſe, continually read the Rethorique
Lecture of Ramme ally? A wiſp, a wiſp, a wiſp,
ripp, ripp you kitchinſtuffe wrangler.* Holla Sir,
ſweeter wordes would do no harme. Doubtleſſe
theſe emphaticall termes of the ally, were layd
aſteepe for ſome other acquaintāce, not for me:
(good fellowes muſt be furniſhed with Oratorie,
meete for their cōpany): but it is ſome mens
euill lucke, to ſtūble in the way, when Will
Summers weapon is ready drawen: and yet more
poſſible for him to ſtay the ſwing of his eger
hand, then for Maulkin to ſtay the dint of her
moodie tongue; that can teach the Storme-winde
to ſcould Engliſh; and pleadeth naturall poſſeſſion
of the Cuckingſtoole. It is good pollicie, to
yeeld to the furie of the tempeſt: (the reſoluteſt
harts are fayne to yeeld to the imperious Iuriſdic-
tion of Stormes, and Shrewes): and the ſtamping
feind, in the Hoat-houſe of her foming Oratorie,
will haue the laſt word. Sweet Goſſip, diſquiet
not your loouely ſelfe : / the dunghill, is your
freehold ; and the Cuckingſtoole, your Copyhold :
I know none ſo rank-minded, to enter vpon
your proper poſſeſſions by riot : and in caſe
thou wilt needes alſo, be the Schoolemiſtris of

Ramme-ally, certainly thou defireft but thy right;
that canft read a Rhetorique, or Logique Lecture
to Hecuba in the Art of rauing, and inftruct
Tifiphone herfelfe in her owne gnafhing language.
Other He- or She-drabs, of the curfteft, or ven-
geableft rankes, are but dipped, or dyed in the
Art : not fuch a Belldam in the whole kingdome
of Frogges, as thy croking, and moft clamorous
Selfe. Euen Martins Vnbrideled ftile, and Pap-
hatchets reaftie eloquence, is but a curtaild iade
to thy long taild Colt. Let the Clocke ftrike :
I haue loft more howers ; and loofe nothing, if
I finde Equitie. Should the Butterwhore, befturre
herfelfe like an arrant Knight, and try all the
conclufions of her cherne, fhe might peraduenture
in fome fort pay thee home with Schoolebutter:
but vndoubtedly fhe fhould haue much adooe, to
ftoppe thy Ouen-mouth with a lidde of Butter,
thou haft fwapped-downe a pounde of Butter
at a peece of a Breakefaft, or elfe there be lyes ;
and art fuch a Witch for a cherne, or a cheefe-
preffe, as is not to be founde in the Mallet of
Witches, or in Monfieur Bodines Dæmonomania.
Three meales of a Lazarello, make the fourth a
Woolner : and it is a crauen frying-pan, that is
affrayd of a Butter whore. No, no ; the butter
whore is thy bondmaide in a bunch of keyes :
and take heede fyrrha, the Cheefeknaue be not her

bondmã in a loade of logges. She commeth not
of the bloud of the threateners : but kitchin-ftuffe,
and a Cole-rake haue in times paft bene of fome
familiar acquaintance ; and it is a badd paier of
Tonges, that cannot make as good fport at a pinch,
as a paier of Bellowes. Though a difh / of buttered
peafe, be no great Warriour, yet a meffe of
buttered artichokes, may perhaps hold you fome
prettie tacke. Onely I barre thoffame hourfonne
vnlawfull termes, fteeped in cifternes of Aqua
fortis, and Gunpowder : and haue at you a gentle
crafh ; when it fhall pleafe the Vrinall, and the
Dairy, to giue me leaue to play, with a butter-fly.
I doe you the vttermoft credit in the world, that
am euer glad to feeke dilatorie excufes, and to
craue a terme *ad deliberandum.* The fortune of
the field, with pike, or penne, is like the lucke
of Nauigation, or the hap of marriage : and I
looue not greatly, to chopp vpon maine-chaunces.
Nothing Venture, nothing loofe ; none of the
worft rules, or cautels for their fecuritie, that can
tell Storyes of hap-hazard ; and haue knowen
fome gallants more hardie, then wife. Humanitie
is defirous of Peace with the beft, and of truce
with the worft : and truly I neuer longed to
fight it out with flat ftrokes, Vntil I muft needlefly
needes : but if there be no remedy by treatie, or
amicable compofition, although I was euer a

floweworme in the Morning, yet I cannot abide
to go to bedd with a Dromedarie. I cannot
maruell enough, how the nimble Bee fhould be
ingendred of the fluggifh Oxe, or the liuely
wafpe of the dead horfe: but Nature is a mira-
culous, and omnipotent workeman ; and I finde
it true by Experience, that I muft learne to
imitate by Example, or preiudice mifelfe by
fauouring other. To preiudice, were a fmall
matter, where the partie leuelleth at no great
matter: but whē a mans credit is affaulted with
bugges-wordes, and his witt beleaguered with
the euer-playing fhott of the Preffe; Wifedome
muft pardon him, whom Follie affaileth; and
Humanitie difpenfe with a neceffary Apologie. I
would I might make it a Pollicie, to make my
aduerfarie much, and much, and much better /
then he is: that I might re-encounter him with
the more reputation, or the leffe difparagement :
but it is his glory, to fhame himfelfe notorioufly,
and he will needes proclaime his owne vanities
in a thoufand fentences, and whole Volumes of
ribaldry; not to be read but vpon a muck-hill,
or in the priuyeft priuie of the Bordello. Let
his Vices fleepe on a downe pillow: would, I
could awaken his Vertues; and ftopp their
mouthes, that wifh me in fober earneft, not to
foile my hands vpon fuch a contemptible rafcall ;

but to let the reckles Villain play with his own
fhaddow : (Truth is my witneffe, diuers honeft
men of good reckoning, and fundry worfhipfull
Gentlemen, haue aduifed me in thofe very termes
exprefly) : but fithence I cã doe him no good
by perfwafion, it were follie to fuffer him to
do me harme by detraction. You that are not
afcertained of the lewd, and vile difpofition of the
man, imagin as fauorably of him, as Charitie
can poffibly conceiue of an impudent Railer, and
a prophane mouth : but you, that can fkill of
learning, and looue Schollerfhip, giue him his
defert ; do Equitie right, and him no wrong,
that wrongeth whom he lifteth. They that haue
leyfure, to caft-away, (who hath not fome idle
howers to loofe?) may perufe his guegawes with
indifferency : and finde no Art, but Euphuifme ;
no witt, but Tarletonifme ; no honefty, but pure
Scogginifme; no Religion, but precife Marlowifme;
no confideration, but meere Nafhery : in briefe,
no fubftance, but light feathers; no accidents,
but lighter colours; no tranfcendents, but lighteft
phantafies that fty abooue the higheft region of
the cloudes, and purpofe to haue a faying to the
man in the Moone. His mountaines of Imagina-
tion, are too-apparent: his defignements of Vanitie,
too-vifible : his plots of Ribaldry, too-palpable :
his formes of / libelling, too-outragious : S. Fame,

the goddeffe of his deuotion: S. Blafe, the idoll
of his Zeale: S. Awdry, the lady of his loue:
and the young Vicar of old S. Fooles, his ghoftly
Father. I haue heard of many notable prowde
fooles: read of many egregious afpiring fooles:
feene many hautie vayneglorious fooles: woondred
at manie bufie tumultuous fooles: but neuer
fuch a famous arrogant conceited foole, the very
tranfcendent foole of the Ship; that hugely
contemneth all the world, but his owne Flim-
flams; and againft all Pollicie, maketh his aduer-
fary more then an Affe, and leffe then nothing;
whofe victory otherwife mought peraduenture
haue feemed fomething. But to ouer-crow an
Affe, is a fory Conqueft; and a miferable Trophy
for fo douty a Squier. There were wayes enough
of aunfwearing, or confuting, with varietie, ·and
reafon; to his owne credite, the fatisfaction of
other, and my contentment: although hee had
not defperately, and fcurriloufly broken-out into
the fowleft and filthieft fcurfe of odious termes,
that Villany could inuent, or Impudency vtter.
Iwis hee mought haue fpied a difference, betweene
ftaring, and ftarke-blinde; betwene raging, and
ftarke-madd; betweene confuting, and rancke
rayling in the groffeft fort. Had hee feafoned
his ftile with the leaft fpice of difcretion, or
tempered his vnmeafurable licentioufneffe with any

moderation in the world; or hadd hee not moft
arrantly laboured, to fhew himfelfe the very brafen
forhead of Impudency, and the iron mouth of
Malediction, without all refpect; he mought
eafily haue found me the calmeft, and tractableft
aduerfary, that euer he prouoked; as reafonable
for him, as for mifelfe, in caufes of Equity; and
as partiall to foe, as to freend, in controuerfies of
Trueth.   But it is the topp-gallant of his braueft
brauure, to be / a Creator of Affes, a Confuter
of Affes, and a Conquerour of Affes : Affes are
borne to beare ; and Birdes to foare aloft.   No
winges, to the winges of Self-conceit; nor any
failes, to the failes of wordes : but hagard winges
are fometimes clipped ;   and hoifed fayles often-
tymes humbled.   Wordes amoũt, like Caftels of
vapours, or pillars of fmoke, that make a mighty
fhowe in the Aier, and ftraight Vanifh-away.
Howbeit Enuie, is a foking Regifter : and Spite,
a Remembrancer of truft.   That would be written
in a glaffe of wine, is otherwhiles founde in tables
of marble, and indentures of wainefcot.   The
Oeftridge can deuoure the ruft of Iron ; and the
gall of prefent Obloquy may be brucked :   but
the note-booke of malice, is a monumẽt of Tuch-
ftone; and the memoriall of Feude, the clawe
of an Adamant.   Pride fwelleth in the penne of
arrogancy : Vanitie bubleth in the mouth of folly :

Rancour boileth in the hart of Vengeance:
mifchief hammereth in the head of Villany : and
no fuch Art memoratiue, as a Crabtree defke.
But in contempt of Pride, I will fpeake one
prowde word : Vaine Nafh, whom all pofterity
fhall call vaine Nafh, were thou the wifeft man
in England, thou wouldeft not; or were thou
the valianteft man in England, thou durft not
haue written, as thou haft defperatly written,
according to thy greene witt : but thou art the
boldeft bayard in Print; a hare-braind foole in
thy head ; a vile fwad in thy hart ; a fowle lyer
in thy throate ; and a vaine-glorious Affe in thy
pen : as I will prooue vpon the carkaffe of thy
wit, and courage, through-out all the Predica-
ments of proofe. I hate malice in mifelfe : but
looue not to be an Vpholfter of ftuffed, and
bombafted malice in other. And bicaufe thou
termeft me an old Fencer ; (indeede I was once
Tom Burleys Schollar); and needeft difpling,
afmuch as any rake-hell / in England : Wherefo-
euer I meete thee next, after my firft knowledge
of thy perfon, (not for mine owne reuēge, but
for thy correction) I will make thee a fimple
foole, and a double fwad, afwell with my hand,
as with my tongue ; & will engraue fuch an
Epitaph, with fuch a Kyrieelefon vpon thy fcull,
as fhall make thee remembred, when Syr Gawins

fcull fhall be forgotten. Some bibber of Helicon,
will deeme it worth eternall record. And if thou
entreate me not the fayrer, (hope of amendment
preuenteth many ruines), truft me, I will batter
thy carrion to dirt, whence thou camft; and fquife
thy braine to fniuell, whereof it was curdled: na,
before I leaue poudring thee, I will make fweare,
thy father was a Rope maker; and proclaime
thifelfe, the bafeft drudge of the Preffe; with
fuch a ftraunge Confutation of thine owne ftraunge
Newes, as fhall bring Sir Vainglory on his knees,
and make Mafter Impudency blufh, like a Virgin.
Thy witt already maketh buttons: but I muft
haue S. Fame difclaime her blacke *Sanctus*; and
Nafhes deuout Supplication to God, to forgiue
Pierces reprobate Supplication to the Diuell. It
muft be roundly done: or I will with a charme
for a full ftomacke, make the gorge of thy
belching Rhetorique, & the paũch of thy fur-
fetting Poetry, fling figures vpward, and downe-
ward. Phy, what neede that be fpoken? True:
there is choice enough of fweeter flowers; & neat
Oratory interteineth neateft Ciuilitie; (what relifh
fo pleafant, as the breath of Suada; or what
fmell fo aromaticall, as the voyce of the Mufes?)
but the mouth of a rude Affe, can taft no other
lettice; and the fpawne of a beaftly dogfifh, will
vnderftand no other language but his owne. Fury

muft be tamed with Fury, according to Homer,
that teacheth the God of the field to ftrike home ;
obftinacy awed with obftinacy; force maftred with /
force; threatnings cooled with threatnings ; con-
tempt aunfweared in his owne toungue: and feeing
the wild Colt is fo vnreafonably lufty, I meane
percafe either to make his courage crowch forward,
or his Art winch backward.   I haue twentie and
twentie charmes, for the breaking of ftubborne
iades, for the biting of mad dogges, for the
ftinging of Scorpiōs, for the darting of Vrchins,
for the haunting of fprites, for the ftorming of
tempeftes, for the blafing of lightning, for the
ratling of thunder, and fo forth ; euen for the
craking of an hundred Pap-hatchets, or a thoufand
Greenes, or ten thoufand Nafhes Peagoofes.   And
in cafe all happen to faile, (for it muft be a
mighty Exorcifme, that can coniure-downe Spite)
I haue a *Probatum eft*, of a rare and powerable
vertue, that will hold the nofe of his, or his conceit
to the grindftone ; and make gentle Villanie
confeffe, all the fhreddes, and ragges of his
flafhingeft termes, are worne to the ftumpes.   The
defperate foole may clawbacke himfelfe awhile:
but it is poffible, he may foone finde by founde
Experience ; He brayeth open warre againft him,
that can bray the Affe-drumme in a morter ;
& ftampe his Iewes-trumpe to Pinduft.   Tom

Drumme, reconcile thifelfe with a Counter-fuppli·
cation : or fuerly, it is fatally done; and thy
S. Fame vtterly vndone world without end. As
fauory a Sainct, by the verdict of that excellent
Gentlewoman, as the cleanely difburfing of the
dirtpurfe of Sir Gargantua, that made King
Charlemaine, and his worthy Chiualry, laugh fo
mightily, that their heads aked eight dayes after.
A meet Idoll for fuch a Beadman. I haue
digreffed from my purpofe, and wandred out-of
my accuftomed way : but when the buttermilke
goeth on Pilgrimage, you muft giue the butter-
whore leaue to play the arrant knight a crafh,
and to make it ganging weeke for once. / Gang-
ing weeke? na, a ganging day, I trow, is a large
allowance; and enough to betire a poore ftragling
wench for all her bragges. Neuer fory laffe fo
pittifully aweary of her ragged petticote, and
dagled taile; the tattered liuery of the confuting
Gentleman. Let it go ; and the wifpe go with
it. I honour the meekeft Humility; but fcorne
the infolenteft Arrogancy vnder my foote; and
fay to the higheft Imagination of Vanity, Thou
art a proude Fopp. When thou carrieft thy witt
loftieft, and prankeft-vpp thy felfe-looue in his
gawdieft colours, thou art but an Affes head,
and a Peacockes taile. Looue other ; and thou
mayft be looued of other for pure Charity : hate

other, and thou art one of the moſt odious paddes
in the world : a Turke, for M. Aſchams Archers
to ſhoote-at ; and a Iewes eye, for Chriſtian
needles. Now a little breathing pawſe will do
no harme.

Were not Malice as wilfull in maintaining abuſe,
as raſh in offering the ſame ; & Arrogancy as
obſtinate in the Concluſion, as violent in the
Premiſſes : I readily could, & willingly would
vndertake a more temperate, and pleaſing courſe :
but the faireſt offer is fowly contemned; the
gentleſt ſuite vnkindly repulſed; ſay I, what I
can, malice wilbe itſelfe ; or do I, what I can,
Arrogancy wilbe itſelfe: and no other impreſſion
can ſinke into the hart of Spite, or the eare of
Pride, but inſtigations of Spite, or ſuggeſtions of
pride. Other motiues, are meere ſimplicities: and
euery treaty of pacification, or parly of reconcilia-
tion, the ſhaking of an aſpen leafe. The Diuels
Oratour, is an Heralde of warre, not a Legate of
Peace: and his Dammes Poet, the rankeſt chal-
lēger at ſhort, or long, that euer ſent defiance in
white, or blacke. To refuſe the tryall, would in
the common opinion ſeeme a ſhame; to accept
the offer, in the beſt iudgements / is a ſhame :
to take the foile, were a diſcredit; to giue the
foile, is no credit. A hard caſe, where Patience
may be ſuppoſed ſimple, and auengement will be

reputed vnwife ; where I cannot hold my peace
without warre vpon warre, nor fpeake without
blame vpon blame ; where I muft either be a
paffiue, or an actiue Affe in Print. I ftand not
vpon the point of honour, or vpon termes of
reputation : but as it is a glory for the inferiour,
to offer the combat, like the Chãpion of prowes,
or the Duellift of courage; fo I would the
fuperiour might refufe that without preiudice,
which he cannot vndertake without difparagement,
or performe without obloquie. To fpoile Pierce
Penniles, were a poore booty : and to make
Thomas Nafh kiffe the rod (by her fauour, that
hath pleafurably made him a *Sultã Tomũboius*, &
another *Almãnus Hercules*, the great Captaine of
the Boyes) were as fory a victory; but only
in her *Bello Euboico*, or in her main-battaile of
Scouldes. Yet feeing he prouoketh me fo mala-
pertly hand to hand; & feeing the infancy of his
fancy will not otherwife be weaned from his cranke
cõceit : better fuch a victory with fome incon-
uenience, (for I hope, I may without arrogancy
prefume of the victory) then continuall difturbance
with more and more mifchief. Hector neuer raged
amongft the Grecians, nor Achilles amongft the
Troians; as Meridarpax, the moft furious, and
thrife-redoubted Captaine of the mife, rufhed vpon
the wofull frogges, in that Heroicall battaile. But

Meridarpax himfelfe in his Impetuous, and mas-
facrous fallyes, neuer made fuch a hauock of the
miferable frogges: as this Swafh-pen would make
of all Englifh writers, howfoeuer garnifhed with
eloquence, or ftored with matter, might he be
fuffred to hewe them downe, like ftockes, or
fhrubbes, without cōtrowlement. He will foone
be ripe, that already giueth fo lufty / onfets; &
threateneth fuch defperate maine carreers, as fur-
paffe the fierceft Caualcads of *Bellerophon,* or *Don
Alonfo d'Aualos.* Nothing curtaileth the courage
of his brauery, or daunteth the fwelling chiualry
in his noftrels, but that excellent learning is not
efteemed, as it deferueth : nor fingular men
aduaunced, according to the merites of their
worthineffe. Might Penniles, fingular Penniles,
be the Preferrer of his owne Vertue, or Iudge of
his owne caufe ; (as he couragioufly contendeth) :
I beleeue, a Veluet coate were fcantly good enough
for his wearing, that now remaineth moft humbly,
and thrife-affectionately bounden to the Right-
honorable Printing-houfe, for his poore fhifts of
apparell, and his rich capp of maintenaunce. An
Anatome of the Minde, and Fortune, were re-
fpectiuely as behoouefull and neceffary, as an
Anatomie of the Body : but this Captain-Confuter,
(like gallant Lobbellinus in a new liuery) neither
knoweth himfelfe, nor other : yet prefumeth he

knoweth all things, with an ouerplus of fomwhat
more, in knowing his Railing Grammar, his Rauing
Poetry, his Roifting Rhetorique, and his Chopping
Logique : with whofe helpe, he hath thwitled the
milpoft of his huge, and omnipotent conceit, to a
pudding-pricke of Straunge Newes. Straunge
newes indeede, that Pierce Penileffe fhould create
more Affes in an hower ; then the braue king of
Fraunce, (now the mightieft Warriour in Chriften-
dome, and a great aduauncer of valour,) hath
dubbed Knightes in his raigne. *The Ironyes*
of Socrates, Ariftophanes, Epicharmus, Lucian,
are *but Carterly derifions* : the Ironyes of Tully,
Quintilian, Petrarch, Pontane, Sanazarius, King
Alphonfus, but the fory *Ieftes of the Counfell-table
Affe, Richard Clarke* : the Ironyes of Erafmus in
his prayfe of Folly ; of Agrippa in his difprayfe of
Sciences ; of Cardan / in his Apology of Nero,
like Ifocrates commendation of Bufiris, or Lucians
defence of Phalaris the Tyrant, but *Good Beare
bite not* : the Ironyes of Sir Thomas More in his
Vtopia, Poemes, Letters, and other writings ; or of
any their Imitatours at occafion, but the *girdes of
euery milke-maide.* They were filly country fel-
lowes that commended the Bald pate, the Feauer
quartane ; the fly, the flea, the gnat, the fparrow,
the wren, the goofe, the affe ; flattery, hypocrifie,
coofinage, bawdery, leachery, buggery, madneffe

itfelfe. What Dunfe, or Sorbonift cannot main-
taine a Paradoxe? What Pefant cannot fay to a
glorious Soldiour? *Pulchrè me herculè dictum, &*
fapienter: or, *Lautè, lepidè, nihil fupra:* or, *Regem*
elegantem narras: or, a man is a man, though he
haue but a hofe vpon his head: or fo forth. *No*
fuch light payment Gabriell, at Pierce Penniles, or
Thomas Nafhes hand. They are rare, and dainty
wittes, that can roundly call a man Affe at euery
third word; and make not nice, to befoole him in
good fullen earneft, that can ftrangle the prowdeft
breath of their pennes, and meaneth to borrow
a fight of their giddieft braines, for a perfect
Anatome of Vanitie, and Folly. Though ſtrōg
drinke fumeth, & Aqua fortis fretteth; yet I will
not exchaunge my Milke-maides Irony, for his
Draff-maides affery. It is not the firft time, that
I haue difputed *de Vmbra Afini*; and prooued the
Fox, the finder; as wily a pigeon, as the cunning
Goldfmith, that accufed his neighbour, and con-
demned himfelfe. A melancholy boddy, is not
the kindeft nurfe for a chearely minde: (the
Iouiall complexion is fouerainly beholding to
Nature): but I know not a finer transformation
in Ouid, then the Metamorphofis of dudgen earneft
into fport; of harfh fower into fweet; of loffe into
gaine; of reproch into credit; of whatfoeuer badd
occurrence into fome / good. I was neuer fo

fplenetique, when I was moft dumpifh, but I could
fmile at a frife ieft, when the good man would be
pleafurable ; and laugh at fuftian earneft, when
the merry man would be furly.   Straunge Newes
wilbe as pleafant as a Cricket, by Cattes panges :
and where fuch a Turlery-ginkes of conceit, or
fuch a gibbihorfe of paftime, as Straunge Newes?
But fillip him, or twitch him neuer fo little ; and
not fuch a powting wafpe in Ramme-ally, or fuch
a winching iade in Smithfield.   Then, *Affe, and
worfe then a Cumane Affe, and foole, and dolt,
and idiot, and Dunfe, and Dorbell, and dodipoul,
and Gibaltar, and Gamaliell Hobgoblin, and
Gilgilis Hoberdehoy ;* and all the rufty-dufty ieftes
in a country, are too-little for his great Confuta-
tion, that is lineally defcended *ab Equis ad Afinos ;*
and taketh-on, like Hob-all-as, a ftout king of the
Saracens.   When I am better grammered in the
Accidents of his proper Idiotifme, and growen
into fome more acquaintance with his confuting
Dictionary ;   I may peraduenture confter, and
pierce the whole Alphabet of his fweet Eloquēce
a little better ; and make fome farther triall of
M. Afchams double tranflation, a pretty exercife
in a fit fubiect.   Meanewhile I am glad, to fee
him fwimme vpp to the beardleffe chinne in a Sea
of hoony, and ypocrafe, that fo lately was plunged
in a Gulfe of other liquor, and parloufly dafhed

vpon the horrible Rocke of defperation. It is
good, they fay, to be merry, and wife.

Poggius was merry, and Panormitan wife :
Marot was merry, and Bellay wife : Scoggin was
merry, and the Lord Cromwell wife : Greene was
merry, and Sir Criftopher Hatton wife : Nafh is
merry, and there be enough wife, though his
mothers fonne be Pierce Penniles. Or if thou
beift wife, or wouldeft feeme no foole, beware of
Cafual / ties, & a new Attractiue. Thy toungue
is a mighty Loadeftone of Affes ; and muft do
afmuch for thine owne naturall eares, as the
Magnes doth for Iron. As good do it at-firft,
as at-laft : and better voluntary confeffion with
fauour, then enforced profeffion with more fhame-
full penance. *Balaams Affe* was wife, that would
not run vpon the Angels fword : *Æfops Affe* no
foole, that was gladd to fawne vpon his mafter,
like a Dogge : *Lucians Affe*, albeit he could not
fly, like the witch his hoftiffe, (whofe miracles
he thought to imitate, had not her gentle maide
coofened him with a wrong boxe) yet could he
Politiquely faue himfelfe, pleafe, or eafe his mafters,
delight his miftriffes, fhewe many artificiall feates,
amaze the beholders, drinke the pureft wine in
Theffalonica, and finally eate rofes, afwell as
thiftles : *Apulius Affe* was a pregnant Lucianift,
a cunning Ape, a loouing worme, and (what

worthyer prayfe?) A golden Affe : *Machiauels
Affe* of the fame mettall, and a deepe Politician
like his founder, could prouide for One, better
then the Sparrow, or the Lilly : *Agrippas Affe*, a
woonderfull compoũd, and (may I fay?) a diuine
beaft, knew all things, like Salomon, and bore all
burdens like Atlas. The great Library of king
Ptolemy in Egipt, reported to haue bene replenifhed
with feuenty thoufand Volumes, not fuch a Library
of bookes, or fuch, or fuch an Vniuerfitie of Arts,
& Sciences, as Agrippas Affe. They that reuerence
the wondrous Prophecies of the Cumane Sibyll,
Amalthea, the chiefeft of the ten infpired Sibylles ;
defende, or fauour the excellent qualities of the
Cumane Affe ; efteemed by Varro, the moft profit-
able feruant of that Country, and by Columella
the moft neceffary Inftrument of all Countryes.
Euery Affe is naturally a well difpofed creature,
and (as the learned Rabbines haue written) a
mirrour of clemency, patience, abftinence, / labour,
conftancy, and diuine wifedome. No fuch Schoole-
mafter for a wild boy, or a rafh foole, as the fober,
and ftayed Affe ; the Countryman of the wife
Apollo, and the feuen wife mafters.

Venerat & fenior pando Silenus afello. Silenus
the tender fofter-father, and fage tutour of the
wanton and frolicke Bacchus, afterward how braue,
and frutefull? What an Orientall worthy? What

an Indian Conquerour? What a feftiuall God?
When Priapus, the fhameleffe God of the garden,
(fo gentility called that leacherous Diuell) attempted
to furprife Vefta fleeping; what an honorable
peece of feruice performed *the honeft Affe,* that
with his lowde braying detected that villanous
affault? What heathen memoriall more fhamefull
to that infamous God, the *the folemne Sacrifice of
that famous beaft,* celebrated by the Lampfacens,
in reuengement, and reproche of that treafonable
enterprife? But what treafon, like the treafon of
Politique Achitophell, and plaufible Abfolon, that
moft difloyally, and defperatly rebelled againft the
facred maieftie of the moft valorous, and incom-
parable worthy king, Dauid? And what reward,
or aduauncement meeter for fuch treafon, then
hanging? And who carried the wife Achitophel
to hanging, but *his owne foolifh Affe?* And who
carried the defperate Abfolon to hanging, but
his owne fober mule? What fhould I furcharge
your memory with more hiftories attonce? He
that remembreth the gouernement of Balaams
Affe, Æfops Affe, Lucians Affe, Apuleius Affe,
Machiauels Affe, Agrippas Affe ; the Cumane
Affe, the Rabbines Affe, Apollos Affe, the feuen
Sages Affe, Silenus Affe, Priapus Affe, Achitophels
Affe, and Abfolons mule; little needeth any other
Tutour, or Counfellour. Some would prefume to

alledge the fingular and peerleffe example / of the Chriftian Poet :

Ille viam oftendit, vili qua vectus afello

Rerum Opifex. Agrippa, Cardan, Trithemius, Erafmus, and diuers other notable Schollars, affecting to fhew the variety of their reading, and the omnifufficiēcie of their learning, haue bene boulder in quoting fuch reuerend examples, vpon as light, or lighter occafion ; but humanitie muft not be too-fawcie with diuinitie : & enough is better then a Feaft. Sweet Apuleius, when thou haft wiped thy mouth with thine owne Affe-dung ; and thine owne Tounge hath fayd vnto thy Pen, Pen thou art an Affe : then fellow-affes may fhake handes, and they clapp their hands that haue heard the Comedie of *Adelphi,* or the two Affes : a more notable Pageant, then the Interlude of the two Sofias, or the two Amphitryos, or the two Mendechmi, or the two Martin Guerras ; or any fuch famous Paire of the true perfon, and the counterfait. But Affes carry myfteries : and what a riddle is this ? that the true man fhould be the counterfait ; and the falfe fellow the true Affe. Or what a Secret in Philofophie fhall I reueale, as vnto the fonnes of the Art : when I tell you, Affes milke is reftoratiue, good for the gowte, for the blouddie flixe, for the cleareneffe of the fkinne : Affes bloud, good for the feauer lurdane : Affes flefh fodden,

good for the Leprofie : Affes liuer rofted, good for
the falling fickneffe : Affes hooues burned to afhes,
good alfo for the fame fickneffe, for the kinges euill,
for woomen labouring with a dead burthen : Affes
bones well-boiled, good againft the empoifonment
of the fea-hare : Affes ftale, good for the raines
of the backe, and a fine decoratiue to bewtifie the
face by taking-of fpottes, and blemifhes : Affes
dung, a fweet nofegay to ftaunch bloud, a fouerain
fumigation to expell a dead birth out / of the
moothers woombe, and a faire emplafter for a
fowle mouth, as it might be for the mouth of
Bawdery in ryme, or of Blafphemie in profe. No
Homericall Machaon, or Podalirius, comparable
to the right Affe; that teacheth the greateft
Empiriques, Spagiriques, Cabalifts, Alchimiftes,
Magicians, and occult Philofophers, to wrap vp
their profoundeft, and Vnreuealable myfteries in
the thickeft fkinne, or rather in the clofeft intrals
of an Affe. I would, fome open-mouthed Liber-
tines, and profeffed Atheifts had as deeply learned
that cunning leffon. Euen the dead carcaffe of
the Affe, ingendreth the flying Scarabe, or foaring
Beetle, the noble and Vnreconcileable feudift of
the Ægle : of whom my braue aduerfary, the
famoufeft dor-beetle of this age, hath learned
to contemne, and depraue the two mounting
Ægles of the heauēly art of Poetry, Buchanan

in Latin Verſe, and Bartas in French meeter :
Whoſe groſe imperfeċtions he hath alſo vowed
to publiſh, with an irrefragable Confutation of
Beza, and our flooriſhingeſt New-writers, aſwell
in diuinitie, as in humanitie ; onely diuine Are-
tine excepted. But no thunderblaſing affright-
eth, or toucheth the right Ægle : and the leaſt
feather of the right Ægle, can ſoone deuoure
the baſtard winges of other enuious, and quarrel-
ous birdes. What carrion Aſſe was the Sire
of this vnappeaſble Scarabe : or what Scarabe
ſhalbe the ſonne and heire of this carrion Aſſe ;
I leaue it wholy to the diſcourſe of the learned
Ægles, that were euer moleſted with the buzzing
flye, and ſhall euer be haunted with the braying
Beaſt. I muſt ſpin-vp my taſke. And bicauſe
the wild-aſſe wanteth a picker-deuant, let him
drinke his owne Vrine, tempered with Spicknard,
as he carouſeth Helicon ; and according to the
tradition of Vitalis de Furno, it will procure, and
encreaſe haire ; as kindly, / as the Artificiall liniment
of Doċtour Leuinus Lemnius for a comely Beard.
And in-caſe he feareth his fellow Greenes ſluttiſh
diſeaſe, let him read the naturall hiſtories of the
Aſſe, and the Sheepe, in Ariſtotle, Pliny, or
Geſner ; and he ſhall finde it one of their
ſpeciall Priuiledges, to be arreſted from the arreſt
of the ſix footed Sergeant, a continuall haunter

of other hairy beaftes, and onely fauorable to the
good Affe, and the gentle Sheepe. Or if haply
he would be fhod with a paire of euerlafting
fhooes, like the talaria of Mercury, (for alas that
any Gentleman of worth, or correctour of the
Lord du Bartas, fhould lye in the Counter in his
bootes for want of fhooes) ; Albertus, and Cardan
will teach him to make incorruptible fhooes of
the durableft part of an affes hide, immortall
leather. And ô fweet Mufes of Parnaffus, are
not the fweeteft pipes, and pleafanteft inftruments
made of Affes bones? or do not the fkillfull
Geographers, Strabo, and Pliny, call dainty Arcadia
in Peloponefus, (the natiue country of the great
Apollo) *the Land of Affes?* Was not the renowned
Pan, the Politique Captaine of the côquerous
Bacchus, & a fuppofed God in the Painim world,
an Arcadian Affe? Was not Prince Arcas, the
braue fonne of king Iupiter, after his death
honored with the glorious memoriall of the *Great*
Beare in heauen, an Arcadian Affe? Was not
the *Little Beare*, his moother Califto, an Arcadian
Affe? Was not her father, the drad Tyrant,
Lycaon, an Arcadian Fox, an Arcadian Woolfe,
an Arcadian Affe? Was not the mighty Atlas,
the father of Maia, and grandfather of Mercury,
an Arcadian Affe? Was not Mercury himfelfe,
the moft-nimble, and fupereloquent God, an

Arcadian Affe? Was not Aftrophill, excellent
Aftrophill, (an other Mercury at all dexterities,
and how delitious a Planet of heauenly harmony,) /
by his owne adoption, an Arcadian Affe? Hiftories
are no fnudges in matters of note : and affes had
neuer leffe caufe to be afhamed of affes.   When
wife Apollo, when Valorous Pan, when employable
Mercury, when furmounting Atlas, when the *Great,*
and *Little Beare* of heauen, when excellent Aftro-
phil, glory in the honorable title of Arcadian Affes,
who would not coouet to be recoonted in that
memorable Catalogue?   What generous, or noble
Antiquitie, may wage comparifon with Statius
Arcadians, *Aftris, Lunaque priores.*   Sweetneffe
itfelfe was the daughter and darling of Arcadia :
and Arcadia the mother, the nurfe, the dug, the
fweet-hart of Sweetneffe itfelfe.   O the fugarcandy
of the delicate bag pipe there : and ô the licorife
of the diuine dulcimers there.   No maruell though
his Mufique be fweeter, and fweeter, that is as fine
an *Afinus ad lyram,* as the famous Difciple of the
worthy Ammonius ; and hath Greenes mellifluous
Arcadia at his fingers endes, the very funerall of
the Counteffe of Pembrookes Arcadia.   His other
habiliments, and complements be innumerable :
and I know not an Affe, but hath fome good
quality, that is, fome fpeciall propertie of an Affe,
either proffitable for commodity, or pleafurable

for delight, as an Affe may be proffitable, or
pleafurable either fimply, or in fome refpect.   It
was not for nothing, that the braueft king, that
euer raigned vpon Earth, Alexander the Great,
euen greater then any Mars, or Iupiter, that euer
brandifhed fcepter in the world; in his Royall
and Valorous iudgment preferred the Affe before
the man, when being folemnely commaunded by
Oracle, to fley the firft liuing Creature he fhould
fortune to meete withall, if after his puiffant, and
conquerous manner he would that day obtaine the
Victory; he happened to meete a good honeft
Coun / try-man, riding vpon an Affe ; whofe pre-
fent facrifice, as a moft acceptable Oblation, made
him Victorious.   Leffe maruell of the Archbifhops
aunfwere, in *menfa Philofophica*, and Pontans
Dialogues, that hauing reuerently, and deuoutly
Preached on Palme Sonday, of the She-Affe,
whereupon Chrift in humility voutfafed to ride;
and after his lowly Sermon mounting vpon his
lofty palfry, was riding his way ; fomewhat
fatherly and gratioufly ftayed awhile, to heare the
old woomans fuite, that came haftely running
towardes him, and boldly taking his horfe by the
bridle ; now I befeech your Grace, quoth fhe, is
this the She-Affe whereupon Chrift in humility
rode ? No, moother, quoth he, but a poore fole
of that rich Affe, and I a humble feruant of

that high Lord. Good enough, quoth the wooman, I knew not before that the gentle She-Affe your Grace Preached of, had fuch goodly foles: yes, mother, quoth the Bifhop, and a great deale goodlier, then mine : and fo departed, leauing behind him an euerlafting memory of that deuout Sermon, and that weighty Communication with the wooman, in honour of the Affe, a frutefull parent of many goodly and pompous foles. I will not trouble Boccace, or Poggius for Tales. He was a naturall foole, that would have giuen his liuery againe vnto his Lord, bicaufe it was embrodered with Affes heades, which made a comely fhowe vpon his garment, and mought ful-well haue befeemed fome richer coates. Could the mill, the plough, the packe, the hamper, the paniar, the cloakebagge, the burden, the fardell, the bagge and baggage, the cudgell, ·the goade, penury, famine, patience, labour itfelfe fpeake; all other Apologies were fuperfluous : they would frame a fubftantiall and neceffary defence of the Affe ; and Experience would declame in com-menda / tion of his perpetuall Exercife, trauaile, induftry, Valour, temperance, fufferance, magnani-mity, and conftancy, the honorableft and inuincibleft vertues in the world. The wifeft Oeconomy maketh efpeciall account of three fingular members ; a marchants eare ; a pigges mouth ; and an Affes

backe. A fhort note, but worth all Tuffers, or
Catos hufbandry. Had I more experience in fome
cafes, I could fay more: & as my experiēce in
thofe cafes may happen to encreafe, or amount,
I will not faile to tender my deuoire. I haue
penned large Difcourfes in prayfe of ftuddy, medi-
tation, conference, exercife, induftry, vigilancy, &
perfeuerance, the worthieft thinges in the circuite
of the Earth, (nothing vnder heauen, equiualent to
labour) : and whatfoeuer I haue addreffed in their
behalfe, I may in fort alledge in honour of the
Affe ; and compile whole Volumes in his commen-
dation, more auailable for commodity, and more
neceffary for Vfe, then the workes of fome great
Commenters in humanity, Philofophy, hiftory, and
other higher Profeffions. He that can kindly play
the right Affe, in ignorance wil finde knowledge, in
pouerty wealth, in difpleafure fauour, in ieoperdy
fecurity, in bondage freedome, in warre peace, in
mifery felicity. Who fo thoroughly prouided for
both fortunes, as he: or who fo ftrongly armed
againft all cafualties, as he? or what Seneca,
Epictetus, Boetius, Petrarch, or Cardan, fo effec-
tuall a Schoolemafter of *Suftine, et Abftine,* as
he? or who fuch an Oeconomer to liue, as he: or
who fuch a Philofopher to dye, as he? or what
Phyfitian for the boddy, like him : or what Lawier
for the fubftance, like him: or what Deuine for

the minde, like him ? or where fuch a Practitioner
of Vertue as he: or where fuch a Fortune-wright,
as he? or finally where fuch an apt fubiect for
the Ciuill, and morall refor / mation of the Prudent
Auguftus, the good Traian, the gentle Marcus
Antoninus, the vertuous Alexãder Seuerus, the
drad Septimius Seuerus, or any honorable Prince,
or Politique Tyrant, that with a reuerẽd autho-
ritie, would eftablifh Vertuous, and awfull orders
of gouernement in his dominions?

But what an Affe am I, that proceede fo coldly,
and dully in the Apology of fo worthy a Creature?
What will you fay, Gentlemen, if I can prooue
with pregnant arguments, artificially drawen from
all the places of Inuention, according to Ramus,
Rodolphes, or Ariftotles Logique ; that the fire-
breathing Oxen, and mighty Dragon, which kept
the moft-famous Golden Fleece, the glorious prize
of braue Iafon, were Affes of Colchos: that the
watchfull, and dreadfull Dragon, which kept the
goodly Golden Apples, in the Occidental Ilands
of the Ocean, called Hefperides, one of the re-
nowned prizes of dowty Hercules, was a Weft-
Indian Affe : that the golden-horned, and brafen-
footed Menalian hart, the fierce Erymanthean
Bore, the hideous birdes Stymphalides, the puiffant
Nemæan Lion, and the feuen-hedded Lernæan
Hydra, which Hercules flew, were Affes of

Arcadia, and other adiacent countryes of Morea:
(for Mænalus, and Erymanthus, were hilles in
Arcadia, Stymphalus a lake in Arcadia, Nemæa a
wood in Argolis, and Lerna a fen in Argolis, an
other fhire of Morea :) that the Serpent with the
golden creaft, which kept the rich fountaine of
Mars in Greece, and was flaine of valiant Cadmus,
was an Affe of Boëtia, fo called *à boue*, where the
Prophet Amphiaraus breathed Oracles : that the
huge Serpent Python *de monte*, ingendred fhortly
after Deucalions deluge, which the Arcadian god
of Wifedome killed with his arrowes, the firft
founders of the / Pythian Games, was a mighty
Affe of the mountaines : that the mounting Ægle,
into which king Iupiter turned, not himfelfe, but
Ganymedes, (whom he tooke with him, as his flying
Page, and vfed as his ftanding cupbearer) was a
faithfull feruaunt, and a perpetuall Affe : that the
hondred-eyed Argus, whom Queene Iuno appointed
the keeper of Io, the faireft creature of the Arcadian
herde, and whom Mercury lullabyed afleepe with
a fweet Syrinx, or Arcadian Pipe, (many Strata-
gemes, and myfteries in that Arcadian Pipe) was
a ·blind Affe of Arcadia: I fkip a thoufand
memorable Hiftories ; that all they, by what-
foeuer noble, or glorious names intituled, that
hauing charge of greateft importance, and in-
eftimable Value, committed to their vigilant and

ielous cuftody, did attonce forgo their treafure,
their honour, and their life (as many great
perfonages for want of circumfpection haue done)
were notorious Arch-affes. If I cannot fubftan-
tially prooue all this, and for a neede euict by
neceffary, and immediate demonftration, that the
great world is a great Affe, afwell *actu*, as *Po-*
tentia; and the Microcofme, a little Affe, afwell
habitu, as *affectione*; fay I am a notable Affe,
afwell *re*, as *nomine*. The Philofopher, that
feeking-about with a candle at high noone, could
not finde a Man in a populous market ; without
a candle would foone haue pointed at a faire
of Affes ; and could quickly haue difcouered a
frutefull generation in euery element, in the water,
on the Earth, about the fier, in the Aier. And
the wife-man, that faid without exception, *Stul-*
torum plena funt omnia ; might eafely haue bene
entreated, to haue fet it downe for a fouerain Maxim,
or generall rule ; *Afinorum plena funt omnia.*
The thundring Oratour Demofthenes, was not
affraide to taunt Minerua, the armed Goddeffe
of fine Athens, for exhibiting fauour to three /
vnreafonable beaftes, the Owle, the Dragon, and
the People: counting the People the moft
importunate and intolerable beaft of the three,
by whofe appointment he was banifhed the dainty
Citty, the onely feate of his raigning Eloquence.

If the people of fine Athens, were fuch a bar-
barous and fenfeleffe brute, as their excellenteft
Oratours, Philofophers, Captaines, Counfellours,
and Magiftrates founde to their coft : and if the
people of braue Roome, the Lady, and Empreffe
of the world, were fuch a bellowing beaft of many
heads, as Horace called it, Tully prooued it,
Scipio fealt it, and Cæfar himfelfe rued it ; what
may be faid of other people? Flooriſhing Greece
in many hundred yeares acknowledged but feuen
wife-mē of fpeciall note ; as the auncient world
acknowledged but feuen miracles, or magnificall
fpeᴄtacles worth the feeing : & Callimachus a
fweet Poet, recording the memorable, and woonder-
full thinges of Peloponefus, termed them Paradoxes.
Vertuous Italy in a longer terme of dominion,
with much adooe bred two Catos, and One
Regulus : but how many Syluios, Porcios, Brutos,
Beftias, Tauros, Vitellios, Capras, Capellas, Afinios,
and fo forth? Other fingularities, meete matter
for Tullyes Paradoxes. The world was neuer
giuen to fingularities : and no fuch monfter, as
Excellency. He that fpeaketh, as other vfe to
fpeake, auoideth trouble : and he that doth, as
moft men doe, fhalbe leaft woondred at. The
Oxe, and the Affe, are good fellowes : the Lib-
bard and the Foxe, queint wifardes : whatfoeuer
is abooue the common capacity, or vfuall hability

a Paradoxe. I will not bethinke mifelfe of the
rigorous fentences of Stoicall Philofophers, or
the biting Apothegs of feditious Malcontents,
or the angry fayings of froward Saturniftes, or
the tumultuous Prouerbes of mutinous people : /
(I haue fmall affection to the reafons, that are
drawen from affection) : but were not the world,
an Vniuerfall Oxe, and man a generall Affe, how
were it poffible, that fo many counterfait flightes,
crafty conueiances, futtle Sophifications, wily
coofenages, cunning impoftures, and deepe hypo-
crifies fhould ouerflow all : fo many opinions,
Paradoxes, fectes, fcifmes, herefies, apoftacies, idola-
tries, Atheifmes fhould pefter the Church: fo many
fraudes, fhiftes, collufions, coouens, falfifications,
fubornations, treacheries, treafons, factions, commo-
tions, rebellions fhould difturbe the Commonwealth?
It is a world to confider, what a world of Follyes,
and Villanies poffeffeth the world : onely bicaufe
the world is a world, *id eft*, an Affe. And would
the Preffe fuffer this fcribling Affe to dominere
in Print, if it were not a Preffe, *id eft*, an Affe ?
Might it pleafe his confuting Afhip, by his
fauorable permiffion to fuffer One to reft quiet ;
he might with my good leaue be the graũd
Generall of Affes, or raigne alone in his proper
dominion, like the mighty Affyrian king, euẽ
Phul Affar himfelfe, the famous fon of the re-

nowned Phul Bullochus. For fo the Gentle-
wooman hath intituled him in a place, or two,
that hath vowed the Canonizatiō of Nafhes
S. Fame, in certaine Difcourfes of regard, already
difpatched to my fatisfaction, & almoft accōplifhed
to her owne intention. It may peraduenture be
his fortune, to leaue as glorious a nephew behinde
him, as euer was the redoubted Lob-affar-duck,
an other noble king of Affyria ; not forgotten by
the faid excellent Gentlewoman, but remembred
with fuch a grace, as bewtifieth diuine wittes.
Kind-hart hath already offered faier for it, &
were it not that the great Phul Affur himfelfe
had foreftalled and engrofed all the commodities
of Affyria, with the whole encomium of Affes /
into one hand; it fhould haue gone very-
hard, but this redoubted Lob-affar-duck would
haue retailed, and regrated fome precious part of
the faid commodities, and aduauncements. He
may haply in time by efpeciall fauour, and ap-
prooued defert, (what meanes of preferment, to
efpeciall fauour, and approoued defert?) be inter-
teined, as a chapman of choice, or employed as
a factour of truft ; and haue fome ftables of Affes
at his appointment, as may feeme meeteft for his
carriages, and conueiances. For mine owne part,
I muft be contented to remaine at his deuotion,
that hath the whole generation of Affyrians at

commaundement ; with a certaine perfonall priui-
ledge, or rather an Imperiall Prerogatiue, to create
and inftall Affes at pleafure. Had I not lately
reuifited the Affyrian Hiftoṛy, with ·the faid
vertuous Gentlewooman, one of the gallanteft
ornaments of her fexe ; I mought perchaunce haue
omitted this fmall parcell of his great honour, and
left the commendation of the Affe more vnperfect:
which notwithftanding I muft ftill leaue moft-
vnperfect, in refpect of his vnfpeakable beau-
defert. Vnto whom for a farewell, I cǎ wifh no
more, then accomplifhed honour ; nor no leffe,
then athleticall health. A fhort exhortation, will
ferue Socrates, to continue like himfelfe. A roach
not founder then a haddocke, or the ftockfifh,
that Pliny termeth *Afellus* : & nothing fo vn-
kindly hurteth an Affe, as the two melancholy
beaftes, cold, and the drowfie fickneffe ; the caufe
why Affes cǎnot abide to inhabite the moft-cold,
& frofen territories of Scythia ; but are glad to
feeke their fortunes in other countryes, & to
colonife in warmer feats. Blame him not, that
fayth ; *The weather is cold, and I am wearie with
confuting :* & in another place ; *Had I my health,
now I had leyfure to be merry : for I haue almoft
wafht my hands of the Doctour.* Now I / fee thou
art a good fellow by thine own cǒfeffion, & wilt
not giue the Affes head for the wafhing : Cold,

and the drowfie fickneffe, are thy two mortall
enemies: when they are fled the Country, like
fugitiue, and difmall birdes, let vs haue a flitch of
mirth, with a fiddle of the pureft Affe-bone: onely
I barre the Cheeke-bone, for feare of Sampfons
tune, more then heroicall. But the fpring-tooth
in the lawe, will do vs no harme, although it
were a fountaine of Mufcadell, or a conduict of
Ypocrafe. Many are the miracles of right Vertue:
and he entreth an infinite Labyrinth, that goeth
about to praife Hercules, or the Affe: whofe
Labours exceede the Labours of Hercules, and
whofe glory furmounteth the topp of Olympus.
I were beft to end, before I beginne; and to
leaue the Autor of Affes, where I found the Affe
of Autors. When I am better furnifhed with
competent prouifion, (what prouifion fufficient
for fo mighty a Prouince?) I may haply affay
to fulfill the Prouerbe, by wafhing the Affes
headd, and fetting the crowne of higheft praife
vpon the crowne of young Apuleius, the heire
apparant of the old Affe, the moft glorious Olde
Affe.

*I haue written in all fortes of humours priuatly
I am perfwaded, more then any young man of my
age in England.* They be the wordes of his
owne honorable mouth: and the golden Affe, in
the fuperabundãce of his rich humours, promifeth

many other golden mountaines ; but hath neuer
a fcrat of filuer. Had Ariftophanes Plutus bene
outwardly as liberall, as Greenes Mercury was
inwardly prodigall, he muft needes haue bene the
onely Orientall Starre of this Language : and all
other writers, old, or new, in profe, or verfe, in
one humour or other, but fory Occidentall ftarres.
Onely externall defects, quoth himfelfe, are caft
in his difh: for inter / nall graces, and excellenteft
perfections of an accomplifhed minde, who but
he ? Come diuine Poets, and fweet Oratours,
the filuer ftreaming fountaines of flowingeft witt,
and fhiningeft Art : come Chawcer, and Spencer ;
More, and Cheeke ; Afcham, and Aftely ; Sidney,
and Dier ; come the deareft fifter of the deareft
brother, the fweeteft daughter of the fweeteft
Mufes, onely One excepted, the brighteft Diamant
of the richeft Eloquence, onely One excepted, the
refplendenteft mirrour of Feminine valour, onely
One excepted ; the Gentlewooman of Curtefie, the
Lady of Vertue, the Counteffe of Excellency, and
the Madame of immortall Honour : come all the
daintieft dainties of this toungue, and doe homage
to your Verticall Starre ; that hath all the foueraine
influences of the eloquent, and learned Conftella-
tions at a becke, and Paradifeth the Earth with
the ambrofiall dewes of his incomprehenfible witt.
But what fhould I dally with hoony-bees ; or

prefume vpon the Patience of the gentleft Spirites,
that Englifh Humanity affourdeth? Pardon me
Excellent mindes : and I will here difmiffe my
poore milkemaide, nothing appliant to the delicate
humour of this minion Humorift, and Curtefan
Secretary. Shall I fay? Phy vpon arrant knauery,
that hath neuer fucked his fill of moft-odious
Malice: or, Out-vpon fcurrilous, & obfcene Villany,
nufled in the boofome of filthieft filth, and hugged
in the armes of the abominableft hagges of Hell.
Be it nothing to haue railed vpon Doctours of
the Vniuerfitie, or vpon Lords of the Court,
(whō he abufeth moft-infamoufly, & abiecteth as
cōtemptuoufly, as me) : but what other defperate
varlet of the world, durft fo villanoufly haue
diffamed Lōdon, & the Court, as he notorioufly
hath done in thefe rafcall termes? *Tell me, is
there any place fo lewde, as this Ladie London? /
not a wenche fooner creepes out of the fhell, but fhe
is of the Religiō. The Court I dare not touch, but
fuerlie there be many falling Starres, and but onĕ
true Diana. Not a wenche,* a very Vniuerfall
Propofition, in fo large, and honourable a Citty :
and *but One,* a very fhort Exception to a generall
rule of the Court. Floorifhing London, the Staple
of Wealth, & Madame-towne of the Realme, *is
there no place fo lewde, as thy felfe?* and Noble
Court, the Pallace of Honour, and Seate of

Maiefty, haft thou *but one true Diana?*   Is it not
right-hand time, the young haddock were caught,
that can already nibble fo prettily?   Was he,
thinke you, lodged in Cappadocia, for fleeping by
the Sunne, and ftudying by the Moone?   Whom,
or what, will not he fhortly confute with an
ouerrunning furie, that fo brauely aduentureth
vpon London, and the Court, all-attonce? Honour,
regard thy good reputation ; and ftaunch the
ranke bloud of this arrant Autor ; as honeft a
man, as fome honeft wooman I could name, that
keepeth her honefty, as fhe doth her Friday faft.
Suffer him to proceede, as he prefumeth, & to
end, as he beginneth ;   and looke for a rarer
beaft in England, then a Woolfe ; and a ftraunger
monfter in Print, then the diuine Ruffian, that
intituled himfelfe, *Flagellum Principum,* and prooued
Peftis Rerum publicarum.   My Toungue is an
infant in his Idiotifme ; and I had rather bleffe
my peftilenteft enemy, then curfe any : but fome
little plaine dealing dooith not otherwhiles amiffe,
where nothing but flat, and rancke grofeneffe
blotteth the paper, infecteth the aier, depraueth
the good, encourageth the badd, corrupteth youth,
accloieth age, and annoyeth the world.   Good
faith is my witneffe, I neither affect to obfcure
any light in an aduerfary ; nor defier to quench
any honeft courage in an enemy ; but wifh euery

gift of heaue, or/earth, of minde, or body, of nature,
of fortune, redoubled in both, euen in the greeneft
aduerfary, and wildeft enemy : in whom I honour
the higheft, and looue the loweft degree of
excellency : but am not eafely coofend by Imper-
fection, branded with the counterfait marke of
perfection. I am ouer-ready to pardon young
ouerfights, and forgiue inconfiderate offences : but
cannot flatter Folly, or fawne vpon Vanity, or
cocker Ignoraunce, or footh-vp Vntruth, or
applaude to Arrogancy, either in foe, or fred.
It cocerneth euery man to looke into his owne
eftate with his owne eyes : but the young man,
that will neither know himfelfe, nor acknowledge
other, muft be told in brief, what the comon
opinion reporteth at large. He hath little witt :
leffe learning : left iudgement : no difcretion ;
Vanity enough : ftomacke at will : fuperabundance
of felfe-conceit : outward liking to fewe, inward
affection to none : (his defence of Greene, a more
biting condemnation then my reproofe) : no reuer-
ence to his patrons : no refpect to his fuperiours :
no regard to any, but in contemptuous, or ceforius
fort : hatred, or difdaine to the reft : cotinuall
quarrels with one, or other : (not fuch an other
mutterer, or murmurer, eue againft his familiareft
acquaintance) : an euer-grudging, & repining mind :
a rauenous throte : a gluttonous mawe : a droken

head : a blafphemous tongue : a fifking witt : a
fhittle nature : a revolting, and rennegate difpo-
fition : a broking, and huckftering penne : ftore of
rafcall phrafes : fome little of a brabling Schollar :
more of a rauing fcould : moft of a roifterly
feruing-man : nothing of a Gentleman : leffe then
nothing of a fine, or cleanly Artift. And as for
termes of honefty, or ciuility, (without which the
fharpeft Inuention is Vnfauery, and the daintieft
elocution lothfome) : they are Gibridge vnto him;
and / he a Iewifh Rabbin, or a Latin Dunfe with
him, that vfeth any fuch forme of monftrous
termes. Aretine, and the Diuels Oratour, would
be afhamed to be conuicted, or endighted of
the leaft refpectiue, or ceremonious phrafe, but
in mockage, or coofenage. They neither feare
Goodman Sathan, nor mafter Beelzebub, nor Sir
Reuerence, nor milord Gouernement himfelfe : ô
wretched Atheifme, Hell but a fcarecrow, and
Heauen but a woonderclout in their doctrine : all
vulgar, ftale, and fimple, that is not a note abooue
Goddes-forbid. Whom durft not he appeach,
reuile, or blafpheme, that forged the abominableft
booke in the world, *De tribus impoftoribus mundi* :
and whom will he forbeare, in any reafon, or
confcience, that hath often protefted in his familiar
hauntes, to confute the worthy Lord du Bartas,
and all the famoufeft moderne-writers, fauing him

onely, who onely meriteth to be confuted with
vnquenchable Volumes of Heauen- and Hell-fier.
Perionius deciphreth the fowle preceptes, and
reprobate examples of his Morall Philofophy, in
an inuectiue Declamation, generally addreffed vnto
all the Princes of Chriftendome, but efpecially
directed vnto the moft-Chriftian French king,
Henry the Second. Agrippa detefteth his mon-
ftrous veneries, and execrable Sodomies. Cardan
blafoneth him the moft-impudent Ribald, that euer
tooke penne in hand. Manutius inuefteth him
the Ring leader of the corrupteft bawdes, and
mifcreanteft rakehells in Italy. His familiar
acquaintance, Sanfouino, doth him neuer a whitt
more creddit, then needeth. Taffo difdaineth his
infolent and infupportable affectation of fingularitie.
Iouius in his Elogies voutfaueth him not the
naming. Doubtleffe he was indued with an
exceeding-odd witt : and I neuer read a more
furpaffing-hyperbolicall / ftile. Caftilios Courtier
after a pleafurable fort, graceth him with a deepe
infight in the higheft Types and Idees of humane
perfections, whereunto he moft curioufly, and
infatiably afpired. His wanton difciples, or Vain-
conceited fauorites, (fuch crowes, fuch egges) in
their fantafticall Letters, and Bacchanall Sonnets,
extoll him monftroufly, that is, abfurdly : as the
onely Monarch of witt, that is, the Prodigall

fonne of conceit; and the mortall God of all
Vertue, that is, the immortall Diuell of all Vice.
Oh, what grandiloquous Epithits, and fupereminent
Titles of incredible and prodigious excellency,
haue they beftowed vpon the Arch-miracle of the
world, Signior Vnico? not fo little as the huge
Gargantua of profe, and more then the heauen-
furmounting Babell of Ryme. But what ap-
prooued man of learning, wifedome, or iudgement,
euer deigned him any honour of importance, or
commēdation of note : but the young darling of
S. Fame, Thomas Nafh, aliàs Pierce Penniles, the
fecond Leuiathan of Profe, and an other Behemoth
of ryme? He it is, that is borne, to glorifie
Aretine, to difgrace Bartas, and to vndooe me.
Say I, write I, or dooe I, what I can, he will haunt,
and trounce me perpetually, with fpritifh workes
of Supererogation, inceffant tormentours of the
Ciuilian, and Deuine. Yet fome-boddy was not
woont to endight vpon afpen leaues of paper :
and take heede Sirrha, of the Fatall Quill, that
fcorneth the fting of the bufie Bee, or the fcratch
of the kittifh fhrew. A Bee? a drone, a dorre,
a dor-bettle, a dormoufe. A fhrewe? a drab, a
hag, a flibber-gibbet, a make-bate, the pickthanke
of Vanity, the pickpocket of foolery, the pick-
purfe of all the palteries, and knaueries in Print.
She doth him no wrong, that doth him right, like

Aſtræa, and hath ſtiled him with an / immortal
penne ; the *Bawewawe* of Schollars, the *Tutt* of
Gentlemen, the *Tee-heegh* of Gentlewomen, the
Phy of Citizēs, the *Blurt* of Courtiers, the *Poogh*
of good Letters, the *Faph* of good manners, &
the *whoop-hooe* of good boyes in Lōdon ſtreetes.
Naſh, Naſh, Naſh, (quoth a louer of truth, and
honeſty) vaine Naſh, railing Naſh, craking Naſh,
bibbing Naſh, baggage Naſh, ſwaddiſh Naſh,
rogiſh Naſh, Naſh the bellweather of the ſcribling
flocke, the ſwiſh-ſwaſh of the preſſe, the bumm of
Impudēcy, the ſhambles of beaſtlines, the poulkat
of Pouls-churchyard, the ſhrichowle of London,
the toade-ſtoole of the Realme, the ſcorning-
ſtocke of the world, & the horrible Cōfuter of
foure Letters. Such an Antagoniſt hath Fortune
allotted me, to purge melācholy, and to thruſt me
vpon the Stage : which I muſt now loade, like
the old ſubiect of my new prayſe. There is no
warring with Deſtiny : and the Lord of my ley-
ſure will haue it ſo. Much good may it do the
puppy of S. Fame, ſo to confute, and ſo to be
confuted. Where his intelligence faileth, (as God
wotteth, it faileth often) he will be ſo bold, with-
out more inquiry, to checke the common ſenſe of
Reaſon, with the proper ſenſe of his Imagination,
infinitly more high in conceit, then deepe in
vnderſtanding : and where any phraſe, or word

prefumeth to approch within his fwing, that was
not before enrowled in the Common-places of his
paper booke, it is prefently meere Inkhornifme :
albeit he might haue heard the fame from a
thoufand mouthes of Iudgement, or read it in
more then an hundred writings of eftimation.
Pythagoras Silence was wont to be a rule for
Ignorance, or Immaturity : (no better bitt for
vnlearned, or vnexpert youth, then Pythagoras
Silence :) but Vnderftand, or not Vnderftand, both
are one : if he vnderftand, it is Dunfery : if he
vnder / ftand not, it is either Cabalifme in matter,
or Inkhornifme in forme : whether he be ripe, or
vnripe, all is raw, or rotten, that pleafeth not his
Imperiall taft. Had he euer ftudied any Prag-
maticall Difcourfe ; or perufed any Treaties of
Confederacy, of peace, of truce, of intercourfe,
of other forrein negotiations, (that is fpecially
noted for one of my Inkhorne wordes) ; or
refearched any actes, and monuments, Ciuill,
or Ecclefiafticall ; or looked into any Lawes,
Statutes, Iniunctions, Proclamations, (na, it is
one of his witty flowtes, *He beginnes, like a
Proclamation :* but few Treatifes better penned,
then fome Proclamatiõs) : or had he feene any
autenticall inftruments, Pragmatique articles, or
other Politique Traicts : he would rather haue
woondered I fhould Vfe fo fewe formall termes,

(which I purpofely auoided, as not fo vulgarly
familiar) then haue maruelled at any, which I vfed.
He is of no reading in comparifon, that doth not
acknowledge euery terme in thofe Letters to be
autenticall Englifh ; and allow a thoufand other
ordinary Pragmaticall termes, more ftraunge then
the ftraungeft in thofe Letters, yet current at
occafion. The ignorant Idiot (for fo I will prooue
him in very truth) confuteth the artificiall wordes,
which he neuer read : but the vayne fellow (for
fo he prooueth himfelfe in word, and deede) in
a phantafticall emulation prefumeth to forge a
mifhapen rablement of abfurde, and ridiculous
wordes, the proper badges of his new-fangled
figure, called Foolerifme : fuch as *Inkhornifme*,
Abfonifme, the moft copious Carminift, thy Car-
minicall art, a Prouiditore of young Schollars, a
Corrigidore of incongruitie, a queft of Caualieros,
Inamoratos on their workes, a Theologicall Gim-
panado, a Dromidote Ergonift, facrilegioufly cõtami-
nated, decrepite capacitie, fictionate perfon, humour
vnconuerfable, merriments vnexilable, | the horri-
fonant pipe of inueterate antiquitie ; and a number
of fuch Inkhornifh phrafes, as it were a pan
of outlandifh collops, the very bowels of his
profoundeft Schollerifme. For his Eloquence
paffeth my intelligence, that cleapeth himfelfe
a *Callimunco* for pleading his Companions caufe

in his owne Apology: and me a *Piftlepragmos,*
for defending my frendes in my Letters: and
very artificially *interfufeth Finicallitie, fillogiftrie,
difputatiue right, hermaphrodite phrafes, declama-
torie ftiles, cenforiall moralizers, vnlineall vfurpers
of iudgement, infamizers of vice, new infringement
to deftitute the inditemēt, deriding dunftically,
banging abominationly, vnhandfoming of diuinityfhip,
abfurdifying of phrafes, ratifying of truthable and
Eligible Englifh, a calme dilatement of forward
harmefulneffe, and backward irefulneffe,* and how
many fundry difhes of fuch dainty fritters? rare
iunkets, and a delicate feruice for him, that cōpiled
the moft delitious Commentaries, *De optimitate
triparum.* And what fay you Boyes, the flatter-
ingeft hope of your moothers, to *a Porch of
Panim Pilfryes, Peftred with Prayfes?* Dare the
perteft, or defteft of you, hunt the letter, or hauke
a metaphor, with fuch a Tite-tute-tate? He
weeneth himfelfe a fpeciall penman: as he were
the headman of the Pãfletting crew, next, and
immediately after Greene: and although he be a
harfh Oratour with his toungue, (euen the filed
Suada of Ifocrates, wanted the voyce of a Siren,
or the found of an Eccho) yet would he feeme
as fine a Secretary with his penne, as euer was
Bembus in Latin, or Macchiauell in Italian, or
Gueuara in Spanifh, or Amiot in French: and

with a confidence prealTeth into the rowte of that
humorous rake, that affecteth the reputation of
fupreme Singularity. But he muft craue a little
more acquaintance at the hand of Art, and ferue
an apprentifhood of fome nine, or ten yeares / in
the fhop of curious Imitation (for his wild Phan-
tafie will not be allowed to maintaine comparifon
with curious Imitation) before he will be hable
to performe the twentith, or fortith part of that
fufficiency, whereunto the cranknefle of his Imagi-
nation already afpireth; as more exquifite, then
the Atticifme of Ifocrates, or more puiffant then
the fury of Taffo. But how infolently foeuer
grofe Ignorance prefumeth of itfelfe, (none fo
hawty, as the bafeft Buffard): or how defpe-
ratly foeuer foole-hardy Ambition aduaunceth his
owne colours, (none fo foole-hardy, as the blindeft
Hobb): I haue feldome read a more garifh, and
pibald ftyle, in any fcribling Inkhornift; or tafted
a more vnfauory flaumpaump of wordes, and
fentences in any fluttifh Pamfletter; that de-
nounceth not defiance againft the rules of Oratory,
and the directions of the Englifh Secretary. Which
may here and there ftumble vpon fome tolerable
fentence, neighbourly borrowed, or featly picked
out-of fome frefh Pamflet: but fhall neuer finde
three fentences togither, worth any allowance: and
as for a fine, or neat period, in the dainty and pithy

Veyne of Ifocrates, or Xenophon, marry that were a periwig of a Siren, or a wing of the very bird of Arabia, an ineftimable relique.   Tufh a point, neither curious Hermogenes, nor trim Ifocrates, nor ftately Demofthenes, are for his tooth : nor painting Tully, nor caruing Cæfar, nor purple-dying Liuy, for his humour.   It is for Cheeke, or Afcham, to ftand leuelling of Colons, or fquaring of Periods, by meafure, and number: his penne is like a fpigot ; and the Wine-preffe a dullard to his Inke-preffe.   There is a certaine liuely and frifking thing, of a queint, and capricous nature, as peerleffe as nameleffe, and as admirable, as fingular, that fcorneth to be a booke-woorme, or to imitate / the excellenteft artificiality of the moft renowned worke-mafters, that antiquity affourdeth.   The witt of this, & that odd Modernift, is their owne : & no fuch minerall of richeft Art, as prægnant Nature ; the plentifulleft woombe of rare Inuention, and exquifite Elocution.   Whuift Art : and Nature aduaunce thy precious Selfe in thy moft gorgeous, and magnificent robes : and if thy new defcant be fo many notes above old Æla, Good-now be no niggard of thy fweet accents, & heauenly harmony ; but reach the antike mufes their right Leripup.   Defolate Elóquéce, and forlorne Poetry, thy moft-humble fuppliants in forma pauperum, cladd in mournefull and dreery weedes, as becom-

meth their lamentable cafe, lye proftrate at thy
dainty foote, and adore, the Idoll-excellency of
thy monftrous Singularity. O ftately Homer,
and lofty Pindarus, whofe witt mounteth like
Pegafus ; whofe verfe ftreameth like Nilus; whofe
Inuention flameth like Ætna, whofe Elocution
rageth like Sirius ; whofe paffion bluftereth like
Boreas, whofe reafon breatheth like Zephirus;
whofe nature fauoreth like Tempe, and whofe
Art perfumeth like Paradife : ô the mightieft
Spirites of couragious Vigour, of whom the
delicate Grecian, worthy Roman, and gallant
Vulgar Mufes learned their fhrilleft tunes, and
hyperbolicall notes : ô the fierceft Trompets of
heroicall Valour, that with the ftraunge Sympathy
of your diuine Fury, and with thoffame piercing
motions of heauenly infpiration, were woont to
rauifh the affections, and euen to mealt the
bowels of braueft mindes : fee, fee what a woon-
drous quaime.

But peace milkemaide : you will ftill be fhaming
yourfelfe, and your bringing-vpp. Hadft thou
learned to difcerne the faireft face of Eloquence,
from the fowleft vifage / of Barbarifme ; or
the goodlyeft frame of Method from the ill-
fauoredeft fhape of Confufion : as thou canft
defcry the fineft flower from the courfeft branne,
or the fweeteft creame frõ the fowreft whey :

peraduenture thou wouldeft dote indeede vpon
the bewtifull and dainty feature of that naturall
ftile, that appropriate ftile, vpon which himfelfe
is fo deepely inamored. I would it were out-of
peraduenture : no man more greedy, to behold
that miraculous Art of emprooued Nature. He
may malapertly bragge in the vaine oftentation
of his owne naturall conceit ; and if it pleafe him,
make a Golden Calfe of his woodden ftuffe : but
fhewe me any halfe page without piperly phrafes,
and tinkerly compofition : and fay I am the
fimpleft Artift, that euer looked faire Rhetorique,
or fweet Poetry in the face. It is the deftiny
of our laguage to be peftred with a rablement
of botchers in Print : but what a fhamefull fhame
is it for him, that maketh an Idoll of his owne
penne, and raifeth-vpp an huge expectation of
paper-miracles, (as if Hermes Trifmegift were
newly rifen from the dead, and perfonally
mounted vpon Danters Preffe, to emprooue
himfelfe as ranke a bungler in his mightieft
worke of Supererogation, as the ftarkeft Patch-
pannell of them all, or the grofeft hammer-drudge
in a country. He difdaineth Thomas Delone,
Philip Stubs, Robert Armin, and the common
Pamfletters of London, euē the painfulleft Chroni-
clers tooe ; bicaufe they ftand in his way, hinder
his fcribling traffique, obfcure his refplendifhing

Fame, or haue not Chronicled him in their Cata-
logues of the renowned moderne Autors, as he
meritorioufly meriteth, and may peraduenture be
remembred hereafter. But may not Thomas
Delone, Philip Stubs, Robert Armin, and the reft
of thofe mifufed perfons, more dif / dainfully
difdaine him ; bicaufe he is fo much vayner,
fo little learneder, fo nothing eleganter, then
they ; and they fo much honefter, fo little
obfcurer, fo nothing contemptibler, then he?
Surely Thomas, it were pollicy, to boaft leffe
with Thomas Delone, or to atchieue more with
Thomas More. If Vaunting, or craking may
make thee fingular, thy Art is incomparable, thy
Wit fuperexcellent, thy Learning omnifufficient,
thy memory infinite, thy dexterity incomprehen-
fible, thy force horrible, thy other giftes more
then admirable : but when thou haft gloried
thy vttermoft, and ftruggled with might, and
maine, to feeme the Great Turke of Secretaries ;
if my eye fight be anything in the Art of en-
dighting, (wherein it hath pleafed fauour, to
repute me fomething), vpon my credit for euer,
thou haft nothing in thee of valour, but a railing
Gall, and a fwelling Bladder. For thy penne is
as very a Gentleman Foift, as any pick-purfe
liuing : and, that which is moft-miferable, not
a more famous neckverfe, then thy choice ; to

thifelfe pernicious, to youth daungerous, to thy
frendes grieuous, to thy aduerfaries pittifull, to
Vertue odious, to learning ignominious, to hu-
manity noyous, to diuinitie intolerable, to autority
punifhable, to the world contemptible. I longed
to fee thy beft amendement, or worft auengement :
but thy gay beft, *vt fupra*, prooueth nothing ; and
thy main worft, *vt infra*, leffe then nothing.
Neuer filly mans expectation fo deluded with
contrary euents vpon the Stage, (yet Fortune
fometime is a queint Comedian, far beyond the
Suppofes of Ariofto) as thefe Strange Newes haue
coony-caught my coniecture ; more deceiued, then
my Prognoftication of the laft yeare, which hapned
to be a true Prophet of fome difmall Contingents.
Though I neuer phanfied Tautologies, yet I
cannot repeat / it enough : I looked for a treaty
of pacification : or imagined thou wouldeft arme
thy quill, like a ftowt champion, with the compleat
harneffe of Witt, and Art : na, I feared the brafen
fhield, and the brafen bootes of Goliah, and that
fame hideous fpeare, like a weauers beame : but
it is onely thy fell ftomacke, that bluftereth like
a Northeren winde : alas, thy witt is as tame, as
a duck ; thy art as frefh as fower ale in fummer ;
thy brafen fhield in thy forehead ; thy brafen
bootes in thy hart ; thy weauers beame in thy
toungue ; a more terrible launce, then the hideous

fpeare, were the moſt of thy Power equiualent to
the leaſt of thy Spite. I ſay not; what aileth thy
Gorgons head? or what is become of thy Samp-
fons lockes? (yet where miracles were promiſed,
and atcheiuements of Supererogation threatened,
they had reaſon, that dreaded vnknowen forces):
but ô blaſtes of diuine Fury, where is your
fupernaturall proweſſe? and ô horne of abundance,
what meaneth this dearth of plenty, this penury
of ſuperfluitie, this infancie of eloquence, this
fimplicitie of cunning, this ſtupiditie of nimble-
neſſe, this obſcuritie of brauerie, this nullity of
omniſufficiencie? Was Pegaſus euer a cowe in
a cage, or Mercurie a mouſe in a cheeſe, or
Induſtrie a ſnaile in a ſhell, or Dexteritie a dogge
in a dublet, or legierdemane a floweworme, or
Viuacitie a laſie-bones, or Entelechy a ſlugplum?
Can liuely, and winged ſpirites fuppreſſe the
diuinitie of their ethereall, and Seraphicall nature?
Can the thunder tongue-tye, or the lightning ſmoo-
ther, or the tempeſt calme, or loue quench, or Zeale
luke-warme, or valour manicle, or, excellencie mew-
vpp, or perfection geld, or ſupererogatiõ combe-
cutt itſelfe? Is it not impoſſible, for Humanity,
to be a ſpittle-man, Rhetorique a dummerell,
Poetry a tumbler, Hiſtory a bankrowt, Philoſophy
a / broker, wit a cripple, courage a iade? How
could the ſweet Mermaids, or dainty Nymphes

finde in their tender harts, to be fo farre diuorced
from their queinteft, and galiardeft minion? Art,
take heede of an aeger appetite, if a little greedie
deuouring of fingularitie will fo foone gett the
hicket, and make thee (as it were) belch the
floouens Oratorie, and (as a man would fay)
parbreake the fluttes Poetry. Pure Singularitie
wrong not thy arch-excellent Selfe, but embrace
him with both thy armes, that huggeth thee with
his fine wittes; and cowll him with thy two corall
bracelets, that buffeth thee with his two ruby
lippes, and his three diamant powers, naturall,
animall, and vitall. Precious Singularity how
canft thou choofe but dote vpon his alabafter
necke, whofe inuentiue part can be no leffe,
then a fky-cooloured Sapphire, like the heauenly
deuifes of the delitious Poeteffe Sappho, the god-
moother of that azure gemme; whofe Rhetoricall
figures, fanguin and refplendifhing Carbuncles,
like the flamy Pyrops of the gliftering Pallace of
the Sun: whofe alluring perfuafions, Amethifts;
whofe cutting girds, adamants; whofe conquer-
ing Ergos, loadftones; whofe whole cōceit as
greene, as the greeneft Iafper; whofe Orient witt,
the renowned achates of king Pyrrhus, that is, the
tabernacle or chauncell of the Mufes, Apollo fitting
in the midft, and playing vpon his Iuory harpe
moft enchauntingly. Is it poffible, thofe powerfull

wordes of antiquity, whofe mightie influence was
woont to debafe the miraculous operation of the
moft-vertuous ftones, hearbes, and ftarres (Philo-
fophy knoweth the incredible force of ftones,
hearbes, & ftarres) fhould be to feeke in a panting
infpired breft, the clofet of reuealed myfteries, and
garden of infufed graces? What lockes, or barres
of Iron, can hold that quickfiluer Mercury, /
whofe nimble vigour difdaineth the prifon, and will
difplay itfelfe in his likenes, maugre whatfoeuer
empeachment of iron Vulcan, or woodden Dædalus?
I hoped to finde, that I lufted to fee, the very
fingular fubiect of that inuincible & omnipotent
Eloquence, that in the worthieft age of the world,
intituled heroicall, put the moft-barbarous tyranny
of men, and the moft-fauage wildneffe of beaftes,
to filence ; and arreared woonderful admiration in
the hart-roote of obftinateft Rebellion, otherwife
how vntractable? Had I not caufe to platforme
new Theorickes, and Idees of monftrous excellency,
when the parturient mountaine of miracles, was to
be deliuered of his mighty burden of Supereroga-
tion? Who would not ride poft, to behold the
chariot of his Triumph, that glorieth, as if he had
woon both the Indyes from the Spaniard; or Con-
ftantinople from the Turke; or Babylon from the
Sophi? But hollà braue Gentlemen, and alacke
fweet Gentlewoomen, that would fo fayne behold

S. Fame in the pompe of her maieftie; neuer poore fuckling hope fo incredibly crofbitten with more then exceffiue defection. I looked, and looked for a fhining Sunne of Singularity, that fhould amaze the eyes, and aftonifh the harts of the beholders: but neuer poore fhimering Sunne of Singularity fo horribly eclipfed. I perceiue, one good honeft aker of performance, may be more worth, then a whole land of Promife. Take heede afpiring mindes, you that deeme yourfelues the Paragon wittes of the world; leffe your hilles of iollity be conuerted into dales of obfcurity; and the pope of your glory, become like this pumpe of fhame. Euen when Enuy boyled his inke; Malice fcotched his penne; Pride parched his paper; Fury inflamed his hart; S. Fame raged, like S. Georges Dragon: marke the Conclu / fion: the weather was cold; his ftile froft-bitten; and his witt nipped in the head. Take away the flaunting and huffing braueries of his railing tropes and craking figures: and you fee the whole galiarde of his Rhetorique, that flowteth the poore Philippiques of Tully, and Demofthenes: and mocketh him, that chaunced to name them once in foure Letters; as he vfed their word Entelechy, now a vulgar French, and Englifh word, once in foure and twenty Sonnets. The wife Prieft could not tell, whither Epiphany were a man-faint, or a wooman-faint, or what the diuell it was. Such an Epiphany to this learned man is Entelechy; the onely quinteffence of excellent, and diuine mindes, as is abooue mentioned; fhewing whence they came by their heauély and perpetuall motion. What other word could expreffe that noble and vigorous motion, quicker then quickfiluer; and the liuely fpring, or rather the Veftal fier of that euer-ftirring Vertue of Cæfar, *Nefcia ftare loco* : a myftery, and a very Chimera to this fwad of fwaddes, that beginneth like a Bullbeare, goeth-on like a bullocke, endeth like a bullfinch, and hath neuer a fparkle of pure Entelechy. Gentlemen, now you know the good nature, and handfome Art of the man; if you happen vpon a feather, or fome morfell for your likyng, (it is a very fory Booke, that yeeldeth nothing for your liking) thanke the true Autor, of whofe prouifion you haue tafted, and fay not but Thomas Nafh has read fomthing, that affecting to feeme an Vniuerfity of fciences, and a Royall Exchaunge of tounges, would be thought to haue deuoured Libraries, and to know all thinges, like Iarchas, and Syfarion, na, like Adam, and Salomon, the archpatrons of our new Omnifcians. If he did fo in verity, it were the better for him, and not the worfe for me : but you fee his / doing, and my fuffering. Neither I, nor my betters can pleafe all : nor he, nor his

Punyes will difpleafe all: but as in the beft fome-
thing remaineth, that may be amended, without
derogation to their credit; fo in the worft there
may appeare fomething, worth the allowance, with
no great cōmendation to their perfon. Were I
difpofed to difcourfe, as fomtime I haue bene
forward vpō leffe occafiō, for the onely exercife
of my ftile, and fome practife of my reading; I
could with a facility declare at-large, that may
briefly be touched. Amongft fo many notable
workes of diuine wittes, excepting the workes of
Gods owne finger; there is not any fo abfolutely
excellent, wherein fome blemifh of imperfection
may not be noted: nor amongft fo many con-
temptible Pamflets, any fo fimply bafe, but may
yeeld fome little frute of aduertifement, or fome
few bloffoms of difcourfe. In the fouerain worke-
manfhip of Nature herfelfe, what garden of flowers
without weedes? what orchard of trees without
woormes? what field of Corne without cockle?
what ponde of fifhes without frogges? what fky
of light without darkneffe? what mirrour of
knowledge without ignorance? what man of Earth
without frailty? what commodity of the world
without difcommodity? Oh! what an honorable,
and wonderfull Creature were Perfection, were
there any fuch vifible Creature vnder heauen?
But pure Excellency dwelleth onely abooue; and

what mortall wifedome can accleere itfelfe from
errour? or what heroicall vertue can iuftifie, I
haue no vice? The moft precious things vnder
the Sunne, haue their defaultes: and the vileft
thinges vpon Earth, want not their graces. Virgill
could enrich himfelfe with the rubbifh of
Ennius: to how many rufty-dufty Waines was
braue Liuy beholding? Tully, that was as fine /
as the Crufado, difdained not fome furniture of
his predeceffours, that were as courfe, as canuas:
and he that will diligently feeke, may affuredly
finde treafure in merle, corne in ftraw, gold in
droffe, pearles in fhell-fifhes, precious ftones in
the dunghill of Efope, rich iewels of learning,
and wifedome, in fome poore boxes. He that
remembreth Humfrey Cole, a Mathematicall
Mechaniciã, Matthew Baker a fhip-wright, Iohn
Shute an Architect, Robert Norman a Nauigatour,
William Bourne a Gunner, Iohn Hefter a Chimift,
or any like cunning, and fubtile Empirique, (Cole,
Baker, Shute, Norman, Bourne, Hefter, will be
remembred, when greater Clarkes fhalbe forgotten)
is a prowd man, if he contemne expert artifans,
or any fenfible induftrious Practitioner, howfoeuer
Vnlectured in Schooles, or Vnlettered in bookes.
Euen the Lord Vulcan himfelfe, the fuppofed God
of the forge, and thunder-fmith of the great king
Iupiter, tooke the repulfe at the handes of the

Lady Minerua, whom he would in ardent looue
haue taken to wife. Yet what witt, or Pollicy
honoreth not Vulcan? and what profounde
Mathematician, like Digges, Hariot, or Dee,
efteemeth not the pregnant Mechanician? Let
euery man in his degree enioy his due: and let
the braue enginer, fine Dædalift, fkilfull Neptunift,
maruelous Vulcanift, and euery Mercuriall occupa-
tioner, that is, euery Mafter of his craft, and euery
Doctour of his myftery, be refpected according to
the vttermoft extent of his publique feruice, or
priuate induftry. I cannot ftand to fpecifie particu-
larities. Our late writers are, as they are : and
albeit they will not fuffer me to ballance them
with the honorable Autors of the Romanes,
Grecians, and Hebrues, yet I will craue no pardon
of the higheft, to do the fimpleft no wrong. In
Grafton, Holinfhed, / and Stowe ; in Heywood,
Tuffer, and Gowge ; in Gafcoigne, Churchyarde,
and Floide ; in Ritch, Whetftone, and Munday ;
in Stanyhurft, Fraunce, and Watfon ; in Kiffin,
Warner, and Daniell ; in an hundred fuch vulgar
writers, many things are commendable, diuers
things notable, fome things excellent. Fraunce,
Kiffin, Warner, and Daniell, of whom I haue
elfewhere more efpeciall occafion to entreate, may
haply finde a thankefull remembraunce of their
laudable trauailes. For a polifhed, and garnifhed

ftile, fewe go-beyonde Cartwright, and the chiefeft
of his Confuters, furnifhed writers : and how few
may wage comparifon with Reinolds, Stubbes,
Mulcafter, Norton, Lambert, and the Lord Henry
Howarde? whofe feuerall writings the filuer file
of the workeman recommendeth to the plaufible
interteinement of the daintieft Cenfure. Who
can deny, but the Refolution, and Mary Magdalens
funerall teares, are penned elegantly, and patheti-
cally? Scottes difcoouery of Witchcraft, difmafketh
fundry egregious impoftures, and in certaine
principall Chapters, & fpeciall paffages, hitteth
the nayle on the head with a witneffe : howfoeuer
I could haue wifhed, he had either dealt fomewhat
more curteoufly with Monfieur Bodine, or côfuted
him fomewhat more effectually. Let me not
forget the Apology of fundry proceedings by
Iurifdiction Ecclefiafticall, or, the Aunfwere to an
Abftract of certaine Actes of Parliament, Iniunc-
tions, Canôs, conftitutions, and fynodals Prouinciall:
vnleffe I will fkip two of the moft-materiall, and
moft-formall Treatifes, that any Englifh Print
hath lately yeelded. Might I refpectiuely pre-
fume to intimate my flender opinion, without
flattery, or other vndecency : methought euer
Doctour Whitgift (whom I name with honour)
in his Sermons was / pithy : Doctour Hutton
profound : Doctour Young piercing to the quicke:

Doctour Chaderton copious : M. Curtes elegant :
M. Wickam fententious : M. Drant curious :
M. Deering fweet : Doctor Still found : Doctor
Vnderhill fharpe : Doctor Matthew fine : M.
Lawherne gallãt : M. Dooue eloquent : M.
Andrewes learned : M. Chaderton methodicall :
M. Smith Patheticall : fundry other in their proper
veyne notable, fome exquifite, a few fingular. Yet
which of the beft hath all perfections? (*nihil
omni ex parte beatum*) or which of the meaneft hath
not fome excellency ? I cannot read-ouer all : I
haue feldome heard fome : (it was neuer my happ
to heare Doctour Cooper, Doctour Humfry, or
Doctor Fletcher, but in Latin) : and I would be
loth to iniury, or preiudice any, that deferueth
well, *Viua voce*, or by pen. I deeme him wife,
that maketh choice of the beft ; auoideth the
worft; reapeth fruite by both ; defpifeth nothing,
that is not to be abhorred ; accepteth of anything,
that may be tollerated ; interteineth euery thing
with cõmendation, fauour, cõtentment, or amẽd-
ment. Lucians affe, Apuleius affe, Agrippas affe,
Macchiauels affe, mifelfe fince I was dubbed an affe
by the only Monarch of affes, haue found fauory
herbes amongft nettles ; rofes amõgft prickles ;
berryes amongft bufhes ; marrow amõgft bones ;
graine amõgft ftubble ; a little corne amõgft a
great deale of chaff. The *abiecteft naturalls* haue

their fpecificall properties, and fome wondrous
vertues: and Philofophy will not flatter the
nobleft, or *worthieft naturals* in their venoms, or
impurities. True Alchimy cã alledge much for
her Extractions, and quinteffences: & true Phifique
more for her corrections, and purgations. In the
beft, I cannot commende the badd ; and in the
baddeft, I reiect not the good: but precifely play
the Alchimift, in feeking pure and fweet / balmes
in the rankeft poifons. A pithy, or filed fentence
is to be embraced, whofoeuer is the Autor: and
for the leſt benefit receiued, a good minde will
render dutifull thankes, euen to his greateft enemy.
ô Humanity, my Lullius, or ô Diuinitie, my
Paracelfus, how fhould a man become that peece
of Alchimy, that can turne the Rattes-bane of
Villany into the Balme of honefty ; or correct
the Mandrake of fcurrility with the myrrhe of
curtefie, or the faffron of temperance. Conceiue
a fountaine of contentation, as it were of Oyle,
or a bath of delight, as it were of nectar ; and
preferre that faffron, or myrrhe, that odoriferous
faffron, or aromaticall myrrhe, before this fouerain
Oyle ; and that Balme, that diuine Balme, before
this heauenly nectar. No naturall Reftoratiue,
like that faffron, or myrrhe, the very death of
contention ; nor any artificiall Cordiall, like that
Balme, the very life of humanity, or fhould I

rather fay? the very life of life. We haue many
new Methods, and platformes; and fome no
doubt as exquifite as fcrupulous: but affuredly
it were an excellent method, and fingular plat-
forme, to honour the wife, and moderate the foole:
to make-much of the learned, and inftruct the
ignorant; to embrace the good, and reforme the
badd; to wifh harme to none, & do well to all;
and finally (for that is the fcope of this, and fome
other Difcourfes) to commende the Fox, and
prayfe the Affe. Martin himfelfe is not altogither
a wafpe: nor Browne altogither a Canker-woorme:
nor Barrow altogither a Scorpion: nor haply Kett
altogither a Cockatrice. Take heede of the fnake
in the graffe, or the padd in the ftraw; and feare
no bugges. Be Martin a Martin Guerra; Browne
a browne-bill; Barrow a wheelbarrow; Kett a
kight; H. N. an O. K; if any found iudgements
finde themfelues beholding vnto them in / any
point of aduifement, or confideration (fingular
men, and namely Scifmatiques, and Heretiques
were euer woont to haue fome thing, or other,
extraordinary, and remarkable) they may without
my contradiction confeffe their beholdingneffe, and
for fo much profeffe a recognifance of their dett.
I thanke Nafh for fomething: Greene for more:
Pap-hatchet for much more: Perne for moft of
all. Of him I learned to know him, to know my

enemies, to know my frends, to know mifelfe, to
know the world, to know fortune, to know the
mutability of times, and flipperineffe of occafions :
an ineftimable knowledge, and incomparably more
worth, then Doctor Gregories *Ars mirabilis*, or
Politians *Panepiftemon.* He was an old foaker
indeede : and had more witt in his hoary head, then
fix hundred of thefe floorifhing greene heads, and
lufty curled pates. He would either wifely hold
his peace : or fmoothly flatter me to my face: or
fuerly pay-home with a witneffe : but commonly
in a corner, or in a maze, where the Autour might
be vncertaine, or his packing intricate, or his
purpofe fome way excufable. No man could
beare a heauy iniury more lightly : or forbeare
a learned aduerfary more cunningly : or bourde
a wilfull frend more dryly : or circumuent a
daungerous foe more couertly : or countermine
the deepeft vnderminer more futtelly : or lullaby
the circumfpecteft Argus more fweetly : or trans-
forme himfelfe into all fhapes more deftly: or play
any part more kindly. He had fuch a Patience,
as might foften the hardeft hart: fuch a fober-
moode, as might ripen the greeneft witt: fuch a
flye dexterity, as might quicken the dulleft fpirite :
fuch a fcrupulous manner of proceeding in doubt-
full cafes, as might putt a deepe confideration into
the fhalloweft phantafy : fuch a fufpicious ieloufy,

as / might fmell-out the fecretest complot, & defeat any practife : fuch an inextricable fophiftry, as might teach an Agathocles to hypocrife profoundly, or a Hieron to tyrannife learnedly. Whereas other carried their harts in their toungues, and their heades in their pennes ; he liked no fuch fimplicity, but after a fmugge, and fleering guife, carried his toungue in his hart, his penne in his head ; his dagger in his fleeue ; his loue in his boofome, his fpite in his pocket : and whē their fpeech, writing, or coūtenance bewrayed their affectiō, (as the maner is), nothing but his fact difcouered his drift ; & not the Beginning, but the End was the interpreter of his meaning. Some of vs, by way of experiment, affayed to feele his pulfe, and to tickle his wily veynes in his owne veyne, with fmoothing, and glofing as handfomly, as we could : but the bottome of his minde, was a Gulfe of the maine, & nothing could found him deepely, but the iffue. I wis elder men had bene too-young to manage fuch an enterprife with fucceffe : and the fineft intelligencer, or fageft Politician in a ftate, would vndoubtedly haue bene grauelled in the execution of that rafh attempt. He could fpeake by contraries, as queintly as Socrates ; and do by contraries, as fhrewdly as Tiberius : the mafter of Philip de Comines, Lewes the French king, one of the bufieft, ieloufeft, and craftieft Princes, that

euer raigned in that kingdome, might haue bor-
rowed the Foxes Satchell of him : and peraduen-
ture not onely Æſops, or Archilochus Fox, but
euen Lyſanders Fox, Ariſtomenes Fox, Piſiſtratus
Fox, Vlyſſes Fox, Chirons Fox, and Proteus owne
Fox might learne of him, to play the Fox in the
hole. For Stephen Gardiners Fox, or Macchiauels
Fox, are too-young Cubbes, to compare with him;
that would ſeeme any thing, rather then a Fox,
and be a Fox / rather then any thing elſe. Legen-
daries may recorde woonderments : but examine
the ſuttelleſt Counſels, or the wilyeſt practiſes of
Gargantua himſelfe, and euen Gargantua himſelfe,
albeit his gowne were furred with two thouſand,
& fiue hundred Fox-ſkinnes, mought haue bene
his Pupill. And I doubt not but he that wor-
ſhipped *Solem in Leone*, after ſome few Lectures
in his Aſtronomy, would haue honored *Solem in
Vulpe*. He once kept a Cubbe for his pleaſure in
Peter-houſe in Cambridge (as ſome keepe birds,
ſome ſquirrels, ſome puppyes, ſome apes, and ſo
forth) and miniſtred notable matter to S. Maryes
Pulpet, with Stories of the Cubb, and the Fox,
whoſe Actes, and Monuments are notorious : but
had the young-one bene as cunning an Artiſt for
his part, as the Old-one was for his : I beleeue, all
the Colledges in both Vniuerſities, or in the great
Vniuerſitie of Chriſtendome, could not haue pat-

terned the young mã with fuch an other Batchelour
of fophiftry, or the old mafter with fuch an other
Doctour of Hypocrifie. Men may difcourfe at
pleafure, and feede themfelues with Carpes, and
Pikes : but I haue knowen few of fo good a
nature, fo deuoide of obftinacy; fo far alienated
from contumacy; fo contrary to frowardneffe, or
teftiueneffe; fo tractable, fo buxom, fo flexible;
fo appliable to euery time, place, and perfon; fo
curious in obferuing the leaft circumftance of
importance, or aduantage; fo conformable to
publique proceedings, and priuate occafions; fo
refpectfull to euery one of quality ; fo curteous
to men of woorfhip; fo dutifull to men of honour ;
fo ceremonious in tendering his deuotion to his
good Lordes, or good Ladyes; fo obedient to
autority; fo loyall to maiefty; fo indifferent to
all, and in all. He was gentle without familiarity,
(for he doubted contempt) : feuere / without rigour,
(for he feared odioufneffe) : pleafant without leuity,
(for he regarded his eftimation) : graue without
folēnity, (for he curred popular fauour) : not rafh,
but quicke ; not hafty, but fpeedy ; not hoat, but
warme ; not eger in fhow, but earneft in deede ;
no barker at any, but a biter of fome ; round,
and found. The Clergy neuer wanted excellent
Fortune-wrightes : but what Byfhop, or Politician
in Englãd, fo great a Temporifer, as he, whom

euery alteration founde a new-man, euen as new
as the new Moone? And as he long yawned to
be an Archbiſhop, or Byſhop, in the one, or other
Church, (they wronged him, that termed the Image
of both Churches, a neuter): ſo did he not arch-
deſerue, to be inſtalled the puling Preacher of
Humility, humility, humility; and the gaping
Oratour of Obedience, obedience, obedience?
Was not euer *Pax vobis,* one end of his gaſping
Sermon, & the very foote of his warbling Song?
Be it percaſe a ſmall matter to temporiſe in foure
alterations of Kinges, and Queenes: but what an
Ambidexterity, or rather Omnidexterity had the
man, that at one, and the ſame meeting, had a
pleaſing Toungue for a Proteſtant, a flattering
Eye for a Papiſt, and a familiar nodd for a good
fellow? It was nothing with him to Temporiſe
in genere, or *in ſpecie,* according to Macchiauels
grounde of fortunate ſucceſſe in the world; that
could ſo formally, & featly Perſoniſe *in indiuiduo.*
He muſt know all the ſinewes of commodity, and
acquaint himſelfe with all the ioints of aduantage,
that will liue, and teach other to liue. *ô fœlix
Cato, tu ſolus noſti Viuere.* Or if Cato were
ouer-peremptory, and ſtoicall, to enioy that felicity,
ô fœlix Perne, tua ſolius Ars viuendi. Doubtleſſe
it were better for the world, by infinite maſſes of
millions, could the barbarous and Tragicall Tyrants,

Saturne, and Mars, / two diuellifh Gods, moderate
their fury, as he could do : or the hypocriticall,
and Comicall Tyrants, Iupiter, and Mercury, two
godly Diuels, temper their cunning, as he could
do. It was in him, to giue inftructions vnto Ouid,
for the repenning of his Metamorphofes anew :
and he better merited the name of Vertumnus,
then Vertumnus himfelfe. His defignements were
myfteries : his Councels, Oracles : his intentions
like Minotaure in the Labyrinth : his actions like
the Stratagemes of Fabius : his defiance like the
wellcome of Circe : his menaces, like the fongs of
the Sirens : his curfes, like the bleffinges of thofe
witches in Aphrica, that forfpoke, what they
prayfed, and deftroyed, what they wifhed to be
faued. I haue feene fpannels, mungrels, libbards,
antelops ; fcorpions, fnakes, cockatrices, vipers,
and many other Serpents in fugar-worke : but
to this day neuer faw fuch a ftanding-difh of
Sugar-worke, as that fweet-toungued Doctor ;
that fpake pleafingly, whatfoeuer he thought ;
and was otherwhiles a fayre Prognoftication of
fowle weather. Such an autenticall Irony en-
grofed, as all Oratory cannot eftfoones counter-
pane. Smooth voyces do well in moft focieties ;
and go currently away in many recknings, when
rowgh-hewne words do but lay blockes in their
own way. He found it in a thoufand experiences ;

and was the precifeft practitioner of that foft, and
tame Rhetorique, that euer I knew in my dealings.
And in cafe I fhould prefer any man of whatfoeuer
quality before him, for a ftayed gouernement of
his affections, (which he alwayes ruled, as Homers
Minerua brideled Pegafus), or for an infinite and
bottomleffe patience, fibb to the patience of
Anaxarchus, or Iob, I fhould iniury him, and
mine own côfcience, exceedingly. Were he
handeled, as London kennels are vfed of fluttes,
or the Thames / of floouens; he could pocket-
it-vp, as handfomely, as they; and complaine
in as fewe wordes, as any chanell, or riuer in
England, when they are moft contumelioufly
depraued. His other vertues, were colours in
graine: his learning, lawne in ftarch: his wife-
dome, napry in fuddes: his confcience, the
weather in Aprill, when he was young; the
weather in Septēber, as he grew elder: the
weather in February, toward his end; and not
fuch a current Prognofticatiō for the fifty yeares,
wherein he floorifhed, as the Ephemerides of his
Confcience. For his fmug, and Canonicall counten-
aunce, certainly he mought haue bene S. Boniface
himfelfe: for his fayre, and formall fpeach,
S. Benedict, or S. Eulaly: for his merry côceits,
S. Hillary: for his good hufbandry, (he was
merry, and wife) S. Seruatius: for his inuincible

fufferance, S. Vincent the Martir : for his re-
tracting, or recanting, S. Auguftine : for his not
feeing all thinges, S. Bernard : for his preaching
to geefe, S. Frauncis, or S. Fox : for his praying,
a S. Pharife : for his fafting, a S. Publicane :
for his chaftitie, a *Sol in virgine :* for his paftorall
deuotion, a Shepheards Calendar : for his Fame,
an Almanacke of Sainéts. But if euer any were
Patience incorporate, it was he : and if euer any
were Hypocrify incarnate, it was he ; vnto whõ
I promifed to dedicate an eternall memoriall of
his immortall vertues, and haue payed fome little
part of my vowes. I twice, or thrife tryed him
to his face, fomewhat fawcily, and fmartly : but
the Piéture of Socrates, or the Image of S.
Andrew, not fo vnmooueable : and I ftill reuerence
the honorable remembraunce of that graue, and
moft eloquent Silence, as the fageft leffon of my
youth. Had Nafhe a dramme of his witt, his
Aunfwere fhould haue bene Mum ; or his
Confutation, the fting of the Scorpion. Other
Straunge Newes, like / Pap-hatchets rapp with a
Bable, are of the nature of that fame fnowt-horned
Rhinoceros, that biteth himfelfe by the nofe ; and
befturre them, like the dowty fencer of Barnewell,
that played his taking-vp with a Recumbentibus,
and his laying-downe with a broken pate in fome
three, or foure corners of his head. He muft

reuenge himfelfe with a learned Difcourfe of deepeft Silence, or come better prouided, then the edge of the rafour, that would be valued as wife, as that Apollo Doctour. Whofe Epitaph none can difplay accordingly, but fome Sprite of the Ayer, or the fier. For his Zeale to God, and the Church, was an aery Triplicity: and his deuotion to his Prince, and the State, a fiery Trigon. And fuerly he was well-aduifed, that comprized a large Hiftory in one Epithite, and honoured him with the title of *The Thrife-learned Deane*. Onely I muft needes graunt, one fuch fecret, and profound enemy, or fhall 1 fay? one fuch thrife-fecret, and thrife-profound enemy, was incomparably more pernicious, then a hundred Hatchets, or Country-cuffes; a thoufand Greenes, or Cunnycatchers; an army of Nafhes, or Pierces Penniles; a forreft of wilde beaftes; or what-foeuer Ilias of profeffed Euils. It is not the threatener, but the vnderminer, that worketh the mifchief: not the open affault, but the priuy furprize, that terrifieth the old fouldiour: not the furging floud, but the low water, that affrayeth the expert Pilot: not the high, but the hidden rocke, that endangereth the fkilfull Mariner: not the bufie Pragmaticall, but the clofe Politician, that fupplanteth the puiffant ftate: not proclaimed warre, but pretended peace, that ftriketh the deadly ſtroke. What Hiſtorian remembreth not the ſuttle Stratagemes of king Bacchus againſt the Indians: of king Midas againſt the Phrygians: of king Romulus againſt the / Sabines: of king Cyrus againſt the Lydians: of many other Politique Conquerours, againſt ſundry' mighty nations, Principalities, Segniories, Citties, Caſtels, Fortreſſes? Braue Valour may ſometime execute with fury: but Proweſſe is weake in compariſon of other practiſes: & no puiſſance to Pollicy; no rage to craft; no force to witt; no pretence to Religiõ; (what ſpoiles vnder colour of Religiõ?) no text to the gloſſe; what will not the gloſſe maintaine by hooke, or crooke? It was not Mercuries woodknife that could ſo eaſely haue diſpatched Argus, the Lieutenant of Queene Iuno, had not his inchaũting Pipe firſt lulled him aſleepe. And was not Vlyſſes in greater ieoperdy by the alluring Sirens, charming Muſicians, then by cruell Polyphemus, a boiſterous Giant? Vndoubtedly Cæſar was as ſingularly wiſe, as vnmatchably valiant; & rather a Fox, then a Lion: but in his wiſedome he was more affrayde of Sylla, thẽ of Marius; of Cato, then of Cataline; of Caſſius, then of Antony; of Brutus, then of Pompey; to be ſhort; of Saturne, then of Mars; of Mercury, then of Iupiter himſelfe. It were a long diſcourſe, to ſuruey the wily traines, and crafty fetches of the old, and new world: but whofoeuer is acquainted with Stratagemes, auncient or moderne, knoweth what an hourde of Pollicies lurketh in the fhrowde of Diffimula- tion: & what wonders may be atchieued by vn- expected furprizes. The profeffed enemy rather encombreth himfelfe, & annoyeth his frendes, thē ouerthroweth his aduerfary, or oppreffeth his foes. *Alexanders,* and *Cæfars* fuddaine irruptions made them the Lordes of the world, and mafters of kinges: whiles greateft threateners got nothing, but greateft loffe, and greater fhame. What fhould I fpeake of the firft founders of Monar- chyes, *Ninus,* and *Cyrus?* of the Venturous *Argo-pilots?* of the worthy / *Heroes?* of the dowtieft *Errant Knights?* of the *braueft men* in all ages? whofe mightieft engin, (notwithftanding whatfoeuer hyperbole of Valour, or fury) was *Scarborough warning;* and whofe Conqueftes were affoone knowen-abroad, as their Inuafions. No power, like the vnlikely affault: nor any mifchief fo peremptory, as the vnlooked-for affliction. He that warneth me, armeth me; and it is much, that a prepared minde, and boddy may endure; but vnfufpected accidents are hardly remedied: and in the fayreft weather of fecurity, to offer the fowleft play of hoftility, is an incredible aduantage. So Cæfar Borgia, the fouerain Type of

Macchiauels Prince, wan the Dukedome of Vrbin, in one day. So the Emperour Charles the Fiftes Army, paffing thorough Roome, occurfiuely facked the Citty, and enriched themfelues exceedingly. So many inuincible ftates haue bene fuddainly ruinated : and many puiffant perfonages eafely vanquifhed. Braue exploites, where the Caufer as honorable, as the Effect admirable. But honorable, or difhonorable, Pollicy was euer a priuy Counfell, whofe Pofie, *Dolus, an Virtus* : Glory a rauifhing Oration : Ambition a Courfer : Looue a hoat-fpurre : Anger a fierbrand : Hope a graine of muftard-feede : Courage an errant Knight : Couetice a marchant Vēturer : Fury a fierce executioner ; whofe word, the fword, and whofe Law, *Non quà, fed quò.* As Monarchies, Princi-palities, and Conqueftes ; fo Pety-gouernements, Segniories, Lieutenantfhips, Magiftracies, Mafter-fhips, Felowfhips, haue their coolerable practifes : and nothing is cunning, that is apparent. The Fox preacheth *Pax vobis,* to the Capons, and geefe : and neuer worfe intended, then when the beft pretended. Horaces, or rather Borgias.

Aftuta ingenuum Vulpes imitata Leonem ; the deepeft grounde / of higheft pollicies, and the very Stratageme of Stratagemes. The glorious Indian Conqueftes are famoufly knowen to the world : and what was the Valorous Duke of Parma in his braueſt Victories, but *Vulpes imitata Leonem*, and a new compounde of old Stratagemes? Iouius Fox in his militar, and amorous Empreſes, may call himſelfe a Fox : but ſome learned Clarkes, and iudicious Cenſours, profound Politiques, like Macchiauell, or Perne, (for Macchiauell neuer diſcourſed with his pen, as Perne deuiſed with his minde) would go very-nigh to call him a gooſe, that gaue for his mott : *Simul aſtu, et dentibus vtor.* And his Griphen in ſome opinions, was neuer a-whit the more terrible, for that luſtie Poſie, a iolly heroicall verſe in a Grammar ſchoole :

Vnguibus, et roſtro, atque alis armatus in hoſtem.

I neuer read that Alexanders Bucephalus, or Cæſars couragious horſe, had any ſuch, or ſuch glorious Poſies : and I beleeue Beuiſſes Arundell was no great braggard with motts. The Troian Horſe, or rather the Grecian Horſe, was not ſuch an Aſſe, to aduaunce himſelfe with any ſuch prowde Impreſe, as *Scandit fatalis machina muros :* but miniſtered ruthfull, and tragicall matter of that hawtie Poſie to the ſtately Poet. Did the flying Pegaſus of the redoubted Bellerophon, before his aduenturous expedition againſt the hideous Lion-dragon Chimæra, that is, againſt the fierce ſauages, which inhabited that fier-vomiting mountaine in Lycia, proude to arme himſelfe with a braue

Pofie ; or boaſt of his horrible mother Medufa,
or of his owne Gorgonean winges ?   Did the fiery
horſes of the Sunne, that is, of the hoatteſt Eaſt-
countryes, threaten Prince Phaeton, or the world,
with a dreadfull Verſe ?

Tunc ſciet ignipedum Vires expertus Equorum.
May not peraduenture the prowdeſt horſe to be
countermotted with a poore fragment of Statius ?
Seruiet aſper Equus.   Or may not haply the
dowtieſt Aſſe be emblemed with a good   old
deuiſe ?   *inſulſo tribulus ſapit aſper aſello.*   The
rowgheſt nett is not the beſt catcher of birdes: nor
the fineſt pollicy, a profeſſed Termagãt.   Although
Lyſanders oxen ſaid nothing, yet the Fox Lyſander
could tell, which of them was a ſluggarde, and
which laborious.   It is not the Verball mott, but
the actuall Impreſe, that argueth a generous, or
noble minde.   Children, and fooles vſe to crake :
Action, the onely Embleme of Iugurth, and the
notableſt fellowes ;   whoſe manner is, *Plurimum
facere ; minimum de ſe loqui :* the honorableſt
deuiſe, that worthy Valour can inuent.   The Tree
is knowen by the fruite ; and needeth no other
Poſie : the gallanteſt mott of a good Apple-tree, is
a good apple ; of a good warden-tree, a good
warden ; of a good limon-tree, a good limon ; of
a good palme, a good date ; of a good Vine, a
good grape ; and ſo fourth : their leaues, their

Prognofticatiõs; their bloffomes, their boafts; their braunches, and boughes, their brauery; their fruite, their armes, their emblemes, their nobility, their glory. I dare not fay that Pittacus was as wife, as he, that beginneth like front-tufted Occafion, (for Occafion is balde behinde), and endeth like Ouids loouer, (for Ouids loouer must not attempt, but where he will conquer) : few refoluter mottes, then *Aut nunc aut nunquam :* and what Valianter Pofie, then *Aut nunquam tentes, aut perfice :* but Pittacus was one of the feuen famous Mafters, and in his fage wifedome thought it a fober leffon, Foretel not, what thou intendeft to atcheiue, leffe peraduenture being fruftrate, thou be laughed to fcorne, and made a notable flowting-ftocke. Perhaps he was an Affe; and fpeaketh like a Foole: (for / who is not an Affe, & a foole with this Thomas Wifedome?) but fome plaine men are of his opinion, and will hardly beleeue that the frãkeft braggards are the doubtieft dooers Were I a collectour of witty Apothegs, like Plutarch, or of pithy Gnomes, like Theognis, or of dainty Emblemes, like Alciat : fuerly Pittacus fhould not be the laft, or the leaft in that Rhapfody. Meane-while it is nothing out-of my way, to prayfe the clofe, or fufpicious Affe, that will not trouble any other with his priuy Counfell, but can be content to be his owne Secretary. There

be more queint experiments in an Vniuerſitie, then
many a politique head would imagine. I could
nominate the man, that could teach the Delphicall
Oracle, and the Ægiptian crocodile to play their
parts.   His Ciuill tounge was a riddle ; his
Eccleſiaſticall tounge a Hieroglyphique ; his face
a viſard : his eyes cormorants : his eares martyrs :
his witt a maze : his hart a iuggling ſticke : his
minde a miſt : his reaſon a vayle : his affection a
curbe : his conſcience a maſke : his Religion a
triangle in Geometry : his Charity a Syllogiſme in
Celarent : his hoſpitality eleuen monethes in the
yeare, as good, as good Friday : for one moneth
or very neere, he was reſident vpõ his Deanry,
& kept opẽ houſe in the Ile, like Ember weeke.
Of an other mans, no man more liberall : of his
owne, no man more frugall.   He deeply conſidered
(as he did all thinges) that good Oeconomy was
good Pollicy : that Learning was to be com-
mended, but Lucre, and Prefermẽt to be ſtudied :
that he ſoweth in vaine, which moweth not his
owne aduantage : that nothing was to be beſtowed,
without hope of vſance : that Loue, or Hatred
auaile not, but where they may preuaile : that
Affections were to be ſquared by occaſion, and
Reaſons to be framed by proffit : that names of
partialities, ſectes, and diuiſions, either in Ciuill,
or Religious cauſes, were but fooliſh wordes, or

pelting termes ; & all were to be eftimated by
their valuatiō in effe : that the true fquire, &
right Geometricall compaffe of things, is habilitie,
the onely thing, that by a foueraine prerogatiue
deferueth to be called *Subftance* : that according
to Chawcers Englifh, there can be little *adling*,
without much *gabbing*, that is, fmall getting,
without great lying, and cogging : that it was
more wifedome to borrow thē to lend *gratis* ;
that the rauens croking loofeth him many a fatt
pray : that the forftalling, & engrofing of priuy
cōmodities, was a pretty fupply of priuy Tithes :
that many a little, by little & little maketh a
mickle : that often returne of gaine amounteth :
that the Fox neuer fareth better, then whē he
is curfed moft : that a filuer picklocke was good
at a pinch ; / and a golden hooke a cunning
fifher of men : that euery man was neereft to
himfelfe, and the fkinne neerer, then the fhirt : that
there were many principles, and preceptes in Art,
but one principall maxime, or fouerain cautell in
practife. *Si non caftè, tamen cautè :* that there was
no fecurity in the world, without Epicharmus in-
credulity, Dions Apiftie, or Heywoods Faft binde,
& faft finde : that Bayard in the ftable, and *Legem
pone*, were fubftantiall points of Law : that many
thinges are hypothetically to be practifed, which
may not Categorically be reuealed : that two frendes,

or bretheren may keepe counfell, when one of the two is away: that *Vnum neceffarium*: and fo forth. For, *Vincit, qui patitur,* would go nigh-hand to open the whóle packe, and tell wonderfull Tales out-off Schoole. Pap-hatchet talketh of publifhing *a hundred merry Tales* of certaine poore Martinifts: but I could here difmafke fuch a rich mummer, & record fuch *a hũdred wife Tales* of memorable note, with fuch a fmart Morall, as would vn- doubtedly make this Pamflet the vendibleft booke in London, and the Regifter one of the famoufeft Autors in England. But I am none of thofe, that vtter all their learning attonce: and the clofe man (that was no mans frend, but from the teeth out- ward, no mans foe, but from the hart inward) may percafe haue fome fecret frendes, or refpeétiue acquaintance; that in regarde of his calling, or fome priuate confideration, would be loth to haue his coate blafed, or his fatchell ranfacked. Befide, what methodicall Artift, would allow the Encomium of the Fox, in the prayfe of the Affe, vnleffe I would prooue by irrefragable demonftration, that the falfe Fox was a true Affe; as I once heard a learned Phifician affirme, if a goofe were a Fox, he was a Fox. Yet fuerly by his fauour who could fharply iudge, and durft freely / fpeake ; He was a Fox, and a halfe, in his whole body, and in euery part of his foule: albeit I will not

deny, but he mought in fome refpectes be a
Goofe, and after a fort (as it were) an Affe:
efpecially for defeating one without caufe, and
troubling the fame without effect, that for ought
he knew, might poffibly haue it in him, to requite
him aliue, and dead. Let the wronged party not
be iniuried : and I dare auowe, he neuer did, nor
euer will iniury, or preiudice any, in deede, word,
or intention : but if any whofoeuer will needes be
offering abufe in fact, or fnip-fnapping in termes,
fith other remedy fhrinketh, he may peraduenture
not altogither paffe vnaunfwered. He thinketh
not now on the booted foole, that alwaies ietteth
in his ftartups, with his Stilliard hatt in his droufie
eyes : but of an other good auncient Gentleman,
that mought haue bene his father for age ; his
tutour for learning ; his counfellour for wifedome;
his creditour for filuer ; his Catechift for Religion;
and his Ghoftly father for deuotion. He once in
a fcoldes pollicy, called me Foxe betweene ieft,
and earneft : (it was at the funerall of the honor-
able Sir Thomas Smith, where he preached, and
where it pleafed my Lady Smith, and the co-
executours to beftow certaine rare manufcript
bookes vpõ me, which he defired): I aunfwered
him betweene earneft & ieft, I might haply be a
Cubb, as I might be vfed ; but was ouer-youg to
be a Fox, efpecially in his prefence. He fmiled,

and replyed after his manner with a Chameleons
gape, and a very emphaticall nodd of the head.
Whofoeuer, or whatfoeuer he was; certes my old
backfrend of Peter-houfe, was the locke of cunning
conueyance : but fuch a lock, as could not poffibly
be opened with any key, but the key of oppor-
tunity, and the hand of aduantage. If Oppor-
tunity were abroad, Iodocus / was not at home:
where Occafion prefented Aduantage, Pollicy
wanted no dexterity ; and the light-footed Fox
was not fo fwift of foote, as nimble of witt, and
quicke of hand. Some, that called him the luke-
warme Doctour, and likened him to milke from
the Cowe, founde him at fuch a fitt ouerwarme
for their feruenteft zeale : and I remember a
time, when One of the hotteft furnace, fhewing
himfelfe little better then a Cowe ; He in a
quauering voyce, and a lightning fpirite, taught
the wild roe his leffon. Haft was not fo forward
to runne to a commodity, but Speede was fwifter
to fly to an aduantage ; and where Haft fomwhat
grofely bewrayed his forwardneffe, Speede very
finely marched in a cloude, and founde the
goddeffe Hypocrifie as fly a Conductriffe, as euer
was fayre Venus to Æneas, or wife Minerua
to Vlyffes, in their queint paffages. We may
difcourfe of naturall Magique, and fupernaturall
Cabale, whereof the learnedeft and credibleft

antiquity hath recorded wonderfull Hiftories : but
it is the rod of Mercury, and the ring of Gyges,
that worke miracles: and no Mathematician,
Magitian, or Cabalift may counteruaile him, that
in his heroicall expeditions can walke in a cloude,
like a Vapour, or in his diuine practifes go
inuifible, like a Spirite. Braue Mindes, and Ven-
trous Harts, thanke him for this inualuable Note,
that could teach you to atcheiue more with the
little finger of Pollicy, then you can poffibly com-
paffe with the mighty arme of Proweffe. Or elfe
in my curious obferuation of infinite Hiftories,
Hypocrifie had neuer bene the great Tyrãt of the
world, & the huge Antichrift of the Church. The
weapon of the Fier, and Aier, is Lightening : the
weapon of the Earth, & Water, Cunning. Was
not he fhrewdly encountred, that was preftigioufly
befieged, and inuifibly / vnderminded with that
that weapon of weapons? What other fupply
could haue feconded, or refcued him, but Death ;
that had often bene the death of his Life in his
worthieft Frendes, and was eftfoones the death of
his Death in his wylieft enemy. Whofe Spite
was intricate, but detected : and whofe Subtility
maruelous, but difuailed: and he that difclofed the
fame, is perhaps to leaue an immortall Teftimoniall
of his Indian Difcoouery. In the meane time, as
the admirable Geometrician Archimedes would

haue the figure of a Cylinder, or roller engraued
vpon his Toombe : fo it were reafon, the thrife-
famous Deuine, fhould haue the three-fided figure,
or equilater[al] Triãgle, imprinted vpon his Sepul-
chre : with this, or fome worthier Epitaph, deuifed
according to the current Method of *Tria fequunter
Tria.*

The Coffin fpeaketh.

*Afke not, what Newes ? that come to vifit wood :
My treafure is, Three Faces in one Hood :
A chaungling Triangle : a Turnecoate rood.*

*A lukewarme Trigon : a Three-edged toole :
A three-oard galley : a three-footed ftoole :
A three-wing'd weathercock : a three-tongu'd fchoole.*

*Three-hedded Cerberus, wo be vnto thee :
Here lyes the Onely Trey, and Rule of Three :
Of all Triplicities the A. B. C.*

Some-body oweth the three-fhapen Geryon a
greater duty, in recognifance of his often-promifed
curtefies ; and will not be founde Vngratefull at
occafion. He were very fimple, that would feare
a coniuring Hatchet, a rayling Greene, or a
threatening Nafh : but the old dreamer, like /
the old dogge biteth fore, and no foe to the
flattering Perne, or pleafing Titius : that haue
fugar in their lippes, gall in their ftomackes ·

water in the one hand, fier in the other ; peace
in their fayings, warre in their doings ; fweetnes
in their exhortatiōs, bitterneſſe in their canuaſſes;
reuerēce in their titles, coouēn in ther actions:
notable men in their kinde, but pitch-branded
with notorious diſſimulation; large promiſers,
compendious performers ; ſhallow in charity, pro-
founde in malice ; fuperficiall in theory, deepe in
practiſe ; maſters of Sophiſtry, Doctors of Hypo-
criſie ; formall frends, deadly Enemies ; thriſe-
excellent Impoſtours. Theſe, theſe were the Onely
mē, that I euer dreaded : eſpecially thatſame od
mā *Triũ Litterarũ*, that for a linſy-woolfie wit,
& a cheuerell conſciēce was *A Per* ſe A : other
braggardes or threatners whatſoeuer I feare, as I
feare Hobgoblin, & the Bugges of the night.
Whē I haue fought-vp my day-charmes, and
night-ſpelles, I hope their power to hurt, ſhal be
as ridiculouſly ſmall, as their defire to affright, is
outragiouſly great. I neuer ſtood ſtifly in defēce
of mine own hability, or ſufficiency : they that
impeach me of imperfection in learning, or practiſe,
in diſcourſing, or endighting, in any art, or pro-
feſſion, cōfute me not, but confirme mine own
cōfeſſiō. It is onely my honeſty, & credit, that
I endeuour to maintaine : other defectes I had
rather ſupply by induſtry, thē cloake by excuſe :
& referre the deciſiō of ſuch points to the arbitre-

m̄et of Indifferēcy : to which alſo I preferre the
Prayſes of my diſpraiſers : & beſeech Equity to
rēder them their due, with a largeſſe of fauour.
Iudgement is the wiſeſt reader of Bookes : and
no Art of diſtinctions, ſo infallible, as grounded
Diſcretion : which will ſoone diſcerne betweene
White, and Blacke : and eaſely perceiue, what
wanteth, what ſuperaboundeth ; what becommeth,
what / miſbecommeth ; what in this, or that reſpect,
deſerueth commendation ; what may reaſonably,
or probably be excuſed ; what would be marked
with an Aſteriſke, what noted with a blacke coale.
As in mettals, ſo in ſtiles, he hath ſlender ſkill, that
cannot deſcry copper from gold, tinne from ſiluer,
iron from ſteele, the refuſe from the rich veyne,
the droſſe from the pure ſubſtance. It is little
of Value, either *for matter, or manner,* that can
be performed in ſuch perfunctory Pamflets, on
either ſide : but how little ſoeuer it be, or may
appeare, for mine owne part I refuſe not to
vnderly the Verdict of any curteous, or equall
cenſúre, that can diſcerne betwixt chalke, and
cheeſe. *Touching the matter,* what wanteth, or
might be expected here, ſhall be particularly, and
largely recompenſed, aſwell in my Diſcourſes,
intituled Naſhes S. Fame, which are already
finiſhed, and attend the Publication : as alſo in
other Supplemēts thereof, eſpecially thoſe of the

aboue-mētioned Gentlewoman, whō after fome
aduifemēt it pleafed, to make the Straunge Newes
of the railing Villan, the cuffionet of her needles,
and pinnes. Though my fcriblings may fortune
to continue awhile, and then haue their defert,
according to the laudable cuftome ; (what fhould
toyes, or dalliances liue in a world of bufineffe ?)
yet I dare vndertake with warrant, whatfoeuer
fhe writeth, muft needes remaine an immortall
worke ; and will leaue in the actiueft world an
eternall memory of the fillieft vermin, that fhe
fhall voutfafe to grace with her bewtifull, and
allectiue ftile, as ingenious as elegant. *Touching
the manner,* I take it a nice and friuolous curiofitie
for my perfon, to beftow any coft vpon a trifle of
no importance ; and am fo ouerfhaddowed with
the floorifhing braunches of that heauenly plant
that I may feeme to haue purpofely preuented / all
comparifon, in yeelding that homage to her diuine
witt, which at my handes fhe hath meritorioufly
deferued. Albeit I proteft, fhe was neither be-
witched with entreaty, nor iuggled with perfuafion;
nor charmed with any corruption : but onely
moued with the reafon which the Equity of
my caufe, after fome little cōmunication, in her
Vnfpotted Confcience fuggefted. They that long
to aduaunce their owne fhame (I alwayes except
a Phenix, or two) may brauely enter the liftes

of comparifon, & do her the higheft honour in
defpite, that they could poffibly deuife in a feruice-
able deuotiō. She hath in my knowledge read the
notableft Hiftoryes of the moft-fingular woomen
of all ages, in the Bible, in Homer, in Virgill,
(her three fouerain Bookes, the diuine Archetypes
of Hebrue, Greeke, and Roman Valour); in
Plutarch, in Polyen, in Petrarch, in Agrippa, in
Tyraquell, in whom not, that haue fpecially
tendered their dilligent deuoir, to honour the
excellenteft woomen, that haue liued in the
world: and commending the meaneft, extolling
the worthieft, imitating the rareft, and approouing
all according to the proportion of their endow-
ments, enuieth none, but Art in perfon, and
Vertue incorporate, the two precioufeft creatures,
that euer flooriſhed vpon earth. Other woomen
may yeelde to Penelope: Penelope to Sappho:
Sappho to Arachne: Arachne to Minerua:
Minerua to Iuno: Iuno to none of her fexe:
She to all, that vfe her, and hers well ; to none
of any fexe, that mifufe her, or hers. She is
neither the nobleft, nor the faireft, nor the fineft,
nor the richeft Lady: but the gentleft, and wittieft,
and braueft, and inuincibleft Gentlewoman, that
I know. Not fuch a wench in Europe, to vn-
fwaddle a faire Baby, or to fwaddle a fowle puppy.
Some of you may aime at her perfonage: and it

is / not the firft time, that I haue termed her ftile, the tinfell of the daintieft Mufes, and fweeteft Graces: but I dare not Particularife her Defcription according to my cónceit of her beaudefert, without her licence, or permiſſion, that ſtandeth vpon masculine, not feminine termes; and is refpectiuely to be dealt withall, in regarde of her courage, rather then her fortune. And what, if ſhe can alfo publiſh more workes in a moneth thē Naſh hath publiſhed in his whole life; or the pregnanteft of our infpired Heliconifts can equall? Could I difpofe of her Recreations, and fome others Exercifes; I nothing doubt, but it were poſſible (notwithſtanding the moſt-curious curiofitie of this age) to breede a new admiration in the minde of Contempt, & to reſtore the excellenteft bookes into their wōted eſtate, euen *in integrum*. Let me be notoriouſly condemned of Partiality, and fimplicity, if ſhe fayle to accompliſh more in gallant performance, (now ſhe hath condefcended to the fpinning-vp of her filken taſke) than I euer promifed before, or may feeme to infinuate now. Yet ſhe is a wooman; and for fome paſſions may challenge the generall Priuiledge of her fexe, and a fpeciall difpenfation in the caufe of an affectionate frend, deuoted to the feruice of her excellent defert; whom ſhe hath founde no leſſe, then the Handmayd of Art, the miftres of

Witt, the Gentlewoman of right Gentleneſſe, and the Lady of right Vertue. Howbeit euen thoſe paſſions ſhe hath ſo ordered, and managed, with ſuch a witty temper of violent, but aduiſed motions, full of ſpirite, and bloud, but as full of ſenſe, and iudgement, that they may rather ſeeme the marrow of reaſon, than the froath of affection : and her hoatteſt fury may fitly be reſembled to the paſſing of a braue career by a Pegaſus, ruled with the reanes of a Mineruas bridle. Her Pen is / a very Pegaſus indeede, and runneth like a winged horſe, gouerned with the hand of exquiſite ſkill. She it is, that muſt returne the mighty famous worke of Supererogation with Benet, and Collect. I haue touched the booted Shakerley a little, that is alwayes riding, and neuer rideth ; alwayes con- futing, and neuer confuteth ; alwayes ailing ſome- thing, and railing anything : that ſhamefully, and odiouſly miſuſeth euery frend, or acquaintance, as he hath ſerued ſome of his fauorableſt Patrons, (whom for certain reſpectes I am not to name), M. Apis Lapis, Greene, Marlow, Chettle, and whom not? that ſaluteth me with a *Gabrieliſſime Gabriel,* which can giue him the farewell with a Thomaſſiſſime Thomas, or an Aſſiſſime Aſſe ; yet haue not called him a filthy companion, or a ſcuruy fellow, as all the world, that knoweth him, calleth him : that in his Pierce Penniles, and

Straunge Newes, the Bull-beggers of his courage, hath omitted no word, or phrafe of his railing Dictionary, but onely *Tu es Starnigogolus*: and hath Valiantly vowed to haue *The Laſt Word*, to dye for't.

Plaudite Victori, Iuuenes hîc quotquot adeſtis :
Nam me qui vicit, doctior eſt Nebulo.

The beſt is, where my Aunſwere is, or may be deemed Vnſufficient, (as it is commonly ouer-tame for fo wild a Bullocke), there She with as Viſible an Analyſis, as any Anatome, ſtrippeth his Art into his doublet ; his witt into his ſhirt ; his whole matter, & manner into their firſt Principles ; his matter *in Materiã Primam* ; his manner *in formam primam* ; and both in *Priuationem Vltimam*, id eſt, *his Laſt Word*, fo glorioufly threatened. I defire no other fauour at the handes of Curteſie, but that Art, and Witt may be her readers ; & Equitie my iudge : to whoſe Vnpartiall Integrity I humbly appeale in the Premiſſes : with dutiful recom-/ mendatiõ of Naſhes S. Fame, euẽ to S. Fame herſelfe : who with her owne flooriſhing handes is ſhortly to erect a May pole in honour of his Victorious *Laſt Word*. Doubt ye not, gallãt Gentlemẽ, he ſhall finde the guerdon of his Valour, & the meede of his meritorious worke. Though my Pen be a flugplum, looke for a quill, as

quicke, as quickſiluer, & pitty the ſoary ſwaine,
that hath incurred the indignatiō of ſuch a quill ;
and may euerlaſtingly be a miſerable Spectacle for
all libelling rakehelles, that otherwiſe might des-
peratly preſume to venture the foyle of their
cranke folly. The ſtay of the Publicatiō, reſteth
onely at my inſtance : who can cōceiue ſmall hope
of any poſſible account, or regard of mine owne
diſcourſes, were that faire body of the ſweeteſt
Venus in Print, as it is redoubtedly armed with
the compleat harneſſe of the braueſt Minerua.
When his neceſſary defence hath ſufficiently ac-
cleered him, whom it principally concerneth to
acquitt himſelfe : She ſhall no ſooner appeare in
perſon, like a new Starre in Caſſiopea, but euery
eye of capacity will ſee a conſpicuous difference
betweene her, and other myrrours of Eloquence :
and the wofull ſlaue of S. Fame muſt either blind-
folde himſelfe with infenſible peruerſitie, or behold
his owne notorious folly, with moſt-ſhamefull
ſhame. It will then appeare, as it were in a cleere
Vrinall, whoſe witt hath the *greene-ſickneſſe* : and
I would deeme it a greater maruell, then the
mightieſt wōder, that happened in the famous
year, 88. if his cauſe ſhould not haue the *falling-
ſickneſſe,* that is encoūtred with an arme of ſuch
force. M. Stowe, let it be enchronicled for one
of the ſingularities, or miracles of this age, that a

thing lighter then Tarletons Toy, and vayner then
Shakerleyes conceit, that is, Nafh, fhould be the
fubiect of fo inualuable a worke: and be it knowen
to Impudency / by thefe Prefentes, that his brafen
wall is battred to Pin duft, and his Iron gate
fhaken all to nothing. It is in the leaft of her
energeticall lines to do it : more eafely, thē a fine
thread cracketh a iãgling Bell. A pretty experi-
ment : & not vnlike fome of her ftraunge inuen-
tions, and rare deuifes, as forcible to mooue, as
feat to delight. The iffue will refolue the
doubtfulleft minde : and I am content to referre
Incredulity, to the vifible, and palpable euidence
of the Terme Probatory. When either the Light
of Nature, and the Sunne of Art muft be in
Eclipfe: or the fhining rayes of her fingular
giftes will difplay themfelues in their accuftomed
brightneffe ; and difcoouer the bafe obfcurity
of that mifchieuous Planet, that in a vile ambition
feeketh the exaltation of his fame, by the de-
preffion of their credit, that are hable to extinguifh
the proudeft glimze of his Lampe. Her rare
perfections can liuelyeft blafon themfelues : and
this penne is a very vnfufficient Oratour to
expreffe the heauenly bewties of her minde : but
I neuer knew Vertue, a more inuiolable Virgine,
then in her excellent felfe : and the day is yet to
come, wherein I euer founde her Witt a defectiue,

or Eclyptique creature. She knoweth, I flatter
not her Fortune: and if I honour her Vertue,
whofe confirmed modeftie I could neuer fee dis-
guifed with any glofe of commendation; who can
blame me for difcharging fome little part of a
great dutie? She hath in meere gratuity beftowed
a largeffe vpon her affectionate feruaunt; that
imputeth the fame, as an exceffiue fauour, to her
hyperbolicall curtefie, not to any merite in himfelfe:
but the leffer my defert, the greater her liberality;
whom I cannot any way reacquite, farther then the
zeale of a moft-deuoted minde may extende; as
inceffantly thankefull, as infinitly debtfull. For
to addreffe a plaufible / difcourfe, or to garnifh a
Panegyricall Oration in her prayfe, as occafion
may prefent ; will appeare to be a tafke of Ciuill
Iuftice, not any peece of Ciuill curtefie, when her
owne filuer Tractes fhall publifh the precious
valour of her golden Vertues, and decipher the
ineftimable worth of the Autor by her diuine
handyworke. At the firft vewe whereof, as at
the piercing fight of the amiableft Bewtie, who can
tell how fuddaine Paffions may worke? or what a
fting, fome tickling Interiection may leaue in the
hart, and liuer of affection? I am euer prone to
hope, as I wifh, euen the beft of the worft: and
although wilfull Malice be a ftiffe, and ftubberne
aduerfary to appeafe, yet I haue feene a greater

miracle, then the pacification of Paper-warres, or
the attonement of Inkhorne foes. There fhe
ftandeth, that with the finger of Induftry, and the
toungue of Affability, hath acheiued fome ftraunger
woonders, vpon as rough, and harfh fellowes, as

The noddy Nafh, whom euery feruing Swafh
With pot-ieftes dafh, and euery whip-dog lafh :

(for the ryme is more famous, then was intended):
and with the fame caufes emprooued, why may
She not directly, or violently accomplifh the fame
effectes ? or what is impoffible to the perfuafiue,
and Patheticall influence of Reafon, and Affection?
It is a very difmall, and caitiue Planet, that can
finde in his hart to encounter thofe two gracious
Starres, with malitious afpectes : which he muft
defpitefully encounter, that will obftinately oppofe
his peeuifh rancour to her fweete Ciuility. In
cafe nothing elfe will preuayle with infatiable
Enuy, and vnquenchable Malice, (for fo I am
eftfoones informed, whatfoeuer courfe be taken
for the mitigation of his rage) : yet I am vehe-
mently perfuaded in Phyfique, and refolued in
Pollicy, that the Oile of Scor / pions will finally
heale the woondes of Scorpions. I know One,
that experimentally prooued what a rod in lye
could do with the curfteft boy in a Citty ; and
founde the Imparitiue moode a better Oratour,

then the Optatiue. It may fortune, the fame man hath fuch a Whipfydoxy in ftore for a Iack-fauce, or vnmannerly puppy, as may Schoole him to turne-ouer a new leafe, and to cry the pittifulleft Peccaui of a wofull Penitent. For my part, whom at this inftant it fmartly behooueth to be refolute, I confeffe I was neuer more entangled, and intricated in the difcourfe of mine owne reafon, then fince I had to do with this defperate Dick ; that dareth vtter, and will cogge any thing to ferue his turne. Not to confute him, in fome refpectes were perhaps better : to confute him, is neceffary. Were it poffible, to confute him in not confuting him, I am of opinion, it would be done : (for Infolency, or any iniury would be repreffed by order of Law, where order of Law is a fufficient remedy : and Silence, in fome cafes, were the fineft Eloquence ; or Scorne, the fitteft anfwere) : and haply I could wifh, not to confute him in confuting him, (for the difcoouery of Cunny-catchers doth not greatly edifie fome bad mindes) : but feeing he is fo defperate, that he will not be confuted with not confuting, I muft defire his Patience, to be a little content to be confuted with confuting, rather after his, or others guife, then after my manner. *Aunfwere not a foole according to his foolifhneffe, left thou alfo be like him : anfwere a foole according to his foolifhneffe, left he be wife in his owne conceit.* They are both Prouerbes of the wifeſt Maſter of Sentences : of whom alſo I haue learned that to the horſe belongeth a whipp; to the aſſe a ſnaffle ; to the fooles backe a rod. Let no man be wiſer then Salomon. The fooles-head muſt not / be ſuffred to coy itſelfe : the colte muſt feele the whip, or the wande ; the aſſe the ſnaffle, or the gode ; the fooles backe the rod, or the cudgell. Let the colt, the Aſſe, the foole beware in time : or he may peraduenture feele them indeede : with ſuch a *Tu autem*, as hath not often bene quauered in any language. If Peace, or Treatie may not be heard, Warre ſhall commaunde Peace ; and he muſle the mouth of rankeſt Impudency, or fierceſt hoſtility, that can do it ; and do it otherwiſe, then is yet imagined : and yet nothing like that inſpired Gentlewooman. Whoſe Penne is the ſhott of the muſket, or rather a ſhaft of heauen, ſwifter then any arrow, and mightier then any hand-weapon, when Curteſie is repulſed, and hoſtility muſt enforce amity : but otherwiſe how gratiouſly amiable, how diuinely ſweete ? Gentlemen, looke vpon the louely gliſtering Starre of the morning ; and looke for ſuch an Oriēt Starre, whē She diſplayeth the reſplendyſhng beames of her bright wit, and pure bounty. Meane-while, if ſome little ſhimering light appeare at a little creuiſe, I haue my requeſt;

and fome pretty conuenient leyfure, to take order
with an other kinde of Straunge Newes in Weft-
minfter Hall. It is fome mens fortune to haue
their handes full of vnneedefull bufineffe attonce:
and for mifelfe, I fhould make no great matter
of two, or three fuch glowing Irons in the fier,
were it not fome fmall griefe, or difcouragement,
to confider, that nothing can be perfe&ly, or
fufficiently performed by halues, or fragments.
Which neceffary interruption hath bene the vtter
difgrace of the premiffes ; and a great hinderance
to my larger Difcourfes, more ample trifles. I
can but craue pardon ; and prepare amendes,
as leyfure and occafion may affourde opportunity.
Learned wittes can fkilfully examine, and honeft
mindes / will vprightly confider Circumftances,
with curteous regarde of Fauour, or due refpe& of
Reafon: in whofe onely Indifferency, as in a fafe,
and fweet harborough, I repofe my whole affiance,
and fecuritie, as heretofore. And fo for this
prefent I furceafe to trouble your gentle curtefies:
of whofe Patience I haue (according to particular
occafions) fometime vnmannerly, but modeftly ;
often familiarly, but fincerely; moft-what freely, but
confideratly ; alwayes confidently, but refpe&iuely;
in euery part fimply, in the whole tedioufly
prefumed vnder corre&ion. I writ onely at idle
howers, that I dedicate onely to *Idle Howers*: or

would not haue made fo vnreafonably bold, in no needefuller Difcourfe, then *the Prayfe, or Supererogation of an Affe.*

This 27. of Aprill: 1593.   Your mindefull debtour, G. H.

FINIS.

Errours efcaped in the Printing.
With certaine Additions to be inferted. *

Page.	faultes.		amended.
26	for angoy,	read	agony.
31	fcholeth,		fchooleth.
49	bewixt		betwixt.
67	railing ftile, without the two prickes, or colon.		
85	very Minifter		euery Minifter.
90	inftringment		infringement.
98	not will		will not.
107	looker-on		lookers-on.
121	fuch fweating		fuch a fweating.
139	or difcourfer		or a difcourfer.
147	thy riot		by riot.
202	fuprifes		furprifes.
205	at the leaft		or the leaft.
219	Orientall		Orient.

KNow alfo, Gentle Reader, that it was the Writers meaning to deuide this Treatife into three bookes: the Second beginning at the *Aduertifement to Pap-hatchet and Martin Mar-prelate :* the Third at, *So then of Pappadocio :* but in the Originall, or vncorrected coppy there was

* These have all been attended to in their respective places.

not any fuch diuifion exprefly fett-downe: neyther
were the Additions following, inferted in their
proper places, but annexed to the end of the
Third booke, noted thus:

In the *Firſt Booke*, page 46. after *Cloude*, infert.
What . . . . maſter. [See p. 93, ll. 13—24.]

In the *Second Booke*, Page 77. after *edifieth*,
infert. Plato . . . . conceites? [See p. 135, ll.
7—18.]

In *the ſame booke*, Page 87. after *Innouation*,
infert. And I . . . . *Poplars.* [See·p. 149, l. 21,
to p. 150, l. 22.]

In the *Third booke*, Page 205, after *Pollicie*,
infert. that Learning . . . . cogging. [See p. 310,
l. 9, to p. 311, l. 8.]

Thefe fower Additions in their feuerall bookes, I
commende to the correction of the curteous
Reader: and fo take my leaue.

FINIS.

TO THE RIGHT WORSHIPFVLL

my very good friend, M. Doctour Haruey.

GOOD M. Doctour Haruey, promiſe I account debte, eſpecially to ſo eſpeciall a frend : and therefore I haue now againe laboured to diſcharge miſelfe of it. I would I were of deſert to ſet-forth your long-deſerued prayſe, and of hability to expreſſe your ſingular habilities, in ſtile, knowledge, and other moſt commendable vertues. What is in my power, the leaſt of your frendes ſhall commaunde : what is not, I can but wiſh : which I would moſt earneſtly wiſh, if that might ſerue, though I neuer ſhould wiſh more. I will not trouble your grauer ſtudies, but pray for your healthes continuaunce : and will moſt willingly performe more, if occaſion ſerue.

Oxford, this 10. of Iuly. 1593.

Yours euer to commaunde,

Iohn Thorius.

Sonet.

*D*Efam'd by One, who moſt himſelfe defameth,
　　Write worthy Haruey: for the wiſe applaude
　　thee :
Shame be his hyer, that fowly himſelfe ſhameth,
And would of thy deſerued right defraude thee.
And | if you force the vndeſerued wrong,
Wherewith ſome ſimple Ignorant diſtaines thee :
You in your Wiſedome may exceede as long,
As he in Folly fooliſhly diſdaines thee.
For ſharpe-eyde Equitie hath deſcride to all,
Th' iniurious vayne, that ſettes his penne to ſchoole :
VVhoſe railing tendes vnto your wiſedomes fall,
And prooues all fonde, to prooue himſelfe a Foole.
VVhich monſtrous Folly would be leaft in haſt :
As Wiſedomes age will make him know at laſt.

　　　　　　　　　　　　Iohn Thorius.

Incloſed in the ſame Letter.

*A*ND that I might not be held laſt in remem-
braunce, though abſent, that in your preſence
haue ſought the ſelfe-proffering cauſe of after-
memory : I haue once more, (as he, that deuoteth
himſelfe, and his poore labours to your good
liking), how badly you may ſee, but how hartely
I wiſh you could ſee, or I could ſay ; writ theſe
my pure deuotions, and Zealous lines : with as

true defire to honour yourfelfe, according to your
worth, as I haue bene wanting the defert, which
your curteous nature hath affourded me. I re-
queft Sir, but your acceptance, and your fauour,
which if I gaine, I haue got more, then my due:
and fo wifhing your continuall bliffe, I ende, as
one with oft prayers defiring to be held,

Your bound by much defert,

Antony Chewt.

Sonet. /

Proceede moft worthy Lines, in your difdaine,
    Againft the falfe fuggeftions you abufe :
    VVhofe rafcall ftile deferued hath to gaine
    The hateful title of a railing Mufe.
Doubtleffe the wifeft, that fhall chaunce to read you,
    In true Iudiciall of a quiet thought,
    Will giue applaufe vnto the wit, that bread you,
    And you fhall winne the good, that you haue fought.
VVinne more : and fince the foole defames you ftill,
    The foole, whom Shame hath ftained with fowle
      blott,
    Performe on him your difcontented will :
Fame fhall be your meede : Shame fhall be his lott.
And fo proceeding, you fhall fo redeeme
    The name, that he would drowne in blacke efteeme.

Subfcribed, Sh: VVy :

for, Shores VVife.

Sur l'Apologie de Monſieur le treſ-doćte &
treſ-eloquent Doćteur Haruey : par le
Sieur de Fregeuille du Gaut.

Celuy qui prouoqué publie ſa defence,
Peut auecques raiſon ſa cauſe déployer ;
La Loy de Talion ne peut moins, qu'ottroyer
Iuſt permiſſion de repayer l'offence.
  Mais celuy qui enflé, a eſcrire commence,
A diffamer autruy, tachant a ſ'employer :
De droit ne peut pretendre adueu ou bon loyer,
Ains l'infame intenté luy vient pour recompenſe.
  I'aime | pourtant par tout vn ſtile moderé,
Meſmes ſi on reſpond au ſot demeſuré,
Car on n'a point raiſon d'imiter ſa ſottiſe.
  Marri ſui mon d'Haruey de te voir prouoqué,
Mais treſ-aiſe qu'eſtant indignement piqué ;
Ta Doćte reſponſe eſt eloquente & raſſiſe.

His Sonet, that will iuſtifie his word, and dedicateth
Naſhes S. Fame to Immortalitie.

A Dame, more ſweetly braue, then nicely fine ;
Yet fine, as fineſt Gentlewomen be :
Brighter, then Diamant in euery line ;
Is Penniles ſo VVitleſſe ſtill ? quoth She.
If Naſh will felly gnaſh, and rudely flaſh :
Snip-ſnap a craſh, may lend S. Fame a gaſh.

Skill *read the Ryme, and put it in* Truthes *purſe :*
(Experience *kiſſeth* Reconcilements *hand*) :
If warning-peece be ſcorn'd, Spite *may heare worſe :*
Though Looue *no warriour be,* Right *leades a bande.*
How faine would Curteſie *theſe iarres ſurceaſe ?*
How glad would Charitie *depart in peace ?*

But if Sir Raſh continue ſtill Sir Swaſh ;
He liues, that will him daſh, and laſh, and ſqwaſh.
   Hæc quoq ; culpa tua eſt : hæc quoq ; pœna
    tua eſt.

An other occaſionall admonition.

Fame rowſ'd herſelfe, and gan to ſwaſh abowt :
Boyes ſwarm'd : youthes throng'd : bloudes ſwore :
    brutes rear'd the howt :
Her meritorious worke, a Wonderclowte :
Did euer Fame ſo brauely play the Lowte ?
I / chaunc'd vpon the Ryme : and wondred much
What courage of the world, or Miſter wight
Durſt terrible S. Fame ſo raſhly tuch.
   Or her redoutable Bull-begging knight.
Incontinent I heard a piercing voyce,
Not Ecchos voyce, but ſhriller then a Larke :
Sith Deſtiny allottes no wiſer choyce,
Paſtime appoſe the Pickle-herring clarke.
Quiet thy rage, Imperious Swiſh-ſwaſh :
Or Wo be to thy horrible triſh-traſh.
    Eſt benè, non potuit dicere : dixit, *Erit.*

An Apoftrophe to the Health of his abufed Frendes.

Liue Father fweet : and mifcreant Varlets dye,
That wrong my parent Hart, and brother Eye.
Deereft of Eyes, contemne thy caitiue foes :
Kindeft of Hartes, enioy thy firme repofe.
Sky, *with a patron Eye afpect that Eye,*
That Eye, efpoufed to the Virgin Sky.
Art, *with a Loouer hart preferue that Hart,*
That Hart, deuoted to the heauenly Art.
Bleffings, *defcend from your Empyreal throne.*
And lend a bounteous eare to fuppliant mone.
   Ambrofiall fpringes of cleereft influence,
   Fountaines reftoratiue of cordiall bliffe,
   Deigne Zeale proftrate your tendreft indulgence,
   And fouerainly redreffe that is amiffe.

L'enuoy.

Volumes of Thankes, and Prayfe, your ftore combine
In paffionateft Hymnes, and Pfalmes diuine.

The Printer's Poſtſcript.

Weet Gentlemē, hauing committed the Premiſſes to the Preſſe, and acquainting certaine learned and fine men with ſome other of the commendatory Letters, and Sonnets of M. Thorius, and M. Chewt: there was ſuch an eſpeciall liking conceiued of two other their writings, that I was finally entreated, or rather ouertreated, to giue them alſo their welcome in Print; as not the vnfitteſt lines, that haue bene publiſhed to interteine laſie howers, or to employ drowſie eyes. Sometime in the braueſt ſhowes there is little performed: and ſometime a poore Publicane may worke as great a worke of Supererogation as a proude Phariſe. I am not the meeteſt to blaſe other mens armes: and they are beſt furniſhed to be their owne tongues, that can ſo well pleade for themſelues, and their friendes. I can but recommende their learned exerciſe, and mine own vnlearned labour, to your gentle acceptation.

To the right worſhipfull, my very aſſured
frend, M. Doɛtour Haruey.

MY ſilence thus long, good M. Doɛtour
Haruey, was not occaſioned either by
forgetfulneſſe, or by negligence : but rather for
want both of conuenient leaſure, and of ſufficient
argument : being very vnwilling either to ſpend
time often in writing of vnmateriall lines, or to
trouble any eſpeciall frend with reading them.
Yet becauſe amitie is maintained by this loouing
kinde of intercourſe ; & becauſe Cuſtome hath
allowed, that Affeɛtion induced, to expreſſe a
carefull memory of the continuance of frendſhip,
by writing euen vpon ſmall, or no occaſion :
though the Letter were ſigned with nothing elſe, /
but, *Si vales, bene eſt : ego valeo* : left longer
ſilence might cauſe me to incurre iuſt reprehenſion,
and that you may receaue ſome ſlender token of
my often thinking on you : I ſend you encloſed
three *Stanzaes*, though ſimple in conceit, or other
regard, yet were they equall to my good will,
they would, vndoubtedly excell, and ſhould be
ſome way ſutable to your right excellent giftes.
If they pleaſe, or not diſpleaſe you, and may ſeeme
worthy, or not altogether vnworthy to ſerue as
foiles with my other Sonnets, which you receaued
before, to thoſe much worthier Verſes, which you

haue of much happier Poets, then mifelfe : you
may therein do your pleafure, whereto onely they
are confecrated. Thus hoping that you are per-
fuaded of me, as of one affectionatly your owne
to vfe, and commaunde at your appointment, I
leaue you with my moft harty, and humble recom-
mendations.

Oxford: the 3. of Auguft. 1593.

Yours alwayes at commaunde,
Iohn Thorius.

Stanzaes.

Among the Greekes, fweet Homers *copious Verfe*
   Foregoing times to Fames fwift winges commended :
The Latins, Virgils *noble worke reherfe :*
   Nor yet in thefe were auncient prayfes ended.
Demofthen's *rich ftile, thorough Greece was blazed,*
   And Tullyes *forcing toungue made Roome amazed*
Our *moderne Age to egall with the paffed,*
   The Italian *pleafing Mufe hath done her beft :*
   The learned French *Pennes haue themfelues fur-*
       paffed :
And worthy Englifh *wittes haue bannifht reft.*
Midft whom, who not emblafon Haruey's *name,*
Wrong him, themfelues, and Englands growing Fame.

Yeelding | fond Naſh thy glory ſhalt not ſtaine,
　But rather ſhalt encreaſe thy pravſe hereby :
　Thv frendes qſall know thy iudgement not ſo vaine,
　But thou diſcernes where true deſert doth fly.
And thy deſert by ſo much ſhall ſeeme greater,
　By how much thou art knowne to know thy better.

Iohn Thorius.

Sir, ſuch a patheticall Aſſe haue I found deci-
phred in your moſt learned and witty Diſcourſe
of that poore Creture, as I know will proue the
eternall Memoratiue of one M. Naſh. Yet I by
Experience haue found more : that it is the nature
of a true Aſſe, (to which Aſſe peraduenture this
was dedicated) that a *greene Figge* being hand-
ſomly tyed to his chappes, he no ſooner ſmelleth
it, but he followes his noſe ſo farre, that he
ſcapeth fayre in vneeuen ground, if he breaketh
not his necke. And this Note I would not but
impart vnto you : as a Caueat worthy to be
remēbred amongſt other ſecrets of that beaſt.
For doubtleſſe your philoſophicall Aſſe will make
Alchimy vpon it. I pray you diſpoſe of it at
your beſt pleaſure. When any other ſuch Memo-
randum fortunes into my hand, you ſhall ſee it :
and ſo in haſt recommending you to your better
ſtudies, I reſt Sir,　　　　　at your ſeruice.

An : Ch.

The Affes Figg.

So long *the Rhennifh furie of thy braine,*
Incenft with hot fume of a Stilliard Clime,
Lowd-lying Nafh, in liquid termes did raine,
Full of abfurdities, and of flaundrous ryme.

So / much *thy Pot-iefts in a Tapfter humour,*
(For thats the Quinteffence of thy Newgate fafhion)
Thy toffepot maiefty, and thy Fame did rumour,
In wondrous Agonyes of an Alehoufe paffion.

So well *thy wydemouth'd, or thy Oifterwhore phrafe*
(Yet Gentry bragges her of thy lowfie degree)
Aptly hath knowne thine Armory to blafe
In termes peculiar vnto none but thee.

So foone *fiue Penniworth of thy grofer witt*
(Yet thou art witty, as a woodcock would be)
More then autenticall, hath learn'd to gett
Thy Mufe intitled, as it truly fhould be.

And now fo neatly *hath thy railing merit*
(I fhould haue faid Ramme-ally meditations)
Procur'd applaufe vnto thy Clarret fpirite,
And fack-fopt miferies of thy Confutations.

That now each Iuy-bufh *weepes her. Teares in ale:*
The Fifh-wiues Commonwealth, *alack forlorne,*

Moornes in ſmall drink, ſharp, ſingle, ſowre, and
    ſtale :
And thy long-booted gentry, *ragged and torne*
Wailes new petitions to the Diuels good grace :
    Although the laſt, God knowes, gott little meede.
    But thow' lt to Hell, when ſhiftes can haue no place,
    Perhaps to Hanging too, when time ſhall neede.
Yet firſt wilt ride, raile, ryme me downe to Hell :
    (Oh but beware ſtrange bugges at ſuch a game) :
    I haue a trick, to teach a Gooſe to ſpell
    Himſelfe an Aſſe, *out-off his* Aſſes *name.*

                              An: Ch.

FINIS.